THE STRANGE CHILD

ANDREA GEVURTZ ARAI

The Strange Child
Education and the Psychology of Patriotism in Recessionary Japan

Stanford University Press · *Stanford, California*

Stanford University Press
Stanford, California

Printed in the United States of America on acid-free, archival-quality paper

Library of Congress Cataloging-in-Publication Data
Names: Arai, Andrea, 1956– author.
Title: The strange child : education and the psychology of patriotism in
    recessionary Japan / Andrea Gevurtz Arai.
Description: Stanford, California : Stanford University Press, 2016. |
    © 2016 | Includes bibliographical references and index.
Identifiers: LCCN 2015041711 | ISBN 9780804797078 (cloth : alk. paper) |
    ISBN 9780804798532 (pbk. : alk. paper) | ISBN 9780804798563 (e-book)
Subjects: LCSH: Education—Social aspects—Japan. | Education—Japan—
    Psychological aspects. | Patriotism—Japan. | National characteristics,
    Japanese. | Recessions—Social aspects—Japan. | Japan—Social
    conditions—1989–
Classification: LCC LC191.8.J3 A72 2016 | DDC 306.43/20952—dc23
LC record available at http://lccn.loc.gov/2015041711

Typeset by Thompson Type in 9.75/13.5 Janson

This book is dedicated to my father, Burton (Bud, Bapa) Gevurtz, who passed away in November 2013. Zichrono l'vracha. May his memory be blessed, and may he be on a beautiful fishing stream somewhere as he loved to be during his life. He was much loved and is very much missed. And to my daughters, brother, and incredible teachers.

Contents

Illustrations

Acknowledgments

This book has taken a very long time to complete. I have been often reminded of just how long by my daughters and friends who do not write academic books. The project developed over time along with the issues and transformations I set out to understand and unravel. For the privilege and pleasure of taking time to research and write this book, I have very many to thank.

My greatest thanks are to my teachers. They inspired, challenged, encouraged, and shared their time unsparingly. It is of them I think each time I enter my own classrooms, prepare my comments, begin discussions, meet with students in office hours. My love of learning, teaching, ethnographic research, and, most recently, collaboration across disciplines and national boundaries is a testimony to the kind of enlightened scholarship of which they are such wonderful examples.

Marilyn (Mellie) Ivy opened up entirely new worlds of anthropological, historical, and conceptual thought and possibility for me. With Mellie, I learned to think differently and really think about modernity, Japan, and so much more. She believed in, supported, and encouraged an older graduate student with two small children every step of the way: from the start of graduate anthropology studies at the University of Washington to the fabulous opportunity to continue at Columbia University, during and after fieldwork in Japan, and over the years since. The ethnographic project at the center of this book owes much to her help conceptualizing strangeness, the child, recession, temporality, and the place of anthropology. Her beautiful and inspiring work is my example. As I became involved in other projects that have added much to the writing of this book, she congratulated me but always reminded, "Finish your own book, Andrea!" If this book provides insights into a complicated set of conditions, is sensitive to their effects, and in any way reads well, it is to Mellie that I owe my ability to have written it.

Ann Anagnost was a hugely important mentor. When I moved from the UW to Columbia, Ann stayed connected in invaluable ways. Her comments and critical feedback on neoliberalism, education, and more have had much to do with how this book developed over the years. It was with Ann that I became involved in my first collaborative project on East Asia, "Global Futures of East Asia." Working with Ann was a gift and a pleasure. I learned enormous amounts about teaching and writing (especially my own) from her. I am very grateful for all the time she devoted to my work and our work together.

Harry Harootunian has been an academic idol of mine for some time. One of the reasons I transferred to Columbia was the chance to work with Harry. I still remember meeting him for the first time in his office at NYU in 1997; the layers of books lining the walls, many of which we began talking about from that first meeting; his boundless curiosity; the pathbreaking nature of his historical scholarship; his interest in my topic. I was enamored then and have not ceased to be since. Harry's insightful comments and questions contributed a great deal to my project. His contribution to this book is throughout.

John Pemberton is the quintessential ethnographer. Walking around New York City with John is like taking a tour through the denaturalization of time and space. His comments and questions about the sounds of the classroom, the body and language, and much more were riveting. "Expect the unexpected," John said as I left his and Mellie's apartment on my way to Japan for my first two years of fieldwork. I took his advice seriously and am very glad I did!

Rosalind Morris pushed me to think harder and further about modernity, violence, media, and the child. She asked about recession, crisis, and "what it looks like" in Japan. Roz graciously agreed to be on my graduate committee, and this book is much better for her contributions to my thinking and questioning.

My initial fieldwork from 1999 through 2001 was made possible by an Itoh Fellowship from Columbia University, a Fulbright Foundation fellowship, and a Wennergren Dissertation Research grant. Follow-up research over many years has been supported by travel grants from the East Asia Center, the University of Washington Japan Program, and the Simpson Center for the Humanities. I offer thanks in particular to Kristi Roundtree of the East Asia Center for her support of my individual and collaborative research and the index of this book.

In Japan, I have so many to thank it would take pages. Given limitations of space, I note only a few here without whose guidance, interest, and hospitality this ethnography and book would not have been possible. At Tokyo University, Department of Education, historical sociologist of education Hirota Teruyuki, agreed to be my advisor. I am grateful to Hirota-sensei for generously sharing his many sources, including me in his seminar (*zemi*), and often taking time out of his busy schedule for discussion and to answer my questions. I traveled many times between Tokyo and Kobe (and later from Kobe to Kochi), staying in Kobe for long periods at a time. The Fujita family opened up their home to me. Fujita Yoshimi fed, drove, made introductions, set up appointments, taped programs, and clipped news stories. At more delicious dinners with Yoshimi, her husband, and their son than I can count, we talked about their experiences of recession, my interviews, observations, and readings. I am grateful for their input and friendship. Thank you to Usunaga Chikako, who features in the final chapter, for giving of her precious time in between an early morning job and working on her alternative space. Thanks as well to the faculty and principal Majima of Imai Elementary School (in the early 2000s) for their hospitality and generosity to my family and to me as researcher. My appreciation to Kawakami Ryōichi for the many hours he graciously granted me. My understanding of "the child problem," related discourses, and classroom environment owes much to him and his Purokyōshi group. We spent holidays and vacations with the Arai family in Komagone, Nagano. I remember with gratitude the now late Arai Isamu, who shared his home with his son and our family during my fieldwork, and our conversations about his pre- and postwar experiences in the education system.

Academic friends and colleagues in the United States have shared time and comments at many points in the writing and revising of this book. Janet Poole read the manuscript and gave feedback and hugely helpful comments on parts of it. Janet spent untold hours on Skype going over ideas and titles and helping me calm down and take my time. Two (and counting) fabulous road trips in Canada and the United States together, talking about our books, lives, and more have reminded us how special and necessary intellectual friendship can be. Gabriella (Gabi) Lukacs has been an amazing Japan anthropology colleague. Ever since she contacted me some years ago about an early piece of mine, she's encouraged me in the cool and funny way that only Gabi can to get my book done. Gabi's comments on the final chapter were more than helpful. Miyako Inoue understood what I was trying to say about the quality of transformations occurring in Japan, told me there was something prescient about my ethnographic project, and kept asking me when the book would be ready.

At the University of Washington, Japan and East Asia Studies colleagues provided the kind of supportive and encouraging environment necessary for writing and revising my manuscript. Davinder Bhowmik has been an amazing colleague and friend, reading and commenting on parts of the manuscript, talking about ideas as I was working through them, and encouraging me in between manuscript revisions to take part in a conference on the environment in Okinawa that provided really necessary and important thinking time. Thanks are also due to Ken Oshima, Ted Mack, Clark Sorensen, Vince Rafael, Azusa Tanaka, and Jonathan Warren for being available for lunch, coffee, and lots of talking over time about Japan, anthropology, education, neoliberalism, and more. My appreciation goes to the faculty and staff of the Henry M. Jackson School Japan Studies program: Marie Anchordoguy, Donald Hellman, Robert and Sadia Pekkanen, Ken Pyle, Martha Walsh, Ellen Eskenazi, my graduate students, and many wonderful undergraduates and exchange students for their support, comments, and questions.

My family has been there for me at all points of my academic career. My brother Brad Gevurtz is the best brother one could ask for, younger in age, but more mature in many ways than his sister. (We often get asked who is older but not because of who looks the part). He takes care of the family in ways much beyond what my Dad would have expected. My daughters Megumi and Michiko were surprised (by my choice of topic), supportive, and maybe proud of their mother, and they are interested now in the why, how, and what it is about. Their father Fumi helped in the first stages of fieldwork, as I was getting used to writing innumerable email, perfecting my formal Japanese, and trying to sort out a complex discursive field. My best friend Meryl Haber is there for me in ways that stretch the bounds of even the oldest friendship (we have been friends since age two!). She has a room ready for me in Portland when I need to get away, walk, talk, and think about ourselves. Thank you also to Barbara Kleine who, in the midst of lots of life's difficulties, helped me to find and keep the focus needed to keep writing this book.

I owe many thanks to Tracy Stober who helped with early copyediting, formatting, and creative thinking about images, covers, and child problems. Tracy's interest in the manuscript and great questions kept me searching for ways to communicate to a broader audience. Michelle Lipinski at Stanford University Press has simply been the best editor I could ever have asked for. Thank you, Michelle, for being so interested in the ethnography, for moving things along, for great explanations, answers, and so much encouragement!

This book is dedicated to my father; my mother Suzanne (Suzy) Gevurtz, who passed away much too young; and to my wonderful daughters.

THE STRANGE CHILD

Introduction
The Strange Child, Education, Neoliberal Patriotism

If we do not know what a child is, then it becomes impossible to invest in their sweet self-evidence, impossible to use the translucent clarity of childhood to deny the anxieties we have about our psychic, sexual and social being in the world.[1]

If the conduct of individuals or collectivities appeared to require conducting, this was because something in it appeared problematic to someone. Thus it makes sense to start by asking how this rendering of things problematic occurred. . . . It suggested that "problems" are not pre-given, lying there waiting to be revealed. They have to be constructed and made visible, and this construction of a field of problems is a complex and often slow process.[2]

Words such as "self-responsibility" are beginning to circulate without being scrutinized thoroughly for their conceptual integrity and their applicability to Japanese society . . . How should Japanese people live in an era in which each individual independently should take risk and take responsibility for his or her action is a contradiction but no one points that out.[3]

This is "the world of recession," she said with a heavy sigh. In the winter of 2007, in an up-and-coming residential area about thirty minutes from the center of Tokyo, a long-time acquaintance and I stopped at a bank machine around the corner from her home. Carefully shielding the number pad as she entered her "secret number" (pin), she cautioned me to do the same. In a country renowned for its lack of crime, her personal security concerns surprised me. Noticing this, she explained, "Secret number thefts are on the rise. This is the world of recession—nothing is as it used to be."[4] This woman's description of the recessionary period that began in the early 1990s epitomized a new sense of social "unease"—an early keyword of recessionary Japan. How a capitalist society had appeared, or had been made to appear, so certain and secure and was now experienced as unfamiliar and uneasy is one part of the ethnographic story this book relates.

"Common sense is not the rule anymore," another friend and mother I had known since the beginning of my fieldwork in 1999 exclaimed around the same time. Using the example of a parent participation day at her children's elementary school, she described with dismay how other parents focused only on their own child's needs. For this woman, and many others with whom I spent time during my decade and a half of fieldwork, which began with what was called "the child problem" (*kodomo no mondai*),[5] shifting parental attitudes toward the school and their own child, often encoded as nationally Japanese, were another sign of the nothing-is-as-it-used-to-be uncertainty and strangeness of the recessionary period.

The opening epigraphs by Jacqueline Rose and Hirokazu Miyazaki point to the specificity of recessionary unease and uncertainty, how and why it took the form of the child problem, and the multilayered effects of which the child problem is a part. These effects transformed the early twenty-first-century language of commonality and requirements for individual development. In *Imagined Communities*, Benedict Anderson famously conceptualized the sense of commonality on a national level with others we shall never know or meet but about whom we have complete confidence in the simultaneity of their existence and activity as "the deep horizontal comradeship of the imagined community of the nation," even as that horizontality is not borne out in income or opportunity.[6]

In a poignant commentary on late twentieth-century Japanese national imaginings and community, the late Masao Miyoshi used the unlikely notion of "uninteresting" to describe the form of horizontal comradeship of late twentieth-century Japan. For Miyoshi, the uninteresting referred to the production of a certainty and knowability beyond question and critique; a totalized and standardized experience of nation and culture, fused and dehistoricized. Miyoshi emphasized the importance of understanding the history of that certainty production, a product of intertwined domestic and international discourses, actions, and contingent events, in order to understand the effects of and on the present.[7]

As Rose emphasizes, the child and childhood are representational forms of the modern subjects' desire for certainty, as much as childhood and children are names for the time and spaces of development of a diverse group of younger human beings. As a representational form, the child is a composite and often contradictory figure, standing for potential and promise as well as deficit and danger. In both of these senses, the child has been employed as a metaphor or symbol of progressive development and developmental time or its inverse, stagnation and failure. Rose's linking of adult certainty to *knowing* what a child is provides one key to what follows here. The child problem of late 1990s Japan was a contingent effect. It emerged out of global historical crossings of knowledge about national identity, cultural difference, and the relation between the two. It was a powerful representation of the outmoding and recessionary replacement of the all-too-certain educationally managed credential (*gakureki*) society and the identity discourse of dependency.[8]

In 1989 through 1991, the Nikkei Stock Exchange fell by 60 percent from a high of 38,916 in 1989 to a low of 11,819 by 1991. Japan's gross domestic production followed suit, declining precipitously. From the famed double-digit growth of the 1960s through the mid-1970s, and a steady 4 percent annual rate during the 1980s, economic growth dropped to 1.5 percent by the year 2000 and dropped to negative rates by the time of the September 11, 2001, attacks in the United States.[9] As Japanese banks and businesses began to fail—for the first time since the Great Depression of the 1930s—terms of financial instability and failure, like bankruptcy and restructuring, identified in Japan with other countries like the United States and China, began to appear with regularity in the Japanese news. The financial plummet was met with domestic and international disbelief. It's just a correction, wrote many international economists at the time; the Japanese will figure it out. When figuring it out macroeconomically with large amounts of government spending did not correct the downward cycle, interest on large risky loans that had been freely allowed during the heyday of Japanese capital surpluses compounded, and that which had seemed so certain and knowable—economic success naturally emerging from the predictability of an educationally managed dependent psychology life course—began to seem insecure.[10]

The financial downturn of the early 1990s, which led to a decade-and-a-half–long recession, constricting of the job market for young adults and restructuring of the lifetime employment system, set the stage for the unease and related effects that I uncover here. Yet, it is important to note that the recessionary unease, the forms it took, and the effects that were produced did not occur all at once. The child (of the child problem), a deeply naturalized representation of national identity and temporal insecurity, made visible a problem while obscuring the history and complexity of the problem's creation. Moreover, this focus on the child deferred questions about the conditions for the production of certainty and seeming prior lack of precarity that had characterized representations and experience of late twentieth-century Japan. *In this book, I uncover a process of social reengineering, enacted through the coming together of education and psychology, the making of problems, and a process of recoding, transforming, and translation of key concepts of national identity and certainty that manage and redirect what the recession laid bare.*

What focused recessionary unease on the child and caused the education establishment and psychological experts to emerge at the forefront of national solutions for a problem that was part media generated and part a conjuncture of political economy and cultural anthropology began with a violent incident in 1997 perpetrated by a fourteen-year-old junior high student. In the spring of 1997, a junior high student in the city of Kobe, known only as Youth A (Shōnen A), an anonymity mandated by Japanese juvenile justice law, murdered and decapitated a sixth grade boy. As the result of a note left on the dead child's body, diaries written, and letters penned to the local newspaper, all suggesting a mature assailant, it took several months for the police to identify the perpetrator as a local youth. As soon as the age of the assailant was revealed, the media descended on Kobe, staying months, interrupting daily life, and ruining property values, as the head of the neighborhood association told me. The media began to describe this violent "heinous" crime as the act of an "ordinary child," elevating concern about strangeness of the formerly certain and secure middle-mass, middle-class Japanese ordinary.

In Chapter Two, I discuss the Kobe Youth A event in detail. I explain how Youth A's violence against younger children was only part of the reason this event became a national problem that needed remedying. How was the problem constructed? What remedies were proposed? Did they fit or reconfigure problems? What do they tell us about the child as figure of temporality and value, the school and national education system's position in Japanese society? The media sensationalized but failed to explore the challenges posed by the youth's deeply articulated violent world; his expressed desire to take revenge on the school system, which he said had turned him into a "transparent being"; and a highly specific set of delusions about the process of identity construction. What emerged after all the years of media coverage, popular publications, and references to this event by the Ministry of Education (hereafter MOE) were pronouncements of child strangeness that created fear but failed to consider the conditions and revelations of the youth's motives or madness. Media generalization of the Youth A event drained it of the particularities of place, post-1995 earthquake Kobe, and time, the recessionary period's effects on salaryman families like Youth A's.[11] Turning Youth A into an example of the quintessential "ordinary child," due to his salaryman father and stay-at-home mother, but gone horribly wrong, left the status of the ordinary unquestioned and reinforced, neglecting the struggles and tensions inherent in maintaining this ordinariness by a family such as Youth A's. Overlooking the specificities of his life and time to turn it into a national problem of the child was the first step in neglecting the relation between the particular and the general. This young man's individual family conditions and the location of recessionary Kobe tell a particular story of postwar development, labor, and credential society of their own, at once particular and situated within national narratives of commonality and conflations of region, class, ethnicity, and gender, into an ordinary or homogeneous Japanese subject.

The strange child was an appropriate figure for the displacements of the world of recession. Strangeness evokes its inverse, the ordinary. If the strange has particular signifying power, if it produces effects of unease, it is because of how the ordinary is imagined and experienced. We should say that a strange child is not the exception but the rule.[12] And, if this is the case, if children are by nature strange because they are on their way to becoming, as Claudia Castenada aptly describes, not yet what only they can become, how does the representation of a strange child surprise and shock?[13] Only if the strange child evokes a set of certainties that the child in modernity came to stand for, including the possibility of a child who is not strange and what has been invested in this unstranging developmental process. How we think about the child and childhood, as the certainty of a sequence of progressive, developmental stages, is a product of the times of capitalist modernity. The articulation and generalization of this strangeness suggests what Benedict Anderson referred to as the configuration or *style* of national imaginings (and I might add management). There is nothing present in the child that mandates directionality, nothing more than some sort of change. In every sense of the word, the child is wild. Thus, the discursive figuration of the strange child and the heightened concern it raised in 1990s and early twenty-first-century Japan alert us not so much to a problem with children but to the societal notions, national narratives, and identity structures child ideas are asked to support. In the case of late twentieth-century Japan, these were a certainty about the replication of a sense of national commonality and temporal experience. What made the child available as a symbol or metaphor of modernity is also what has made the child the locus of problems when the certainty of the national trajectory was in question and reform-minded officials sought to shift the terms and responsibility for individual and national futures.

From Incomprehension to Independence

Junior high school history teacher Ryōichi Kawakami and his teachers' group, the Professional Teachers' Association (*Purokyōshi no kai*), began publishing widely on the strange child and the "collapse" of the school in the mid-1990s. For Kawakami, the focus of strangeness was child (student) bodies out of order:

> Over the past ten years, the change in students is stunning. Everyone criticizes the overregulation of kids, but are kids so pure and all teachers sadists? The school's role was to prepare kids for society; give them the ability to manage on their own for which they need to absorb basic strengths. Lately kids have become weak. The lifestyle has changed, and so has the body. *Words are no longer absorbed by the body.* This is really a frightening thing. We can't get through to these children; they're incomprehensible [*tsūjinai; wakaranai*], and we don't have a clue what they're thinking.[14]

Kawakami's articulation of "the body that no longer absorbs language" is evocative of the position of the body and training in the production of national commonality. He connects students' bodily comportment, or the sudden lack thereof, with shared forms of communication understood as Japanese. What sort of language and body is this? Language not absorbed by child bodies is a routinized form of everyday communication that signifies a set of relationships—between adult and child, teacher and student—of order and authority. Kawakami (as I discuss in Chapter Four) described this relationship of the body, language, and social order located in the schools and education system as a "sacred" one. In this formulation of the national community and national identification, the body, trained and culturally inculcated, occupied a central position in national representation (as in the "national body" of the prewar period) and everyday interaction—one that the recessionary period was eclipsing. The representations of strange child and collapsing school are the discursive forms of a failure or transformation of this certainty of communication on the one hand and revelatory of a cultural inculcation supposedly so thorough on the other that it could fix the meaning and defy the arbitrariness of language itself. Language absorbed by bodies is a language without *différance*—a neologism created by Jacques Derrida to represent the temporal delay inherent in the linguistic act. The project of managing meaning, creating a language that would be absorbed without delay, is in many ways not language (an arbitrary system of differences) at all. If it could be produced, it would mean complete identification: a nonindividuated, consensual subject. In a language situation of such pure identity, words need almost not be spoken.

Kawakami's strange child figuration evokes and reveals. It evokes a space opened up between the fantasy and expectation of seamless communication. It reveals the terrain of the production and the unproduction of the seemingly comprehensible child. In Chapter Four, I describe individual meetings with Kawakami, observations in his classroom, and participation at the professional teachers' weekly meetings. I explore the production of comprehensibility in terms of the everyday physical and mental training and its relation to the disciplines of high growth and prosperity of the 1950s through the 1980s. I uncover the coming apart or collapse of its production in the coming together of education and psychology language and policies and the new rationales of governance that shifted responsibility to the individual for his or her own training and self-development.

The child problem displaced the troubles of the economic downturn and the fissures the downturn opened up in national identification onto the young. Recessionary government institutions and officials turned the child problem into a political rationale and a language of recession, based in the neoliberal principles of "rolling back" services and protections and "rolling out" less direct forms of government intervention.[15] By the end of 2006, the first Shinzō Abe government (2004–2006) appropriated the social unease that the problematizing of the child and schools created to justify a set of revisions (for the first time in sixty years) to the Fundamental Law of Education (hereafter FLE) of 1947. Emphasizing self-development, independence, and individual responsibility, the revisions also included a language of cultivating a "heart" to love one's country. In the following pages I refer to this seemingly impossible individualized collectivism as *neoliberal patriotism*.[16]

As Hirokazu Miyazaki highlights, words like *independence* and *self-responsibility* circulated in Japanese society in the beginning of the twenty-first century without scrutiny for the way they were used or the effects they produced. At issue for Miyazaki was uncovering the process of substitution and erasure: independent for dependent, group for individual, and the erasure of a long-cultivated association of Japanese with dependency and groupism. Miyazaki exposes not only a history of national identity representations, made in and beyond Japan, but their connection to education and psychology. What has been obscured is what dependence was and did, how independence dismisses it, the temporality of this dismissal, and how independence circulates and is deployed. What is the independent self in the context of twenty-first-century Japan? How does it signify, operate, and relate to the past? What new forms of training are necessary? Where does one obtain them? Who is responsible? What is the relationship of this independence to the insecurities and uncertainties of education and labor faced by families and children across Japan? What expectations on young and old accompany the new independence?

Contrary to recent political rhetoric, there is nothing inevitable or simple about this shift from dependent to independent that took place as a result of the coming together of educational discourse, policy, and psychological experts on the child problem from the 1990s on. Many have suggested that becoming independent was a long-awaited next step for Japan and the Japanese, a step that represented a fuller, more complete modernity. A long-term debate about the nature of modernity lies within this sort of conclusion. But a more complete modernity, as it were, a modernity of fuller rights as well as responsibilities, was not inherent in the rationale behind the new independence of the recessionary period circulated by the MOE and psychologists of identity and written into the FLE. The rationale for the promotion of independence and concurrent demotion of dependence as national identity discourse was connected to a form of governance known as neoliberal. Neo-liberal rationales or logics, in the realms of education, psychology, and human capital development in Japan on which I focus in this book work from within existing ideas of the individual and national identity. Altering their meaning from the inside, neoliberal discourses of self-development, strong individuals, skills, abilities, and independence reflect a changed relationship between society and government. Risk and responsibility trump rights and protections in the world of this new or neoliberalism.

In Chapter One, I discuss the coming together of education and psychology within the recessionary conditions of unease and uncertainty and the neoliberal substitutions that resulted. I am looking at psychology here because of its particular connections in Japan with discourses of national identity, as well as the new legitimacy gained by clinical psychologists during the recessionary period, a legitimacy that meant they would be turned to for solutions for a particular problematizing of the young. In this book, I ethnographically follow the trail from the child problem to the replacement of one identity discourse for another and the emergence and circulation of an entirely new language of strong, independent, responsible, and risk-bearing selves by educators and clinical psychologists.

Neoliberal rationales transformed a whole history of Japanese cultural and national identity representations. The present shift to independent Japanese selves, rationalized by a problem with the child and a parallel language of emotion and "the heart," is the product of intertwined histories and complex crossings of knowledge (Chapter One). This shift is responsible for a range of effects, one of which has been the forgetting of earlier projects of social engineering at home and abroad and between city and countryside.[17] Another is summed up by Tomiko Yoda as obscuring "the disruptive effects of the Japanese capitalist regime's withdrawal from the system of social management."[18]

Writing and Rewriting Japanese Education

Interest in Japanese education in schools, child rearing in homes, and the relation between the two with Japan's economic success grew tremendously in the latter part of the twentieth century. The school and home became a focus of comparative research in anthropology, psychology, education, and popular writing within and beyond Japan. Both the beginning of high-growth economic policy in the late 1950s and the end in the early 1970s brought changes to education policy, aimed at producing the workforce of a highly productive and accelerated economy. This included controversial governmental efforts to revise the 1947 FLE. Picking up where the Naka-sone government of the mid-1980s had tried and failed, the first Abe government (2004–2006) succeeded in the first revision of the FLE in sixty years. The revision removed key language of educational rights and inserted new language of "hearts that love Japan."[19]

This book has benefited from this earlier period's ethnographies of education and the issues they raise of comparison, method, identity discourse, cultural nationalism, and what all of these have to do with Japanese schooling. The focus on how young Japanese are raised and educated and attempts to use educational practices to create generalizations about national identity were heavily influenced by changing views of culture in the American cultural anthropology of the early to mid-twentieth century. In the late 1940s and early 1950s, shifting geopolitical formations of power in a decolonizing world occurred alongside anthropological theories of cultural difference and modernization theory's "objective" stages and sequences of measurable economic advancement.[20] Two important and related results emerged from this conjuncture that had significant effects on the writing, research, and educational policy of the child and childhood. First, differences between Japan and the United States (as representative of the West) were national-ized, culturalized, and posed along psychological lines. Second, imperial Japan's multiethnic empire-state (from 1905 through 1945) was discursively converted; that is, it was reinscribed historically into a single-ethnic homo-geneous entity by the American Occupation forces in Japan and Japanese leaders.[21] Through recourse to postwar ideas of culture and modernization, the past was demonized and separated from the present, even as moving out of Japan millions of former imperial subjects—for whom Japanese was their formal language and nationality—and then moving equal numbers of Japa-nese settlers back to Japan would take many more years.

This historical context is key to how academic knowledge, writing, and popular policy on Japanese education, psychology, and childhood developed. One of the main distinguishing features of research in the 1950s through the 1980s on childhood, psychology, and education in the home and school is comparative: Japanese as culturally dependent, Americans as culturally independent, Japanese as groupist, Americans as individualist.[22] Key dichotomies in this literature of comparison were written as such, as many of its authors acknowledge, because Japan seemed to be doing something right (that the United States was doing wrong) educationally. Look at the orderliness of the Japanese classroom, the competitiveness of their test scores and workforce! According to a national best seller in the United States at the time, every Japanese worker was worth three Brits (British citizens).[23]

Several early English-language studies that began to unpack these dichotomies were Thomas Rohlen's ethnography of three Japanese high schools, Merry White's *The Japanese Educational Challenge*, and Catherine Lewis's *Educating Hearts and Minds*. Rohlen's study was pathbreaking for its comparison among Japanese schools, rather than across national boundaries, and the challenge Rohlen posed to the taken-for-granted ideas about quality and equality for all in the Japanese system. White was interested in questioning stereotypes of childhood; Lewis's focus was in the preschool experience in which she found a less disciplined, "whole child" approach compared to the United States. White and Lewis both frame the differences between the United States and Japan as "rooted in deep psychological and cultural realities" that we need to understand. Rohlen is more focused on beginning a discussion of social class at a time when few in Japan used this term. The strength of all three, particularly for the situations we meet in the 1990s, is their long-term fieldwork and, in the case of Rohlen's high schools, his extended observations inside the classroom. As I found in my own work over a number of years, ongoing participant-observation in schools and classrooms, and exam preparation schools (*juku*) as well, made all the difference in understanding the gaps among ideology, problem discourse, and everyday experience.

By the late 1990s and again in the 2000s, the work on childhood, education, and psychology had changed a great deal. Anne Allison sheds very different light on the "whole child" practices that Lewis and others had praised.[24] Allison's focus is on the role of the mother, whose job it was to make ordinary and "continuous" the routines and disciplines of the everyday in such a way that summer break might be time away from, but not time off, schooling.[25] Norma Field's "The Child as Laborer and Consumer" was a pathbreaking look at problems associated with schooling in Japan, which according to Field mandated a level of discipline of mind and body resulting for many mothers and children in peril to their health. Margaret Lock and Shoko Yoneyama's specific focus on "bullying" and "school refusal" demonstrated the inability of some to conform to the demanding homogenizing routines of ordinary and unending exam study. Roger Goodman's original work on "returnee" children in the 1980s era of internationalization opened up this schooling experience to different scrutiny and conclusions about leaving and coming back to a total education system like Japan's. All challenged the natural orderliness of Japanese educational settings in different ways. Field, Lock, and Yoneyama, in particular, introduced theories of power into the discussion of Japanese education, including a focus on discipline as a form of power that is "productive" rather than "repressive."[26] Productive power is a form of influence that operates by creating and managing populations, rather than by diminishing and separating.

This book has also been strongly informed by a number of recent ethnographies by Amy Borovoy, Mary Brinton, and David Slater focused on the difficulties faced by young Japanese born at the end of the 1980s, the sudden changes in education and work they have had to negotiate, and, in the case of Borovoy, how the waning of dependency discourse is playing a part in this transformation. As I describe in detail in Chapter Six, these are changes with which their parents' generation is wholly unfamiliar.

The work on Japanese education by Japanese researchers in the 1990s has been diverse and deep. During this period of tremendous unease, in which education was suddenly blamed for social and personal issues emanating from the recessionary environment, researchers like Teruyuki Hirota, Takehiko Kariya, Ryoko Tsuneyoshi, Manabu Sato, Hidenori Fujita, and Teruhisa Horio protested, published, and spoke out against the new recessionary language of independence, responsibility, and educational liberalization.[27] Unlike education ministry spokespeople and the psychologists enlisted to reframe and neoliberalize postwar education, these researchers have been concerned with the unfulfilled promise of the FLE to make education a "right," not a duty; provide equal access to all; and keep the state from overmanaging teachers and the curriculum.[28] As Kariya and Sato have argued repeatedly, their efforts to improve on the postwar system are antithetical to turning all Japanese into entrepreneurs of themselves. Demonizing educational practices like the exam system to recategorize liberalization as progress is a ploy, they claim. But the child problem, which draws its power from a history of modern temporal effects and the recessionary psychologization of national identity, has proved a powerful justification for change.

This book adds to and extends this work. It combines an ethnography of the practices, policies, and experiences of Japanese education in the home and school with a keen attention to language, complex crossings, and historical specificity, the hallmarks of which have been called the linguistic and historical turns in anthropology. Some of my colleagues have described this book's long-term ethnography as "predicting" changes happening at the time. This of course has not been the case. What has occurred, as a result of my focus on the anxious and productive figure of the child problem and its educational and psychological effects, is that I found myself in situations in which new realities were taking shape. This was the case with the shifting of the age of adulthood in the juvenile justice law; the turn en masse to private educational services; the reception of the new heart language; the revision of the FLE at the end of 2006; and the shift in the child problem discourse to the arena of labor and the recessionary generation.[29]

It is my intention that this book shed new light on the research on education and its relation to nation and modernity; the child, childhood, youth, and families living in recessionary times; nationalism, neoliberal patriotism, and psychology of identity; and more. I hope the combination of long-term ethnographic work, historicization, and conceptual engagements that make up this book will be read and used by anthropologists and sociologists of Japan, East Asia, and beyond, as well as by all those in the humanities and social sciences whose work benefits from what ethnographic work reveals and is sensitive to the complexities of contemporary life and society.

Ethnography at its best is descriptive and revealing. It devotes time to the taken-for-granted, to how things have come to be the way they are. Ethnography uncovers and accounts for the unexpected and is deeply interested in the texture of everyday life and the historical quality of change.[30] The ethnographic project that has materialized in this book is a result of reading and thinking across disciplines and theoretical terrains, of following out what Gilles Deleuze referred to as the "little lines of convergence."[31] Here these lines involve: how education and psychology came together under the conditions of a long recession, how the recession itself took on a quality much beyond a financial event; how geopolitical contingencies brought American cultural anthropology's culture and personality approach together with modernizations' stages and objective measures, and how the changing nature of liberalism (what Donzelot would say is not liberalism at all) reworked liberal notions of independence from the inside out in the Japanese context.

If this ethnography is revelatory to others, as it has been personally for me, it will be in its ability to evoke the particularities of these lines, figures, and displacements.[32]

The recessionary focus on the problem with the child circulated so widely and became such a source of social concern in Japan in the late 1990s that when I said I was studying the strange child and the child problem no further explanation was required. That there was something suddenly and incontestably wrong with the Japanese child and schooling seemed increasingly agreed upon, and everyone was looking for answers. Unease about the Japanese child, schools, and homes—the sites of individual development—was exacerbated by media repetition of stories of seemingly out-of-control (collapsing) classrooms and youth violence. The concern that ensued over the child was from the start about much more than children, the schools they attended, and the homes in which they were being raised. *What I set out to understand was how the young and the places of their development had become the figurative and pragmatic focus of social unease, an unease that went far beyond the times and spaces of children's contemporary lives and that shifted recessionary concerns from financial practices and the contexts that have made these practices possible to the potential of individual development.*

This book makes the following arguments. The child problem turned the child, youth, school, and home into the problematic focus of a dramatically changing economic environment, obscuring the pragmatic consequences of the financial downturn for individual lives and social institutions. The moral panic associated with the child and education was a product of historical and cultural investments in both over time. The problematization of the child and school, perpetuated by media commentators, government officials, and a range of new psychological experts, provided the rationale for neoliberal education and labor reforms and for the reformulation of dependence and homogeneity—former cultural ideologies—into neoliberal logics of independence, self-responsibility, and self-development.

I uncover the contemporary and historical forces that came together to produce the child problem in 1990s Japan: how the child and strangeness were paired, how this discursive figure circulated, and how it involved shifts in educational discourse and a rise of a new psychology of identity that negated dependency and the national character it had come to define from schools to homes to workplaces. Under the conditions of a nagging recession, education and psychology coming together enabled a highly particular process and a representational form of neoliberal globalization to emerge.

This book tracks discourses of unease and strangeness that began with the child problem and transformed over the first decades of the 2000s to include the young men and women these children became, their schools, job market, and workplace. The young people born into recession are immersed in a world of completely different requirements for their own development and life making. Negotiating a past they do not know and the present for which they are being made responsible, they articulate distress, embody the confusion of a transforming environment of expectation and lack of preparation, and encounter contradictory requirements of life. As roles are reversed, older generations are at a loss to understand this world of recessionary effects and the child that is its representational form. I attend to the plight of the recessionary generation, young Japanese adults who must learn to navigate the economic conditions of recession. These children and youth of recession live in the midst of a world of recession, in which nothing is as it used to be. The young are both the subjects and objects of this recessionary world. They exist in their own time, in which, out of seeming impossibility, possibilities, alternatives, and new spaces of life also emerge.

A long-term, multisite, cross-regional ethnography of the effects and representational forms these effects have taken following the 1990s downturn of the financial sector in Japan, this book tracks these forms and effects— beginning with discourses of the child problem and the collapsing school. I map the undoing and replacement of an ideology of cultural difference, an ideology created over time *in* Japan and *about* Japan. I show how the dependency narrative of cultural difference has been replaced by way of a *neoliberal twist*. This twist has replaced the heavily loaded notion of dependency for a seemingly more neutral independence. The effects traced in this ethnography show otherwise. The terms *independence* and *independent individual* took on completely new meanings circulating in the recessionary climate of the end of the twentieth and beginning of the twenty-first centuries. Associated with an individualized and psychologized language of self-development, risk, and inner frontiers, the ascendance of independence has performed neoliberal, neonational, and neocolonial work. Initiated by the education ministry, as we will see in Chapters Two and Three, dealt with by the schools (Chapter Four), and appropriated by the private education industry or cram schools (*juku*) (Chapter Five), young and old in Japan, often unknowingly, became the objects of increased expectations and fewer protections.

The effects and substitutions I reveal in this book demonstrate the intersection of education and psychology and the longer-term effects on schooling, families, government policy, and the new generation. These effects also reverberate with effacement and separation within the present and between the present and the past. Initiated in the social management projects of the postwar developmental economy and credential society, the changes of the late 1990s to early 2000s created what we might think of as a second-order shift that further obscured the violences and extractions of capitalist modernity.[33] The Fukushima disaster, to which I return in Chapter Six and the conclusion is the most recent example. As we now know, the disaster of Fukushima was foretold by many in the Tohoku area. Others in rural and regional Japan had questioned the free subsidies and promises that doubly exploited the countryside, as nostalgic and economic resource—a location from which to generate the energy and economic gains for distant Tokyo.[34] Left now in irradiated ruin, the Tohoku area stands for the history of turning space and time into a resource frontier.

This book returns to the postwar social engineering project and the too often obscured environmental costs of the high economic growth period (1960 through 1972) to take adequate account of the present reengineering of society through an intersection of neoliberal language, governance, and neo-national tropes that represent a shift to a new form of devotion, rather than a return to notions of former empire and intact nation. *Recessionary effects, the conditions of their production, and how Japanese of different ages and across different regions live and articulate these effects are the concerns of this book.*

The Chapters That Follow

In Chapter One, I discuss the "complex crossings" of knowledge and power that comprise the intertwined historical context of Japanese discourses of identity, cultural anthropology, psychology, and the idea of the child in modernity and Japan. This context is critical for understanding how recessionary unease and uncertainty that exceeded a concern over financial futures coalesced in the representational form of the "the child problem" in 1990s Japan. Solutions for this problem, which was always already about more than the lives of children in all their diversity and steeped in neoliberal rationales of governance, deposed and replaced Takeo Doi's theories of dependent national character. The responsibilitized independence of Hayao Kawai and others that replaced dependence began to circulate in the late 1990s and 2000s as if it were the necessary and inevitable next step of Japan's modernization in a global age. In fact, independence and related terms of recessionary Japan signified a transformation in the relationship of responsibility and risk for the individual, a retraction of state institutions from key public support (and the idea of public itself), at the same time that new forms of intervention were introduced. I explain how seemingly contradictory or conflictual ideas and programs came together and comprise the vocabulary of the new generation's life with the notion of *neoliberal patriotism*. At the end of the chapter, I move from a discussion of context and ideas to a discussion of two films that exemplify the before and after of these transformations in recessionary Japan.

In Chapter Two, I describe the MOE's education reform pitch to the public. I situate this public outreach within the political economy of the early to late 1990s, explaining the media's role and what Japanese educators have had to say about the changes. This chapter connects the MOE reform campaign with the Kobe Youth A incident. I move beyond the media reporting on the Kobe incident to Youth A's violent acts within the local environment of how families, schools, and young people in Kobe were affected by the 1995 Kobe earthquake and recession. I look carefully at the relation between Youth A's acts of violence and his efforts to communicate his identity struggles and deteriorating mental state and its connections to past and present forms of control and identity construction. I discuss my conversations with those who knew him but whose explanations did not make it into the media, notably his defense lawyer (who wrote his own book about his encounters with Youth A) and who generously shared time with me, as well as members of the neighborhood association, his teachers, and friends. My goal here is to show how educational changes were rationalized by incidents of youth violence and the new individualizing and responsibilitizing discourse of independence.

Chapter Three goes into detail about Hayao Kawai, one of the foremost authors of the terms of reform: independence, heart, emotions, and his key contribution, *inner frontiers*. In this chapter, I describe how clinical psychologists like Kawai were brought in as experts on the Japanese child to persuade the public that less support and a shift in focus to the independent heart (and new kind of patriotism) on the part of the MOE were better for the public. This chapter details my fieldwork with and at Kawai's events. He gave regular public lectures during this time, which I attended. He was also appointed to chair several high-level committees on reforming education. He authored a major report I discuss at length, entitled "The Structure of Japan in the 21st Century," that blends his Jungian psychology with neoliberal logics.[35] The inclusion of clinical psychologists at this level was unprecedented on governmental committees, which were made up for the most part of ministry officials and business leaders.

In Chapter Four, I discuss my ethnography of schools and classrooms, including Kawakami's junior high and the Professional Teachers' Association meetings. This chapter describes their view of the strange child as "incomprehensible" and "a body that does not absorb language." Long-term observations at Kawakami's junior high, Imai elementary, and other schools provided me a different form of engagement with the powerful discursive constructs, *classroom* and *school collapse*, of the early 2000s. A great deal of change has occurred in the realm of education and the family and education and work from the late 1990s through the first decade of the 2000s and into the present. Changes in curriculum, hours of instruction, shifting discourses of identity, social management, and human capital development have produced a range of effects at all levels of society. My observations took me from so-called collapsing classrooms to those that were said to be orderly and manageable, participation at teacher's meetings, after-hours get-togethers, Parent–Teacher Association (PTA) gatherings, community meetings, and much more. This extensive participant observation helped me to understand the ideological space between on-the-ground economic realities and discourses of collapse: how the ordinary child and homeroom teacher were singled out and why Kawakami and his group worried about the body and its training, whereas others were focused on the heart, neoliberal patriotism, new flexible labor regimes, and the corporate restructuring that accompanied educational changes.

In Japan, a private supplementary education system parallels the public school system.[36] This private school industry had a big stake in the recessionary period. The managers of these private industry schools capitalized, literally, on the changes in discourse, role, and policy of the MOE. In Chapter Five, I discuss my observations in exam preparation cram school classrooms, conversations with teachers and managers, and participant-observation at parent explanation sessions and "expos." Held at large conference centers, these expos were organized by the large chain cram schools to showcase materials and approaches. Presenting themselves as much-needed support in an era of independence, these chain schools enticed parents to enroll their children at younger ages. One of the main appeals to parents at the time was improving student mental attitude and physical stamina, something the private education industry blamed the public school system for neglecting.

Chapter Six focuses my discussion of recessionary environment and neoliberal reconfigurings on the younger generation. This chapter investigates these young people's strategies of survival in the midst of transforming relationships of responsibility, risk, and national identification. I focus on the changed perception and experience of temporality of the recessionary environment from the credential society of their parents and its status in the world to an entirely new *vocabulary of their lives*, of altered expectations and requirements that they must navigate on their own because the past and past supports are little guide. In this chapter, I also explore the recessionary generation's changing relationship to formerly marginalized areas outside the major metropolitan centers of Tokyo and Osaka and the alternative spaces and livelihoods created by some who "migrate" or "turn" to these locales. The child, the young adult, and the countryside share a common fate of being the objects of devaluation and revaluation at different times in Japan's modern history.[37] What I seek to show in this last chapter is how the overturning of the previous developmental timeline of the credential society has affected the recessionary generation's notions of the time of their lives. For some, there is a new sense of time that includes the revalorization of spaces of life and spaces outside major urban centers. The young who live in this new time are rethinking the spaces and places of their lives.

Fieldwork with members of the first recessionary generation—those who are part of what the Japanese and international press have referred to as the "lost generation"—has been a pleasure. I found that many of these young adults have a keen understanding of what is changing but often felt ambivalent toward both the disciplinary power structures of their parents' generation and the neoliberal rationales of governance and globalization's naturalization of international competition, for which they were instructed to accept and prepare.

I use the frame of alternative futures and spaces in the second half of Chapter Six to reflect what I learned and witnessed in the spaces of mutuality and creative negotiation with past and present some of these young people are creating. New approaches to life making reveal an explicit critique of the extractive practices of capitalist modernity, both human and environmental. In this final chapter, I discuss how, in the era of recessionary effects and the aftermath of the Fukushima triple disasters, the new generation no longer views personal exploitation, local cultural destruction, or environmental sacrifice as inevitable. I explore what comes out of this world of recession, with its shifts in discourse and requirements, its displacements of the past, and social engineering projects of the present. How are possibilities opened up as others are foreclosed?

Chapter One

Historical Crossings and Recessionary Effects

The child problem was a social category built up of examples provided by the media, popular commentators, educators, psychologists, and the government. What made this late 1990s social category so potent were cultural and institutional investments in the period of childhood and the idea of the child stretching back to the Meiji modernity project and forward to mid-twentieth-century anthropological knowledge about culture and personality. This combined production of knowledge linked the Japanese child's development to national identity, forcefully influencing late twentieth-century discourses of dependency. For a non-Western place like Japan, equalizing itself with the West at the end of the nineteenth century meant confronting Japan's temporal position as child—measured in civilizational and social evolutionary terms—against the "adult," civilized, *full-in-time* West. Moving out of what Stefan Tanaka has called Japan's "self-incurred immaturity" required a wholesale transformation of the archipelago's times and spaces.[1] National unification (post-1860) was thus a project of the conversion of the cultural, temporal, and natural diversity that had characterized Tokugawa (1603–1867) society and politics. The social and cultural development of the child became representationally and practically conflated with the late nineteenth-century national unification of temporality and spatiality, as well as postwar standardization and homogenization. As children moved through the new education system, the child's development was seized upon as evidence of national advancement from heterogeneous temporalities into a homogeneous progressive time.

This transformation of the population involved mass movement from rural to urban spaces in the Taisho and early Showa periods (1912–1945). As David Ambaras shows in his insightful discussion of the history of juvenile delinquency in early to mid-twentieth-century Japan, young rural workers in the urban environment became the focus of state management and concern. Summing up this past in light of late twentieth-century social anxieities, Ambaras writes, "If today's Japanese are losing their ethical moorings . . . they have been losing them for a long time—indeed for as long as authorities have been trying to anchor them."[2]

Key theorists and historians of the modern category of childhood— Jacqueline Rose, Claudia Casteneda, Carolyn Steedman, Denise Riley, Stefan Tanaka, and Karatani Kojin—each situate issues of youth management and control within the new times of capitalist modernity and the structures and timelines of comparison that modern nation-states began to impose on each other. These authors pose key questions about the historically new attention—financial, emotional, and ideological—focused on the young. They show how the time of physical maturation became a metaphor for progressive human development and the quality of the national development of particular nation-states.

How did individual development become synonymous with the progression of national development for a non-Western state like Japan? In "The Discovery of the Child," Karatani Kojin argues:

> Although the objective existence of children seems self-evident, the "child" we see today was discovered and constituted only recently. . . . Of course children have existed since ancient times, yet "the child" as we conceive of it and objectify it did not exist prior to a particular period. The question is not what is elucidated by psychological research about children but what is obscured by the very concept of "the child."[3]

As Karatani emphasizes, the child category, a historically specific body of knowledge about the period of growth newly named childhood, was not a Japanese invention but part and parcel of the practical, geographical, and temporal remaking of localities, and the territories of others, into national and imperial spaces. Forming children into citizen-subjects of the imagined communities of nation-states meant reconceiving the time of their growth as a time of national-cultural inculcation and training. Attention, investments, and emotional connection to the developmental time of the child in Western nation-states also became a means of justifying Western tutelage in other locations. Ashis Nandy and Hugh Cunningham reveal the utility of comparisons between the child of the poor at home and the childlike colonial abroad. The applicability of this child knowledge was not lost on nation-states in need of a figure that could stand for future growth, development of the state, and the timelessness of the nation. The child became the bodily and mental material of national cohesion and change.

In Japan, reconceptualizations of time and space meant that existing ideas and lived practices of temporality and spatiality became associated with a prior time. Localities were made the focus of this redefining and reallocating to an earlier temporal moment, as would be the case for Taiwan, Korea, and China several decades later. The transformative time of child to adult, formerly associated with the customs, locality, and the immediate spaces of the child's birth, was ascribed the role of representing the directional time of national progress. In other words, this time of growth, formerly locally defined and celebrated, which stood for itself, underwent a conversion. The Japanese child came to stand for the temporal values of a nation seeking to move itself out of *the time of the child* into which Western timelines of progress had inscribed it. To serve as an analogy for the new time, the child and childhood had to be transposed from their immediate time and space to a representational figure of the ever-forward in-common time (a key feature of Benedict Anderson's "imagined communities") that all Japanese were moving through and into. Applying this new time to Japan, Tanaka tracks how the category of the child emerged along with schools, clocks, calendars, and, of course, industry and the military. All played a part in charting, measuring, and inculcating the concept of in-common time and the practices of a shared identity. Conceptualizations of childhood and education changed again with the policies and ideologies of imperialism, total war, and ideological inculcation in Japan in the early twentieth century. The Meiji national education system played a major role in the inculcation of empire under the names of "family-state" and "national body."

In the 1940s and 1950s, Japanese childhood and education became the focus of a new anthropological approach to culture known at the time as "culture and personality." Ruth Benedict's *Patterns of Culture* (1934) provided conceptual underpinning for the idea that the mental makeup of different peoples was the result of their social environment and transmission during childhood, rather than of their racial or biological heritage. For Ruth Benedict and Margaret Mead, culture was plural, psychological, and relative, rather than singular and hierarchical.[4] Mead notes that their work was responsible for the introduction into everyday speech of the phrase *in their culture.* Childhood for the proponents of culture and personality was conceptualized as a "laboratory" for the study of cultures as "integrated," "articulated," holistic, and ultimately patternable by the knowing anthropologist.[5] The pattern of a culture synthesized and essentialized difference. Each culture became understandable as a separate and bounded whole. In the process, however, diversity and contradiction were converted into coherence.[6]

This anthropological approach meshed well with the immediate postwar needs of the U.S. government for a definitive view of their former enemy, Japan.[7] The trajectory later turned on itself, however, as the Japanese claimed and appropriated the discourse on their national character, unique personality, and non-Western psyche. During the period of the 1940s when fieldwork in Japan and other non-Western locations became impossible, Mead and Benedict came up with a program for the "study of culture at a distance." Honed during their work in the field in the prior decade, the idea was to consolidate what they had learned and apply their new analytic tools to postwartime needs. In this way, culture and personality became psychological studies of the "national character" of those societies with whom the Allies were (or had been) at war:

> If culture was indeed "personality writ large," then collective psyche of an entire nation—its distinctive configuration of temperament, values, *Weltanschauung*—could be illuminated from the analysis of its literary, artistic, and religious creations.[8]

Benedict's *Chrysanthemum and the Sword: Patterns of Japanese Culture* is the most famous example. Commissioned by the U.S. Office of War Information in the mid-1940s, it continues to hold sway among psychologically informed approaches to the study of Japan. In *Chrysanthemum and the Sword,* Japanese child rearing becomes the key to the pattern and personality of Japanese culture that, as Benedict notes, a focus on the adult could never disclose: "Japanese childrearing makes clearer many of their (Japanese) national assumptions about life which we have so far described only at the adult level."[9] One of the central characteristics of childhood and its contribution to understanding the configuration of culture in Japan, according to Benedict, was the uniqueness of the mother–child relationship. In "The Child Learns," (chapter 12), Benedict focuses on this special mother–child bond, establishing through it Japanese distinctiveness and difference from the West (for which the United States serves as her main example). Childhood, which in the West is a time of restriction and the forming of individuality, in Japan is characterized by freedom and learning dependence on others (starting with the mother), an unindividuation that will later be called groupism.[10]

Benedict's characterizations of Japanese national character and culture influenced anthropologists and others writing and thinking about Japan well into the late 1990s. Praised by many for rendering comprehensible "the most alien enemy," Benedict's *Chrysanthemum and the Sword*, which she wrote without going to Japan or speaking Japanese, became (for Japan) what Sonia Ryang has called "a face saving alibi."[11] Benedict's *Chrysanthemum* and its personality as culture approach provided the vocabulary for an emerging genre of native national identity writing in Japan by Japanese that began in the late 1950s and developed into a full-blown Japanese authored national character literature by the early 1970s.

Doi's Dependency and Kawai's Independence

In the 1950s work of Takeo Doi, the child's development, beginning with the earliest relationship with the mother, is made fully exemplary of the uniqueness of interpersonal relations in Japanese society and culture. A Freudian psychologist by training, Doi gained his insights about Japanese culture during his own "anthropological" experience as a student of psychology in the 1950s in the United States. Doi's "discovery" of *amae* (rendered in English as "dependency" and "indulgence") repeats the Benedictian culture and (or as) personality, a patterning of national character approach, with a reverse essentialist difference.[12] In the writings of Doi, Benedict and Mead's *in their culture* took on a new force in the Japanese postwar high-growth economic climate of the late 1960s and early 1970s. In his first and most famous book, *The Structure of Dependency (Amae no Kōzō)*, Doi, like Benedict, neglects the historical trajectory and histories of modernity, imperialism, and colonialism of the Japanese nation-state, as well as the pre- and postwar processes of rapid modernization, urbanization, and the nationalization of local cultures. *Amae*, maintained Doi, was the foundation for Japanese socialization processes and interpersonal relations, as well as the explanation for cultural coherence and continuity.[13] The ongoing repetition of this difference was provided by the body of research on cross-cultural child development, socialization, and early education, in which, for the most part, historical moments and their specific meanings were generalized to create a sense of continuity and stability.[14] Dependency, according to Doi, was an old principle, expressed in the uniquely Japanese term of *amaeru*, from the root *amae* or sweetness. Doi popularized the verbal form extending the word *sweet* to the innocent reliance on others. As the contingencies of history would have it, Doi's theory met fertile discursive ground in Japan that the "culture and personality" school of anthropological theorization about Japanese culture had made available.

The recessionary period, which began in the early 1990s, marked the waning of Doi's culturalist theory of dependency. Doi had depicted Japanese culture as national character, though the operations of the nation-state are hardly mentioned. He had characterized the Japanese as members of a consumer capitalist society who somehow retained a deep and culturally inflected psychological difference, despite the fragmenting and individuating processes of consumer capitalism. One of the key components of this psychological difference, according to Doi, was a non- or anti-individual dependency. The persistence of Doi's dependency through the early 1990s was due at least in part to its neglect, borrowed from earlier psychological theories of culture, of the complexities of modernity in Japan, among them the complicated trajectories of individual and collective.

Yoshino Kosaku and Tessa Morris-Suzuki argue that Doi's influence, was a product of its time, not to mention the sheer number of his publications, over twenty self-authored volumes. Kosaku refers to this time in the early 1970s as the second moment of Japanese postwar cultural nationalism and the genre of writing known as *Nihonjinron*, or Japanese discourses on Japaneseness. Kosaku calls the late 1940s and 1950s the first moment or the "introspection boom," a time that coincides with translations and commentary on Ruth Benedict's *Chrysanthemum and the Sword* and the (1945–1952) American Occupation's remaking of Japanese educational and constitutional systems.

The first moment was also characterized by the introduction of modernization theory into Japan and East Asia as Michael Latham and Victor Koschmann cogently outline.[15] Latham shows how modernization theorists borrowed from Benedict's patterns and personalities. Western modernizers in Japan and elsewhere saw in the idea of holistic cultures the potential of "a spectrum" along which the "traditional" might move toward the "modern" rather than an "immutable barrier" between "savagery" and "civilization."[16] The modernizer's task was to carefully guide non-Western nations along the proper developmental path to capitalist modernization. In the case of Japan, this required a turning away from and redefining of the prewar past. In American modernizing terms, Japan's prewar period was a nonmodern feudal time, a "dark valley" that could and should be moved (temporally) beyond. In this conception, Japan's occupation of and war in Asia was simply backward, never mind the fascism of the national body, family-state, and pure blood lines, rather than colonial and imperial.

The second moment identified by Kosaku is characterized by a focus on groupism, verticality, and dependence versus Western individualism, horizontality, and independence.[17] Tessa Morris-Suzuki describes how cultural nationalism of this second moment was inflected with policy and technology narratives as well. In her *Beyond Computopia*, she describes the search for a "unifying theme" by Japanese industry that would share discursive space with Doi's dependency for the low-growth late 1970s. The narrative and industrial shift that emerged in post-1973 in Japan was at the time called the "information society" (what we now refer to as the knowledge economy). Former Prime Minister Nakasone, a champion of the information society narrative, admonished American heterogeneity and lauded assumed Japanese homogeneity and groupism for its superior information flow.[18] A technical fix for postindustrial conditions, the information society narrative in Japan borrowed from Doi's dependency theory and other cultural nationalist ideas, wedding them to a utopian vision of human capital development, which by the mid-1990s had come to a crashing halt.

The change in status of Doi's theory of dependent selves during the recessionary period has been noted by a number of writers. Its replacement and displacement by Hayao Kawai's *independence* has not. Kawai's independence (Chapter Three) deemphasizes homogeneity, shared bodily training, and creates a new notion of collectivity. (Kawakami's worries about the decline of bodily comportment and communication, often referred to as *shitsuke*

(Chapter Four), are a reflection of this shift). *Shitsuke*, often rendered as "manner training," was closely associated with postwar industrial society and the culture of dependency.

In the mid-1990s, Kawai, a clinical psychologist in Kyoto (not far from Kobe) and author of many Jungian-inspired books about Japanese national identity, was enlisted by the MOE to reinvent Doi's dependency theory for the recessionary period. It was precisely dependency's consensual model of homogeneous character that educational officials and Kawai's psychology fixed on for transformation. For Kawai, this was a first opportunity to turn what had been his formerly marginalized position in western Japan into a central one and, in so doing, to promote his long-time interest in Jungian psychology. As Kawai notes in many books and public lectures, an independent heart is part of an inner frontier and the individual's own responsibility. In the world of Kawai's inner frontiers, there are no limits. Everyone has "his or her own story." Kawai as a Jungian was a believer in the often wholesale application of folktales and myth, in place of history, to everyday reality.

The recessionary period has been a time for new theories about the individual and social psyche. In 1999, the MOE, long criticized by the public for the excessive pressure of the exam system and called to do something to address the child problem, began to talk about reforming education to make it "suitable" (*fusawashī*) for the supposed changes in the child. The introduction of Kawai's thought into education ideas and policy coincided with the Japanese government moving out of the role of educational guidance. Prior to the 1990s recession, junior high and high school graduates were "guided" to jobs out of high school as a result of a special system of employment security offices designated for this purpose.[19] These and other social supports were in the process of change at that point, as was the very language of expectation and the requirements of the credential society. As Takehiko Kariya points out, by the late 1990s, credentials were on the verge of giving way to discrete skills and risk-bearing individuals in a new inherently unequal "learning capital society."[20]

In Chapters Two and Three, I extend Kariya's discussion to show how the Japanese government targeted education for psychologizing and neoliberalizing. With the help and advice of Kawai, the MOE created and circulated a set of new terms: strength to live, independence, self-development, responsibility, and inner frontiers. Kawai provided the Japanese government and the MOE a formula for converting prior postwar forms of cultural nationalism into neoliberal ones. Out of this meeting of education and psychology, within the shifting national character and subject-producing mandates of dependency to independence what I call *neoliberal patriotism* emerged. *Neoliberal patriotism* is an effect of the particularity of the introduction and application of neoliberal rationales of governance into the Japanese social, institutional, and discursive environment. Its productivity and strength are a result of a *twist* or inversion. The secret of the twist is not to reinvent but to resituate and recirculate former identity terms (or oppositional terms of identity, such as *independent* and *heart*) in the context of social class separations taking place amidst the economic liberalizing of the recession. The "heart" (*kokoro*), with its deep lexical and historical associations with Japanese national and cultural identity discourse, was a wise choice for transformation.[21] Reassociating the heart away from its postwar set of associations with Doi's dependency and toward independence, Kawai and the MOE sought to create not only a different national-cultural vocabulary but to alter the ways Japanese individuals imagined and experienced their own emotional development and the conditions of their national attachment. The following is an early example of how Kawai framed this change:

> Up until now we have counted on tacit understanding [*ishin denshin*] . . . but in this age of internationalism and globalization, what we need is Japanese heart [*kokoro*] and the independence to meet the global standard.[22]

Many in the early 2000s interpreted this language of the heart as a return to previous moments when the Japanese government alternately demanded and required individual, regional, cultural, and bodily sacrifices in the name of national unity—from the Meiji period's "civilization and enlightenment" to the imperial ideology and campaigns of the "East Asian Co-Prosperity Sphere" and finally "the peace and prosperity" program of the postwar.[23] The call for a unified national emotion or sensibility was a common thread at some point in most of these national projects and the ideologies that accompanied them. The return in the twenty-first century to a language of the heart therefore appeared similar to neonationalist calls like those of manga artist Yoshinori Kobayashi to repair a severed collectivity in the face of recessionary policies of division and separation. Kobayashi's concern with deteriorating national devotion caused him and others to excavate tropes of war, shorn of their historical specificity and often accuracy, in the case of

Japan's previous wars and occupation of parts of Asia, as necessary examples of collective identification and mutual sacrifice. Unlike Kawai's new heart language, Kobayashi's patriotic impulse does not, however, individualize, nor does it emerge from the trajectory of psychologically informed ideas of culture, following Doi and others. Kobayashi's project(s) (he has several) bend and conflate historical events and references to create a space, however inflammatory and discriminatory, for selectively shared identification. Kawai and the MOE want it both ways. Their language of the heart is individualizing and selectively collectivizing: Raise yourself and (self-) develop a heart that loves your country;[24] national allegiance without former supports, protections, or complaints.

The Kawai and Kawakami projects were also far apart.[25] The history of training and social management that created the communal subject-body, whose demise Kawakami fears, runs counter to the new independent heart language, emotional educational programs, and morals curriculum I witnessed over the period of my fieldwork.[26] For Kawai and other recessionary reformers, the key has been to *reengineer* the discursive realm of the social subject in two related ways: inverting, repurposing, and deploying former terms of cultural collectivity in changed ways and contexts and disparaging former terms and educational practices. What resulted was the particular inflection and temporality of neoliberal rationales of governance I refer to as *neoliberal patriotism*: a retracting, though not shrinking, of the state, and its coincident reintervention in new forms and different places.

The rationale for the 2000s version of heart language, associated terms of individualism, self-strengthening, and the education reform program was the child problem. Problematizing the Japanese child and then seeking to fix the child with this new language and reformed education was a reaction to much more than the problems that children across Japan were facing regionally, economically, ethnically, and by gender due to the long economic downturn.

What (Neoliberal) Independence Looks Like: A Satire of Recessionary Effects

Recession in Japan has produced a series of effects: the rendering of the familiar strange; strangeness assigned to the form of the child; schools and education made the psychological objects of government reform; the young generation's lives saturated with neoliberal value production and its requirements. Kiyoshi Kurosawa's 2008 film *Tokyo Sonata* stages this strange new ordinary at the dinner table and between parent and child, teacher and student, boss and subordinate. The main characters—salaryman father, housewife mother, and older and younger brothers—live a contemporary life full of sudden changes for which they appear completely unprepared. The mother and father in *Tokyo Sonata* cling to their roles and the common sense of their generation, only to be forced to acknowledge when they reach their sometimes fatal limits (the antithesis of the seemingly all open *frontiers within* I discuss in Chapter Three) that the recession has altered the future irreparably and the former ways of the past are obsolete.

Some have compared *Tokyo Sonata* to the 1983 family parody *Family Game* (*Kazoku Geemu*), directed by Yoshimitsu Morita and recently in serial form. But whereas the 1980s film accentuates the ironies of a family dominated by the commonsense subordination of all life to the credential society narrative of school and work success, *Tokyo Sonata* depicts a time of shared experience and identification unraveling.[27] In *Family Game* the sacrifices and abuses of the postwar developmental narrative (good home → top school → lifetime job → managed life-course) are exposed outright. *Tokyo Sonata* evidences how the violence of the world of recession has turned inward, bearing down on the individuated, independent subject, who because independent only has themselves to blame. *Tokyo Sonata* does not romanticize silence and forbearance as examples of national character. Rather, the film situates its characters and their actions and reactions fully within the changing scenes of the recessionary period, eerily so at times: sudden employment redundancy, the reserve army of young part-time labor, full-time housewives presented with a future without the security of male full-time breadwinners, and young children who seem more prescient than their parents.

As the film opens, the father, Mr. Sasaki, is at the office. His activities and relations with others suggest a middle management lifetime employee. He is suddenly called into the boss's office, where he is asked what he will do once he leaves the company! Literally unable to speak, Sasaki packs his few belongings and exits the office. We see his replacement, an impeccably dressed young Chinese woman with nearly flawless Japanese, who will work for half of Sasaki's salary. The scene is a terrifying enactment of replacement on many levels: Japan taken over by a China that can produce not only cheap but quality labor; the destruction of the lifetime employment seniority system; the rendering meaningless of the developmental time of Sasaki's generation; and a change in representation itself, as Sasaki encounters recessionary language and expectations.

Sasaki descends from the office into the park below. With nowhere to go and nothing to do for the first time in his adult life, he notices other men his age sitting in the park in the middle of the workday. This is the beginning of Sasaki's reeducation. Paying new attention to the conversations of men idling in the park, he overhears one of the ragged-looking older men warning a younger well-attired companion to head over to *Hello Work* (the new employment offices) "unless you want to end up like me." We see the salaryman—the one-time icon of Japan's twentieth-century economic success and so-called economic miracle—reduced to the status of the precariat, the disposable and exchangeable part-time labor force, known as the *furītā*, regularly ridiculed for their inability to find work. The flexible labor regime and its neoliberal lexicon of discreet and mobile skills suddenly confronts Sasaki, a product of the credential and seniority society of the past. From one scene to the next, we witness the temporal and cultural devaluation of the salaryman and all he has stood for.

Some of the starkest moments are those in which Sasaki appears incapable of either comprehending or responding to what is being asked of him by younger people in positions of authority. The story of *Tokyo Sonata* flips Kawakami's dread about the young bodies that do not absorb language. It is indeed as if the systems of representation and authority have shifted to such a degree that the past is no longer recognized by the present. Sasaki's adult body, representing the fulfillment of a system of cultural and national training, seems just as redundant as his former position in the company. He and his timeline have been rendered valueless and meaningless. As Sasaki is standing in another park sometime later, watching rows of restructured men march off to nowhere, we hear him say, "The lifeboats are all gone, all gone . . ."[28]

After showing this film a number of times in classes at the University of Washington, I notice that my students are most affected by the young in the film. Despite the fact that we talk at length about the system of lifetime employment, the role of the public school system, cram schools, the family, and the developmental narrative, they have little sympathy for adults, like Sasaki.

They expect the salaryman father to "get over" being restructured and just do something about it. They are unaware for the most part how they have come to think this way, how their own society's neoliberal transformations over several decades of restructuring, liberalization, and rationalization have become their mind-set. They do not easily recognize and cannot identify with the violences of a life made redundant, of the strangeness of a world turned upside down for a lifetime employee like Sasaki, and the excruciating difficulties of translating his credentials—the epitome of the temporality of credential society and a life lived according to the orderliness for which Japan became so praised—into discrete skills.

My students more easily identify with the young characters in the film who make it on their own and have little connection with the protections or once imagined guarantees. One of the scenes that exemplifies the position of the young in *Tokyo Sonata* takes place at the home of a former colleague of Sasaki's, also an unemployed worker, who asks Sasaki to his home in an effort to keep up the elaborate, but tragic, secret he is keeping from his family about his unemployment. Though the two men attempt to keep the loss of their jobs a secret, the friend's elementary school–aged daughter not only seems to know what is going on but articulates it better than the adults. With a small towel in her hand, she comes up silently behind Sasaki, as he stands at the sink in the bathroom and whispers, as she hands him the towel, "It's tough for you too, isn't it, Mr. Sasaki?"[29] How and what does she know? The next time we see the young girl, she is dressed all in black, standing with a relative in front of her now-vacant family home—her parents have committed suicide.

There is also the Sasaki family older brother who volunteers for a fictitious U.S. military program for young Japanese adults who cannot find work in Japan. And then there is Kenji, the Sasaki's younger son. He seems out of place in the ordinary arenas for children his age. Standing up to his teacher, he forcefully defends himself against the teacher's spurious disciplining in front of the class, causing a minor revolt among the other students. Suddenly Kenji becomes interested in piano lessons. Defying his father's wishes, he finds a broken toy piano and begins to practice. Within a very short time (the span is unclear; one to two years at most) he has become a piano prodigy. His teacher is amazed. She asks if anyone else plays piano in the family. If so, it must be nature rather than culture. Suddenly transformed into a mature pianist (even his hand position is that of a long-studied player), he excels at the entrance performance for a renowned music school, seemingly overturning the relationship between time and value that in many ways has been a central theme of the film all along. At the end of Kenji's performance of Claude Debussy's "Clair de Lune," the audience is left with a sense of the separation of individual and national time. The separation is made further evident by the figures of the young who are not products of any developmental, progressive scheme of reproduction but are instead set adrift in a sea of uncertainty to make it on their own. *This is the time of prodigies*: those who find their own latent potential. For the others, the world of recession is a time in which the sacrifices of adults and children—women as mothers, men as workers and fathers, and children as educational laborers—no longer add up to the perceived lifetime guarantees of the past.

In "Neoliberalizing Space," Jamie Peck and Adam Tickell characterize the shift that occurred in Britain and the United States during the governments of Thatcher and Reagan in the 1980s as "rollback" neoliberalism. This was a new form of liberalism with little connection to examples of liberal governance like the New Deal in the United States. This new liberalism removed legal impediments to mass layoffs, downsizing, and the defunding of the public sector, inverting notions of individual responsibility, "freedom," and the "individual" to mean the bearer of risk for personal futures. In 1980s Japan, then Prime Minister Nakasone had similar ideas about rolling back in the midst of a low-growth economy. Facing pollution scandals, currency issues with the United States, and a post–oil crisis world, Nakasone felt the need to reorient the Japanese export-based economy toward a knowledge, or information, economy and society. Seeking to introduce neoliberal notions into Japan's education system and other sectors of public life, he and his special committee on education reform first came up with the phrase "low-pressure education" (*yutori kyōiku*).[30] Low-pressure education was intended to reduce the burden on the Japanese government for the progressive distribution of education resources, a policy that provided equal education facilities for all regions of Japan. The least well-off received the most funds.[31] As sociologists of education in Japan argued at the time, and throughout the 1990s, real reform would be aimed at the hypercompetitiveness of the education system and not its progressive aspects—the hard-fought results of the teacher's union's postwar campaigns for educational and social equity.[32]

Nakasone did not succeed in pushing through the defunding and individualization of risk that took place in the United States and Britain in the
1980s. This all changed in the 1990s as recessionary uncertainty gave way
to "the child problem," which became a source of national concern and a
convenient rationale for reform. As Takehiko Kariya, Hidenori Fujita, Hirota Teruyuki, and other Japanese sociologists of education have argued,
withdrawing support and guidance runs contrary to the necessary goal of
updating the Japanese educational system to meet the postbubble needs of
all children and families in Japan equally. These scholars have opposed the
wholesale reform of Japanese education, as if the entire system was a problem. In Chapter Two, I situate the MOE's criticisms of schooling within the
long and important history of national education's role in the struggle over
equity, rights, and the role of education in a capitalist economy.

Peck and Tickell help us understand the global reach, changes in and
national inflections of neoliberalism as rationales of government originally
understood as a system of removing or dismantling and deregulating social
services and support. They admit to being surprised at what followed. An-
ticipating the demise of a system that took things away from the public, especially in Britain, Peck and Tickell describe what they call neoliberalism's
extraordinary "transfigurative capacity."[33] What they called "rollback" was
followed by what they refer to as "rollout," or the active building up of the
state in selective ways, as they put it, to "find a way to contain" the dispos-
session of all those people out of work and left to fend for themselves.[34]

In *Tokyo Sonata*, director Kiyoshi Kurosawa seems to capture what I
describe in the following chapters as an "all-rolled-into-one, rollback and
rollout" neoliberalization in Japan. Well-known and expected systems of
support in schools and work were rolled back following the collapse of the
bubble economy of the 1980s.[35] Simultaneously, the language of strength and
independence, self-responsibility and skills, was rolled out. Ability was made
discrete and measurable. Hence the emphasis in *Tokyo Sonata* on abilities and
skills (*nōryoku*). Finding ways to obtain these skills has become the individual's problem, as the restructured father of *Tokyo Sonata* learns.[36] Deregu-
lated labor leaves the older son without a job and nowhere to look besides
the military. The younger son ends up completely on his own. In the world
of an all-rolled-into-one mind-set, only prodigies—the epitomes of "self-
development"—survive, leaving no sense of how to reproduce the timeline
of their development on a national scale.

Jacques Donzelot, in a powerful essay, "Michel Foucault and Liberal Intelligence," helps to elaborate on the particularity of this "new" or "neoliberalism":

> Neoliberalism is not a revival of old liberal themes; it carries a shift in the role of the State and conception of exchange. Neo-liberals do not introduce unregulated space for laissez-faire; they produce conditions for competition. Government acts on society itself, so it can be regulated by the market. *Homo economicus* has only competitors. Situated in a game, he applies himself to increasing his successful outcomes in a system of inequalities. . . . The entrepreneur in the game is eminently governable . . . because he governs himself, modifies his conduct (the conduct of conduct). So one can make him responsible for it.[37]

In line with how new modes of economic rationality made their way into Japanese professional and personal life and the staging of this by director Kurosawa, the importance of the physical body comes back forcefully. The child is also a child body. It is this body that was the focus of Japan's and other countries' national projects. Junior high teacher Kawakami (Introduction and Chapter Four) makes this clear in his horror at "bodies that don't absorb language" and in the image of the "strange child"—a body transforming from a uniformed school child into a small monstrous creature. What is important here, returning to what I have previously discussed, is that the remedies, reforms, and the government-inspired psychologically informed language welcomes the transformations in these bodies. This is one reason for the absence of teachers on the big education reform committees. Administrators and psychologists are appointed, but no one from a physical school site. This lack of teachers on high-level committees is due to government replacing the trajectory of the child body with one of emotions and "the heart"—a notion that borrows from the sense of a unified population but is not invested in the training or creation of the individual or this unity. It is up to the individual, as we see from the opening moments on of *Tokyo Sonata*.

Tokyo Sonata also responds to the earlier notion of the irresponsible bodies of the present. The priorities of unified, disciplined bodies, the body politic of the Meiji period's slogan, "creating people," or "the national body" (*kokutai*) of wartime ideology, and the disciplines of postwar homogeneity, groupism, and manner training (*shitsuke*) have shifted. *Tokyo Sonata* reveals

a present in which time and finances are no longer directed at the standardization of the body; a time in which a common language of the body is absent. Father Sasaki's second humiliation at an interview for a much lesser
job returns us to the issue of incomprehensibility. Asked by a much younger
interviewer to articulate his skills and abilities, a basic question of human
capital *self*-development, Sasaki is dumbfounded and speechless. It is as if the
words and world of representation to which he belongs have collapsed. In
a surprising inversion of the temporality of the strange and incomprehensible student, here it is the developmental past embodied in the senior employee, made strange. When asked, "What are your skills?" Sasaki freezes.
In a last-ditch effort to close the gap in representation, Sasaki walks over to
the younger interviewer and whispers his former company title. Unaffected
by a name that stands for a trajectory disparaged by neoliberal rationales, the
younger man laughs, and the interview is over. The scene is a double parody of the seemingly natural way in which a regime of self-development has
replaced and deposed dependency and its form credential society, and the
callousness of self-development and independence to other forms and lived
experiences of value.

Making sure the game continues, as Donzelot explains, the entrepreneur
of the self must continue to compete and therefore do the work of the state
on him- or herself. "What can you do?" the young interviewer in *Tokyo Sonata* asks. Sasaki's response of his position in the company falls on deaf ears.
Neither the body nor the mind of the young interviewer comprehends. It is
the language of the changed conditions of individual development, of independence, portable flexibility, individual responsibility, and, in the Japanese
context, a heart of latent potential. It is a language that shifts responsibility
to the individual to, as Donzelot puts it, work on him- or herself, to constantly improve and excavate his or her own frontiers.

Abenomics' World of Recession, Post-Fukushima

In the May 18, 2013, issue of *The Economist*, Prime Minister Shinzo Abe was
featured as "Super-Abe" sailing through the air with a blue cape. Was this
depiction intended to suggest some kind of return of Japanese invincibil-
ity? If so, following the cataclysmic disasters of Fukushima, it was strange
to see. Abe's first term (2004–2006) had been marked by a major pension

scandal and the controversial revision of the 1947 Fundamental Law of Education. As it turns out, the Super-Abe image had little to do with either. It referred instead to Abe-nomics, the name given to the prime minister's second-term economic plan for moving beyond nearly a decade and a half of deflation and recession. According to *The Economist*'s four-page spread, Abe-nomics includes strategies of "rebranding" and "reawakening." The magazine praises Abe and his government's strategies for kick-starting an off-economy, urging "inward-looking youth" to take on global challenges—why they might turn inward under these conditions is left unexplored—and repair "wounded national pride." The magazine expresses concern and surprise, however, over Abe's "backward looking nationalism," "an unwelcome remnant" of an earlier time, and an obstacle, as it were, to Japan's forward-moving liberalizing path.[38] *The Economist* fails to consider how liberalization might go hand in hand with a new nationalism within the conditions of recessionary Japan. Overlooked, moreover, is that Abe's second-term growth strategy obscures the sacrifices—human and environmental—of earlier growth agendas, doubly so the sacrifices required by neoliberal reforms of education and labor, which have created a patriotism that nationalizes and individualizes.

During the winter and spring of 2012–2013, I returned several times to Kobe. During these visits, I met with a group of women I knew to talk about what the recession meant to them. Many things had changed since the beginning of my fieldwork there at the end of 1990s. More than a decade had passed since the Youth A incident, and this group of women was focused on what they called "no more leeway" (*yutori ga nai*). What was once imagined as the Japanese middle-class consciousness of "work hard and things will get better" (at one time over 90 percent of Japanese polled identified as middle-class) has shifted into a recessionary consciousness of no latitude and no protection. In the good relaxed times, the year's end brought a bonus and work was regular, one of the women said:

> Things have gotten cheaper. "Is that price okay?" Cheap things are scary, department stores are empty, but education costs haven't gone down. Kids don't know the bubble period. There's a sense of uneasiness all around, of foreboding. Even if you want to become a full-time housewife, you can't anymore. What in the world should we do? We can't give them advice, even if parents think something is good.[39]

Others in the group talked about "raising kids for global times." The women clarified "global rearing" as "if you get restructured, you can start again." This is not only a problem of the head, they went on, but of the body, of having the physical stamina and perseverance to keep going in the face of uncertainty. The husband of one of the women avoided restructuring by quitting his lifetime employment position to start a small business. It's been hard, he said. "What you expect and what is expected have completely changed":[40]

> Where are the limits? The Japanese way was identified with lifetime employment; now it's an early retirement system. Slimming down. Lots of bankruptcies this year. Individual ability is mobile now; people have to take it with them. Those with strength can move. It's a money game now, people move often. . . . How to adapt?

For many I talked to and spent time with from the late 1990s through 2013, the recession had altered individual and national relationships in such a way as to make them unrecognizable. Over the course of my fieldwork, discursive terms that regularly reinforced common understandings of Japan's postwar developmental system seemed to be falling by the wayside. Terms of commonality were being replaced with a recessionary language that put the self-responsibilitized individual at the center.

These were not the kinds of answers that the housewives in Kobe, the woman at the cash machine, and the mother at school participation day (in the opening of the Introduction) or my businessman friend in Kobe anticipated in raising questions of their own such as, "What are the new limits?" They hoped for government and corporate guidance and preparation in an era of change. What they got instead, along with other parents, teachers, managers, and young people, was an entirely new language and conditions of life that rendered the past redundant.[41]

The first Abe administration (2004–2006) appointed various spokespeople to explain or, more pointedly, sell these new ideas to the Japanese people. Education ministry officials took to the airwaves to justify how changes in government involvement would be better for all—more freedom for the individual and less financial burden for the government. The child problem, as ostensible problem, seemed to demand a remedy. It was one of the reasons the MOE message was easy to sell.[42] As government support receded, recessionary language flooded the public sphere, and the private schooling industry stepped in. How this happened, the ways the education industry appealed to anxious parents trying to navigate the shift from dependence to independence, is the focus of Chapter Five. The supplementary school industry took advantage of the shifting burden of responsibility and lack of preparation for the changes, belittled the government for stranding the public, and promoted itself as the new expert in securing individual futures.

According to their parents, young Japanese born from the end of the 1980s on have little connection with the twentieth-century past of their parents and grandparents. This is a source of serious concern to older generations. Those raised prior to recessionary times hardly recognize the young who inhabit them.[43] For the youth born into the beginning of the recessionary 1990s, the stability of the 1960s through the 1980s and so-called guaranteed futures of the credential society and its developmental narrative are unavailable and unrecognizeable. Though that time and its conditions are no longer present in their lives, they continue to experience the burden of its erasure. Bankruptcy, restructuring (*ristora*), and the recessionary language of self-development are the new terms of their time. For their parents, these are strange terms that suggest somewhere else, like the United States or China, not Japan.[44] As one of my young interviewees related to me, "My parents want me to graduate from a good school and get a good job, so I won't be stuck being a part-time worker, but why should I go to all this trouble? Even if I get into a good company, it will probably go under."[45]

Other young people are frustrated by the media representations of lethargic youth, of the things that the young are said to be deficient in as a result of their lack of effort to discover their own inner frontiers. Even as the young are required to live in completely new economic and social conditions, they have been publicly criticized and often demonized for not reproducing the supposed national character of past generations. As several of my young interlocutors put it, "Why are we viewed so badly when we are working so hard?"[46]

In the following chapters, I expand on the effects of the recessionary period, the forms they take, what these forms reveal, what they further obscure, and the arenas of education and psychology they bring together. Effects are changes that emerge as a result of a conjuncture of long-invested ideas—in the case of the present study, the child, education, psychology of dependency, Japanese cultural difference—with the modernity projects of which these ideas are a part and internationally created events of consequence, in this case recession.[47] Managing these effects has been the work of successive Japanese governments since the early 1990s. Creating a new language of recession and policies to match, government officials and the new experts they enlist have tried to divert attention away from the extractive practices of human labor and environmental destruction of the present and past eras of capitalist modernity.

In the next chapter, I turn to the MOE's pitch to the public, how the MOE language of ending competition and responsibility appropriated the social panic of the child problem and the Youth A incident, and Japanese education scholars' opposition to misrepresentations of the past justifying present changes. Proposing remedies steeped in a language of new life energies (*ikiru chikara*), the MOE plan for education and social reform seemed to offer a new freedom from direct control by the government but did not include a discussion of the new requirements of this shift for many in Japanese society.

Chapter Two

The Ministry of Education and the Youth A Incident

Terrible times have befallen Japan. To get at the root of these problems, we need to focus on the inner self or heart of these children.[1]

Neoliberal discourse is deceptive. It replaces politics and society with emotion and psychology.[2]

In an unprecedented broadcasting of the new direction of Japanese education in the twenty-first century, MOE spokesperson Ken Terawaki was featured in a ten-part television series on school problems and proposed solutions for ending the competition in schools.[3] Appearing opposite commentators on education from both sides of the political spectrum, Terawaki responded calmly to critiques of the MOE's third major reform of education, similar in scope to reforms undertaken in the immediate postwar era and the late nineteenth century. Ultraconservatives claimed that the current plan amplified the freedoms and individualism of the 1947 FLE, whereas liberals questioned the integrity of promises for twenty-first-century change in light of the MOE history of imperial to industry-based approaches to national education.

Terawaki began by reviewing for his listeners the revised MOE position on the postwar education past. He focused on how "education from above" had created a population of docile adults. In retrospect, he explained, past educational control was flawed and now outmoded. What the government was promoting for the new century was a larger view of citizenship. The goal of Japanese education in the twenty-first century would be to create globally aware individuals who would not wish to foist responsibility off on others or expect the schools or the government to take care of them. This discursive shift was an early sign of the critique of dependency within the educational establishment and a new connection between educational discourse, policy, and clinical psychology.

The changes occurring in the education system, explained Terawaki, are far more dramatic than anything in the last fifty years. What this amounts to is that "in the end the Ministry of Education will become almost 'unnecessary.'" It means the end of schools having to do what the MOE says if they want funds.[4] It also means that the public will be more involved in education. When there are education problems from now on, the public will not have to turn to the MOE but can rather solve them on their own by developing the *strength* (a keyword of ministry reformers) that is now lacking:

> Japanese kids say they feel they don't amount to anything. They are irritated and angry all the time. They exist in a narrow world, say they don't like themselves, think that others don't care if they live or die, and don't believe their lives will ever amount to anything. In this environment, there is probably a kid nearby you that could commit the same kind of violence as that of Youth A, the fourteen-year-old, third-year junior high student from Kobe.[5] According to a survey of junior high students conducted by the MOE, following the Kobe Youth A incident, one in two kids is frustrated or wants to smash someone.[6]

Terawaki elaborated at length on the MOE slogans of ending competition and strength to live in order to mitigate what might have been construed as a burden on local schools and communities:

> In the past, many in Japan thought that the competition of exams was necessary for Japanese vitality, but the MOE thinks this is mistaken. The fight-to-win type of competition of the twentieth century is over. The twenty-first century is one of symbiosis. This means that everyone will now make the best of his or her own strong points. Those who do well under competition will not be the only ones praised. Those who don't get good marks on school exams will be viewed in terms of other areas in which they excel.[7]

In these remarks on television and elsewhere, Terawaki skipped neatly over the FLE language of educational freedom as a protected right, as he sidelined the MOE's 1950s efforts to undo this rights language and recalibrate education to the high-growth economy.[8] In 1947, the FLE had inaugurated a major break from the Imperial Rescript on Education (1890s through 1945) that had inscribed the Japanese and their colonized populations as dutiful members of an imperial "family-state." Terawaki and others' self-responsible global individual language did not mean a return to the FLE rights-bearing individual nor did it seek to thoroughly erase the role of the state. Instead, the goal was substitution and the vehicle the strange child. In other words, the larger view of citizenship that Terawaki and the MOE were promoting meant less direct intervention in the form of funding and guidance and new kinds of indirect intervention in the realm of emotion and personality, supposedly required given the problem with the child.

Terawaki similarly did not situate the problems and social unease he identified within the changing conditions of life for families following a decade of economic downturn, the first stages of liberalization, and shifting ideologies of national character. Perhaps one of the reasons for this is that *liberalization* in the context of the 1990s in Japan (earlier in the United States and Europe) stood for different forms of power and competition embedded in corporate restructuring and the rolling back of former credential society predictabilities. Employment security had become a real concern for families in Kobe and elsewhere like the baby boomer (*dankai no sedai*) father of Youth A to whom I return in the second half of this chapter. Terawaki raises questions but sidesteps the answers. Why are kids frustrated and angry? Could it have something to do with the shifting economic and ideological terrains of life? Where did Terawaki and others get the psychocultural language with which they identify problems and propose solutions?

In his book on the topic of ending the competition in schools, Terawaki begins to integrate the new terms of emotion and psychology into the MOE's 180-degree change of course for Japanese schooling. The focus is clearly on the problems of the young and the responsibility of the family:

> Terrible times have befallen Japan. To get at the root of these problems, we
> need to focus on the inner mind or heart [*kokoro*] of these children. We need
> to raise children with energy who will be able to go anywhere in the world and
> solve problems. Moreover, the Kobe wounding and killing of children incident
> has shown us that Japanese adults have become hopeless. This is not a problem
> for the schools but rather a problem that concerns education in the homes and

in the larger community. What we need now is the lifelong education of the whole society. If we do nothing, the situation among the youth could lead the society (and the world) into ruin.

So this is why we are instigating these reforms; everyone will learn what is necessary to live his or her life. The twenty-first century will be harsh, and children will have to learn things that were neglected during their parents' generation.[9] This is our way of preventing things like the Kobe incident from happening again, and this is strength for life (*ikiru chikara*).[10]

Taking aim at adults of his own baby boomer generation (Terawaki was born in 1953), it seems precisely the social engineering of his own catch-up society, once used widely as an example for non-Western development, that has become the object of ridicule and reform. Terawaki's message is careful to circumvent the forms of control of that past to think about the present and future. Neither does he offer any specific guidance for the young and their parents in understanding the social, cultural, and economic mechanisms that led to prior forms of competition. His explanation simultaneously replaces and displaces a system that catapulted Japan to worldwide fame and fortune, about which many were critical but conflicted. What are the effects of this doubled enactment on the history of difference and national identification?

Led by spokespeople like Terawaki, the MOE's public information campaign in the early 2000s had three main purposes. The first was persuasion; the second outsourcing and diverting of responsibility; the third creating the conditions within which a type of educational change would be seen as necessary and inevitable, even though it was not the one that teachers, parents, and intellectuals had requested for sometime. It was not a simple task. Persuading the public of the need for a particular kind of turnabout in educational approach, given the centrality of the educational institution in Japanese society, meant reframing public concern over the downturned economy, highly publicized violent incidents, and problems associated with the young.

The late 1990s was not the first time of national concern over schools and school-aged children. During the mid- to late 1980s, the media focused on a range of school-related problems, among them inner-school violence, bullying, and what is known in Japan as school refusal (*futokō, tōkōkyohi*).[11] What was different at the end of the 1990s and in the early 2000s moment was the conjuncture of a transforming political economy—recession and liberalization—and the discursive reframing of problems facing society in the wake of these political and economic changes in representational figures like the strange child, independence, and responsibility.

In the second opening epigraph, Manabu Sato refers to the deception and illusion surrounding changes in educational discourse. As Sato explains, the end of the Cold War brought a combination of decentralization, deregulation, and, by the early 1990s and the financial plummet of the 1990s, dramatic downsizing in the form of "slashed education budgets, reduction of public schools and a 30 percent reduction in curriculum."[12] The downsizing in education and liberalizing of the labor market between 2001 and 2006 under prime ministers Koizumi and Abe led as well to what Sato calls an "alienation of learning" and a "cultural politics in and out of the schools."[13] By alienation of learning Sato is referring to how neoliberal policies "endangered the human right of learning" by erasing the labor market for high school graduates (between 1992 and 2002) and creating what he calls a "third world country" inside Japan. According to the OECD (2005),[14] over 17 percent of Japanese children live in poverty, and over one-half of Japanese young people have no full-time work. Sato faults the media for over-publicizing problems with youth and "manufacturing crises" around them (Chapters Three and Four), leading to moral panic and cynicism in the adult population. Created or not, highly publicized problems beg solutions. As Sato notes, the neoliberal solution is privatization (Chapter Five). What then is the deception and illusion? Neoliberal discourse replaces politics and society with economics and psychology. Responsibility equals accountability. Human rights equal freedom of choice. Neoconservatives settle for emotive words in place of philosophical or historical discussion.

Roger Goodman and Keita Takeyama add to Sato's call for critical terms to counter the meanings generated within neoliberal and neoconservative discourses. Writing about the how, what, and why of Japanese education reform, Goodman cautions against too quickly assuming that Japan is simply moving in the direction of the United States or England. Of reform language, he adds, we should not assume that reform language means the same in all contexts: "Terms are multivocal, different groups, different meanings."[15] Keita Takeyama alerts us to the problem of thinking that Japan is a "global exception," hardly neoliberal at all. Why? According to exception theory, neoliberalism has little appeal in East Asian countries. Takeyama refers us to the earlier "immobility thesis" of Leonard Schoppa, used as an example by exceptionalist thinkers, about the unsuccessful efforts in the 1980s by past Prime Minister Yasuhiro Nakasone to downsize and privatize Japanese education in line with the rollback changes going on in Britain and the United States. Building on Sato's and Goodman's arguments, Takeyama counters the exceptionalists by directing us to think about "the ways that disciplinary power operates in neoliberal times."[16] (Neoliberal) disciplinary power liberates by assigning responsibility. It focuses government attention on the family. In this new politics of education, neoliberal and neonational are *complementary*; the MOE has formed tactical alliances with nationalist forces in the Liberal Democratic Party (LDP).[17]

This chapter discusses *how* this complementarity got its start in the 1990s. I describe ethnographically the particular conditions of the onset of a neoliberal disciplinary power that gave rise to the discursive figures of the strange child and child problem, shifted the focus of attention from the body to the heart and brought psychology together with education to create specific forms of neoliberal and neonational alignment. By looking at present conditions of alignment, this chapter takes account of the work that independence and other keywords of neoliberal educational and psychological discourse have done and the *neoliberal patriotism* of historical crossings and present conjunctures that has resulted. In the rest of this chapter, I explain how the MOE first and, in following chapters, others in psychology, the academy, the media, and private industry contributed to, and in some cases capitalized on, the social panic of the Youth A and other child-related events. I explain how these contributions and capitalizings required delocalizing and decontextualizing. And I begin the work of showing how contradictory terms and ideas were made to seem reasonable and how parents, teachers, and some intellectuals would be antagonistic to a lessening of competition that many had called for over a decade.

Dependency as postwar cultural characterization was both an ideological construct and a social value. It defined historically specific forms of commonality and control in the late twentieth century. It echoed back to prewar communal ideologies but also forward to service and sacrifice to the twentieth-century high-growth state. The dismissal of dependency by the MOE and others was made to seem like a necessary next step for the Japanese state and population toward fuller modernization and globalization with global individuals in the lead. In fact, the substitution of dependency for discourses of strengthening and independence was not so much a release from power and control but an exchange of one form for another, which "deceptively," according to Sato and others, seemed free of state control.

It is important to note the historical nature of this substitution. In the switch of discourse and cultural constructs is also a shift in the structure and requirements of capitalist modernity. Dependency defined a groupist model that seemed to promise a social existence less exposed to the ravages of the market than a Western individualist one. But the global individual who would not want to turn to or expect government help is one who is fully exposed to market and other forms of risk. Couched in a language of global progression, Terawaki's pitch seemed like an answer to parents' and teachers' organizations and academics' critique of the contradictions of a groupist dependent society with brutal forms of individualist competition imposed by the postwar education system. The independent global individual was not free from competition but fully exposed to all forms. For this shift to operate under the radar of many, as it did, for it to seem natural, necessary, and inevitable, depended on turning the child into a problem such that the only viable response seemed to be to fix the child, through strengthening, resocializing, individualizing, and making independent.

The Kobe Youth A Incident and the Terms of Translation

To understand how "the end of competition" became one of the namesakes for a future signified by new risks and responsibilities, we need to return to the summer of 1997 and the harrowing discovery that a mysterious set of attacks against elementary-aged students in the city of Kobe, both frightening and fatal, were perpetrated not by "an adult driving a big black sedan," as the media and other pundits originally concluded, but by an "ordinary" junior high student thereafter known as Youth A. Although dozens of books, articles, and television specials have been produced by professional analysts and laypeople alike, the incident's role as a trigger event or catalyst of reform discourse has been left generally unexplored. In the aftermath of the Youth A incident, a new category of psychological knowledge was created through which this event and other relatable problems could thereafter be defined, delimited, and viewed, obscuring the conditions in which the events took place.

Figure 2.1. Tomogaoka Junior High in Kobe.
Photo by author.

In May 1997, a third-year junior high student strangled and decapitated a sixth grader, Jun Hase (thereafter known as little Jun or *Jun-kun*), leaving the decapitated head at the foot of the gate of Tomogaoka Junior High School with a note taunting and blaming the school system (Figure 2.1). Later, it was discovered that this killing was not the first but the most violent in a series of attacks against other children that took place over the course of four months in and around Suma Ward, one of the more established new town areas in the city of Kobe. This culminating event placed Suma Ward under police surveillance, turning it into an object of media fascination. Exacerbating matters, the attacker, whose identity remained unknown for several months, followed this final act with carefully articulated descriptions of the perverse pleasure he derived from killing and the school system he held accountable for these acts by robbing him of his existence. The announcement of the capture and arrest of the perpetrator initially sent a wave of relief through this overwrought area of Kobe, only to be drowned out by the realization that the author of these acts and accusations was none other than a local fourteen-year-old junior high school student.

Horrific as it was, the decapitation itself was not what triggered the media frenzy and social panic that ensued. Rather it was the term (and idea) of "ordinary child" that the media adopted to describe Youth A and the youth's unchildlike taunts and threats to the authorities. He placed the first of these in the mouth of the murdered sixth grader. The note read: "Everyone, the game starts now. Just try to stop me. I really love killing."[18] In a follow-up letter to the local newspaper, he wrote of the revenge he planned on the school system for making him into a "transparent existence" (*tômeina sonzai*).[19] He swore revenge against those who did this to him and gave himself a range of new names, the first of which was written in English letters, "SHOOL (school) KILLER."[20] What followed was a seemingly inexorable public panic, the intensity of which social scientists have since been at a loss to explain. In the casting about for blame and a locus of responsibility, attention immediately turned to the education officials in the city of Kobe and the community in which it had taken place, in spite of the watchfulness of Japan's neighborhood associations and localized policing.

Education officials at the city and prefectural level were now faced with the daunting task of finding an explanation that would satisfy an anxious public and at the same time shift the responsibility, if only in part, away from the school. The MOE, headed at the time by Takashi Kosugi, convened high-level committees almost immediately to consider the questions of responsibility incessantly posed by the media and increasingly on everyone's mind. How had this situation developed? Did the school know about this student's problems? Did they communicate them to the family? What was their nature? Was this youth an aberration or, more chillingly, an example of deeper shared trouble of the ordinary, a challenge to the system as a whole of which he was a product? How and where should responsibility be located?

By the end of the summer of 1997, a short two months after the arrest of Youth A, Kosugi published a book describing the official interpretation of the Youth A incident. In his *In Search of the Lost Emotional Education*, the Youth A event serves as an urgent example of the need for a reform plan (still tentative at the time), with a focus on "relaxing" the pressure in the schools and refocusing on what Kosugi, and the psychological experts he enlisted (Chapter Three), determined were the inadequate social skills and cultural knowledge of young Japanese. (As I discuss in Chapter Four, *relaxed education*, or *yutori kyōiku*, was a term picked up from the Nakasone era and remade in the 1990s, targeting public schools because private schooling was not under the mandate of the MOE.) The plan for relaxing education, fewer hours and less curricula, included a diminished financial role for the central government and a compensatory shift in the responsibility for educational success to the individuals and families, whereas emotional education meant a new kind of MOE involvement.

The central education board of the city of Kobe, in conjunction with the larger prefectural board, was the first to face these difficult questions and the first to be required to provide some kind of answer to them, or at least an approach that could be articulated as the official position. As Toru Sasai, one of the central figures on the Kobe school board, described to me in detail, the immediate problem was that he and other education officials felt at a loss to explain what had happened with Youth A. What they were missing, he suggested, were *terms of translation*. They had to find a means of redefining this event in a way that would address the issue of the ordinary child, which included the particular status of the ordinary in late twentieth-century Japan, and shift the responsibility for missing (and producing) it away from the school. He acknowledged that this was not the first serious violent incident perpetrated by a junior high student. In the 1980s, schools nationwide had been plagued by bullying, inner-school violence, and a number of incidents of youth attacks on teachers and parents. Yet the Youth A incident presented them with a particular problem of categorization and context because it failed to conform to one of the existing categories of class, race, age, and because of the conditions of recession and social uncertainty in which it had occurred.

Feeling overwhelmed, the Kobe school board decided to seek expert advice. I happened to be in Mr. Sasai's office when this conversation took place and calls were made to the Kyoto psychologist Hayao Kawai, whose involvement I discuss in Chapter Three. Among the theories that had circulated in the media following the beheading of little Jun was the question of the psychological health of the attacker. Had the perpetrator been, as anticipated, an adult, the psychiatric community would have been turned to along with other criminal experts. But because of Youth A's youth, the board knew that it would require an expert who could address the incident in such a way that the education establishment would be absolved and the potential fallout of this event would be minimized.

By the time the city of Kobe completed its own report on the Youth A incident in March 1998, it and the youth had been placed within the larger context of school problems. Psychological references dominated the text, the center of responsibility had shifted from the school to the home, and the conclusion was that this event was a result of the mistaken (and on its way to being replaced) project of dependency and homogeneous training for academic competition. The report added a section on the family, suggesting what becomes more fully articulated in later reports, and the 2006 revision of the FLE, that adults, rather than the MOE, need to take more responsibility for their children. Parents, it suggested, have neglected their civic responsibility of making sure that the young become fully integrated and respectful members of society, formerly the express responsibility of the period of compulsory education.[21]

As a result of ceaseless media coverage and popular commentary, the Youth A incident became a concrete referent for the child problem. The ordinary became strange as a local event was transposed into a national symbol of the problem with the child, schools, and the times and spaces of sociocultural development. These transpositions seemed to lift the event and the youth's troubled articulations, like so much during this time, out of the time and spaces of the recessionary struggles of on-the-edge middle-class families like Youth A's and the ongoing deprivations of Kobe following the 1995 earthquake. The overlooking of recessionary challenges and sidestepping of Youth A's own articulations of his "troubled subjectivity" removed his individual struggles, which pulled him into a world of delusion and ultimately violence, from the larger economic and political contexts of their complex formation.[22]

Yumiko Iida has associated the violent acts and writings of Youth A with the violence perpetrated by the millennialist cult Aum Shinrikyō (Supreme Truth). The cult became infamous in the mid-1990s for its Armageddon-like attack on the Tokyo subways with poison sarin gas. What shocked Japanese society in particular about these well-planned cult attacks was the revelation that its top members included the nation's brightest minds, graduates of the best departments of the elite University of Tokyo. Gaining entrance to the science faculty at the University of Tokyo involves literally years of nonstop after-school cram school preparation and until the late 1990s guaranteed lifetime employment at a top company. In the publications of Aum, Iida finds a combination of images of pop culture apocalypse and hyperrationality. In the writings of its lower-level members, she identifies a search for a "safe home" from the lack of attachment and isolation of a society narrated as inclusive and dependent but infused with competitiveness and consumer capitalism.

Iida suggests that Youth A as well encountered this paradoxical nexus within which individual identity construction became an ongoing struggle that ended in violence against others. She situates Youth A's descent into violence within the "salient hardships" faced by Japanese youth—conditions of "fragmented, disembodied and claustrophobic subjectivity."[23] Treated as isolated incidents, the seeming incomprehensibility of their acts became an excuse for educational reform remedies.[24] Without excusing the violence, Iida suggests we see it as a "mirror for the immanent problems of contemporary Japan" of the young made into the subjects and objects of the uncertain conditions of recessionary life characterized by liberalization on the one hand and what Iida calls the "unsurprising calls for recovery of the collective unity of Japan," on the other. Both of these are problems, rather than solutions.

What was especially poignant about this conflation in the case of the Kobe event and Youth A was that the very processes that made it possible for an event and its young perpetrator to become a symbol of national trouble are the processes that also allowed this incident to be emptied of its specificity and thus of the possibility of actually understanding the problematic or monstrous world that the youth encountered and in some sense revealed.

You Have the Right to Be Held Responsible

Overall, my explorations and conversations with those close to, and most directly affected by, the Youth A incident in and around Suma Ward revealed much of the same disconnect between the tensions and problems of individuals and families and of the education experts, local and national policy makers, and other powerful political pundits. I originally spent several months over the course of 2000–2001 in and around the new town where Youth A and his family had lived (they moved following his arrest), talking to the local neighborhood association, teachers, administrators at his junior high, and family friends and exploring the sites of the incident that had become the sites of foreboding, viewed and reviewed in hundreds of publications nationwide. During this time, I was struck by how much of the local reality of disappointment and disillusion, loss of livelihood, and tension and anxiety over the future had been effaced in the massive reporting and outpouring of popular and expert commentary. The Youth A incident was converted into a trigger event. Contained and controlled by the discourse of which it became a part, Youth A became the quintessential strange child framed by psychological and political terms and remade as the needed example to further the reforms.

In Kobe, the past and present heads of the various neighborhood and community associations I visited took great pains to describe and demonstrate for me the fallacy of the idea that the areas where the incident had taken place—Tomogaoka, Kitasuma Danchi, and Tainohatta, part of larger Suma Ward—were typical of the estranged atmosphere and lack of close community ties and cooperation said to be characteristic of "new towns." It was in fact basically incorrect to include this ward in the new development category reserved for the term *new town* because Suma Ward, though it was added on later than established areas of Kobe, which developed outward from the port into commercial districts and small urban neighborhoods, has been in existence for over three decades and had produced community organizations and neighborhood ties as strong as anywhere else in Japan.[25]

From friends and others who knew Youth A and lived close to his junior high, including his defense attorney, I was told that a lot of "mother bashing" had gone on in the early aftermath of the identification of her son as the perpetrator. Youth A's mother, they told me, had been strict in the rearing and concern for the educational success of her oldest son. The word they used was *nesshin*, a term associated with education, which refers to an intense level of parental, usually gendered female, involvement and commitment to a child's success on the highly competitive entrance exams. From the late 1990s on, with all the reform talk of relaxed education, the private education industry (Chapter Five) ramped up its appeal to urban parents in particular to enter their children in cram school at earlier ages, starting in third grade, to prepare for entrance exams to private junior high schools (outside the control of the MOE).[26] "Why was it always the mother who got the blame?" locals with whom I spoke complained. As the neighborhood association head at the time argued, why didn't the father know anything about what was going on? The principals and teachers, for their part, mentioned having been informed by the boy's elementary teachers that he had problems: They had talked to his mother about seeking counseling, but they were unaware as to whether she had followed through; they acknowledged that they had no way of compelling her to do so.

Yoshikuni Noguchi, the defense lawyer, wrote his own account of his team's investigation, his repeated meetings with the family, and his thirty-some meetings with Youth A.[27] In his book, he paints a more complex picture of the family, community, and nation at the time, shedding different light on the massive media commentary and teachers' and neighbors' reflections, as well as on the language of emotions and policies being formulated to address them in the reforms. Attorney Noguchi told me that the idea of "ordinary" no more fit this family and their son than any other. He described the youth as weak and sensitive and the mother as driven by her fears of falling behind. Although the family had managed to be considered part of the greater middle class during times of economic prosperity, the recession had put their lifestyle at risk. Retaining it had seemed to require breakneck efforts. The father, a junior high school graduate, devoted himself to his work, and the mother took it as her charge to make sure that her children would do at least as well or better than the father, often, according to Noguchi, adopting forceful means of fulfilling this goal. This, in the midst of what those in the less fortunate neighborhoods of Kobe described for me as a desperate situation for many families and those in the more fortunate areas described as an atmosphere of constant competition for their children's place in the educational hierarchy, was exacerbated by the MOE talk of relaxed education and the end of the resources and ideological investment required in the production of a homogeneous workforce.

Emotional Education

By historical accident, the city of Kobe, which had been the site of a devastating earthquake in 1995, from which many of the neighborhoods had not at the time of my visits in 2000–2001 yet recovered, had also become a testing ground for various psychological methodologies and new programs to solve the child problem. It is not possible within the confines of the present chapter to do justice to the devastation that the 1995 earthquake caused the city of Kobe.

The critical commentary on this natural disaster points to the political disaster that it also was, once it became painfully clear that the famed efficiency and responsibility of the central government for its citizens did not extend to adequate emergency help or even to the ability to allow outside emergency staff and medicine to reach the afflicted. Although the focus of this event in its aftermath became the psychological effect on the inhabitants, and the beginning of the usage of the idea of trauma and scars to describe the long-lasting effects, many in Kobe with whom I spoke pointed out that the long-lasting effects of this disaster were the shaking of their certitude in the government beyond easy repair and the impairment of the local economy.

If the Youth A incident could not be explained in structural terms, perhaps this was a problem of what the media had begun to call the problem of the "inner mind" of the child.[28] The foremost expert in the Kansai region on the individual and collective Japanese psyche, whose work had heretofore been confined for the most part to a specialized readership and his inner academic circles at Kyoto University, was the Jungian psychologist Hayao Kawai. Kawai was known in these circles for his interest in applying his Jungian approach to the reading of the "Japanese personality" and Japanese culture.[29]

It was a short step from the contact made by the central education committee of Hyogo prefecture with Hayao Kawai to the forming of a committee on educating the heart of the child (*kokoro no kyōiku*), afterward officially rendered as "emotional education," for which Kawai was chosen to be the director. The final report, issued in October 1997, was called "Toward a Solid Emotional Education."[30] From this time on, Kawai also became closely involved in the deliberations and high-level committees of the MOE's reform program. From the opening statement of the final report of this committee, there is an emphasis on the personal that sets the tone for the remainder of the text. Kawai emphasizes that the inhabitants of Hyogo Prefecture, who have recently experienced the tragedy of the loss of life following an immense natural disaster, know the importance of respecting life, consideration or compassion for others, and mutual help.

Following on this theme, Kawai moves quickly to the Kobe killings and woundings of younger children by Youth A, stating that these incidents clearly demonstrate the need to understand the current conditions in which the young find themselves, in particular their emotional or psychological development. Although "emotional education" is the official rendering of *kokoro no kyōiku*, it is arguable that the English terms chosen do not cover the range of references included in the Japanese term *kokoro*, in particular in its pairing with education. The word *kokoro* incorporates a wide lexical and connotative area. It can be used to suggest the thoughtful and reflective mind, (rather than the logical and rational) and the heart, as the locus of emotion and feeling and has often been invoked to suggest a shared mentality (of the former mind and heart) and a sense of shared aesthetic. Calling for an education of the *kokoro* suggests a gap or lack of development, where there should not be one, that can and should be filled or completed pedagogically. What were these pedagogies? To whom were they directed, and whom did they mean to benefit?

What guided Kawai and the MOE in their creation of emotional education was the sense that the postwar focus on economic growth and the abundance that resulted had stunted these faculties of the *kokoro* at the individual level, leading to the depletion of the once taken-for-granted collective Japanese heart. Kawai blames his own generation for neglecting to provide the young with a strong example of *kokoro* development. What are the signs of this seeming failure? Kawai points to a decrease in vitality, compassion for life and respect for tradition among the young. The focus on compassion, mutual understanding, and life skills, included in the various catch phrases of emotional education, was supposed to underemphasize competition as well as teach individual responsibility. To understand the urgent need for emotional education articulated repeatedly by the MOE and psychologists like Kawai, we need to remember the context of this pedagogy of emotion. Teaching emotional development meant fortifying oneself emotionally for the challenges of globalization. What globalization has to do with the strengthening of emotion is the subject of the next chapter, in which I engage with how a focus on psychosocial health became a means of reenfolding the problems of identity and national subjectivity in a discourse that paired neoliberal disciplinary power with a shift in the form of cultural nationalism.

In its final report, the committee headed by Kawai set out five tenets for understanding the child better, creating the basis of a plan to address the present situation among the young educationally.[31] On the basis of these understandings, and in light of the challenges that the Youth A incident presented to the MOE and the nation as a whole, the committee came up with recommendations for the content of "emotional education."[32]

From the direction set out in this report, it was not a big step to the deliberations on "the state of the child's heart" set out by a special session of the central education committee convened by Minister Kosugi at the time of the Youth A incident. The central committee made recommendations to be included in the education reforms for incorporating a program of moral education based on direct engagement and experience. Proponents of emotional education insisted on the need to refocus attention on the lack of a coherent moral standard among the young. This lack had caused the young to lose their sense of consideration for others, which according to Kosugi had been a natural part of past generations' collective emotions.

One of the earliest measures that was enacted to restore the seeming lost sense of moral grounding and replenish the energies of the young was a program first piloted in the city of Kobe exactly one year following the Youth A incident.[33] Known as "trial week," this program targeted Youth A's age group (second-year junior high students) at the time he began to wound and kill elementary students. Prominent among the stated aims of this program was to provide second year junior high students with direct experience in their communities, with a goal of (re)instilling compassion for others, something Youth A's violence seemed to deny. During one week in June, one-half of all second-year students at junior highs across the city of Kobe and Hyogo Prefecture participated in this one-week program.[34] Setup and arrangements for trial week were left to individual schools, and within the schools the burden for the arrangements, of which there were many, fell to homeroom teachers.[35]

In an article in a popular monthly magazine, entitled "Hyogo Trial Week and Children," the journalist Katsuyoshi Sōri argued that if this program really intended to promote deeper ties between the young and the larger community, there would be a stronger effort to involve the community in a discussion of the best ways to do this.[36] He suggested that if the aim of this program was really to contribute to the development among the young of a more compassionate view of others through an education with a greater emphasis on direct experience, then it would be more effective to apply teachers' time and energies in the service of building better everyday ties to the community and breaking down barriers in the school system, rather than putting all this effort into one week.

At the core of the reform process for Terawaki and others was the need to remake the Japanese public. It is time, they said, for the public, which up until now had registered its dissatisfaction with the way the government ran things, to assume more of the responsibility for its own management. In the following chapter, I investigate the relation between the different aspects of the educational reform at the end of the 1990s and "The Structure of Japan in the Twenty-First Century," a key publication that provided the ideological scaffolding for ending competition, relaxing curriculum, and efforts to manage emotion at a time when classrooms seemed increasingly unmanageable. I delve further into the complexity of the reforms, revealing dual (or dueling) discourses that cloak the economic limitations of the recessionary period in a discourse of responsibility and its changing modalities of power. One line of this discourse derides the competition of the past, promoting a plan for the creation of a less stressful environment in which everyone can proceed at his or her own speed and succeed in his or her strongest areas. The other, emphasizes the need to meet the challenges of globalization through the creation of a new individual who is independent and responsible. I show that any apparent conflict between these dual discourses is obscured through the language of the newly legitimized clinical psychology of Kawai, which owes its due to Doi's dependency and other 1970s–1980s psychological discourses of national identity.

Chapter Three

Frontiers Within

Neoliberalism needs frontiers. . . . It thrives on the borders between the known and the unknown, the possible and the (yet) impossible.[1]

The frontier is not a natural or indigenous category. It is a traveling theory, a blatantly foreign form requiring translation.[2]

In the neoliberal mode the State takes on new tasks and functions . . . It entails shifting the burden for social risks of poverty, illness and unemployment into the individual's domain. This agenda becomes visible as a technique or positive art of governance.[3]

In the late 1990s, the Japanese Ministry of Education (MOE) appointed the Kyoto University Professor of Clinical Psychology and Director of the International Center for Japanese Studies, the now late Hayao Kawai, as special advisor for the 2002 education reforms (*kyōiku kaikaku*). In June 2001, I attended a public talk of Kawai's entitled, "The Condition of Japanese Culture: Education in a New Age."[4] Arriving at a cultural assembly hall on the outskirts of Tokyo, I found the foyer crammed with people looking over the huge variety of Kawai's publications, fifty of which had been published between 1995 and 2001.[5] It was one of many demonstrations I witnessed of the appeal that Kawai and his message about the child, education, and Japanese culture were attracting.[6] Hundreds purchased books that day, including the hot-off-the-press title by the same name as Kawai's talk. Kawai wrote in an informal manner, much the same way as he spoke, a style that played on his academic and regional marginality. As already noted, Kawai was from the Kansai region (south central Japan, probably best known for the cities of Kyoto, Osaka, and Kobe), and he seemed well attuned to the effects on his Tokyo audience of shifting from standard Japanese into the Kansai dialect. This ability to switch vernaculars helped Kawai blend a wide variety of personal and national subjects and histories.

Kawai's prominence as psychological expert on Japanese education and national identity grew dramatically in the 1990s.[7] By the end of the decade, the Japanese government, represented by the MOE, had begun to promote a new approach to education and a slew of terms with which to explain it. Kawai was central to this approach and new language about the child, school, and recessionary period.[8] In Chapter Two, I outlined how the MOE turned to Kawai for a set of terms with which to respond to the Youth A incident and the child problem that emerged in its wake as a full-blown social issue. The terminology he helped develop psychologized the child problem and recoded education reform into an individual project of self-development and responsibility for value production.

Kawai sought to replace the dependency theory of national character. In the talk I attended and in key writings, he articulated his notion of independence as one of latent potential. Adopted as a central part of education reform discourse and present in the revision of the Fundamental Law of Education (FLE), Kawai's independence was based on a strategy and temporality of development other than dependency's. Dependency depends. Independence individuates. Independence names the individual as the site of risk and responsibility. The individual Kawai and the MOE began to imagine would be responsible for discovering his or her own potential. To Kawai, this discovery and responsibility were like a frontier within the individual and without limits. The potential was something the individual would be put in charge of discovering and developing on his or her own. Kawai named this project of independence "the frontier within." The frontier within, unlike Doi's dependency, was not reliant on the institutional management and guidance of the prerecessionary development narrative of which salaryman Sasaki (*Tokyo Sonata*) was a product.[9]

Individualizing the Japanese Heart

Seating approximately 2,000, the hall was filled to capacity the day I attended Kawai's talk . The host praised Kawai's many contributions and affiliations. He insisted that Kawai's was a voice too long ignored and insisted that we consider Kawai alongside other major theorists of modernity like Maruyama Masao.[10] The host explained that something had been missing from the thinking of Maruyama and other postwar intellectuals. What they lacked that Kawai's thinking manifested was "Japanese spirit" (*Nihon no seishin*):

> In Japan's race after modernity, spirit was replaced by natural science, objectivity, and talk of action and reaction. But when we began to read your [Kawai's] books, we realized what was missing.[11]

Full of conviviality, Kawai took to the stage. He drew his listeners closer with the informal register of his speech and its emphasis on his non-Tokyo origins. This is a point that Kawai used to his advantage in his discussion of transformation and difference. Kawai's talk loosely traversed the past several decades, when problems were relatively simple and the students who could not keep up with the breakneck speed of the curriculum—"those who fell through the cracks" (*ochikobore*)—were the center of educational controversy. At that time, the MOE's position was "the more knowledge absorbed the better." In the aftermath of the juvenile crime incidents of the last several years, claims of home and school collapse, and out-of-control strange kids, the focal point of concern has shifted, said Kawai:

> People are truly anxious about these problems and the direction of the nation and its culture in the twenty-first century. As a result . . . many people are asking, what will become of Japanese culture?[12]

Over the next hour, Kawai tacked back and forth among issues of education, the family, myth and religion in Japan, as well as the changes needed to face the future of globalization. He enthralled his audience with his seeming command of the issues. Beyond his cleverly crafted puns, down-to-earth presentation, and some chiding of the bureaucracy over past impositions of top-down education, Kawai's goal seemed to be to establish links among the child problem, the continuity and stability of Japanese culture, and the realities of globalization:

> Japanese culture has somehow withstood the onslaught of modernization throughout the twentieth century, but the current crisis of our children and schools, and the challenges from without of globalization, make it imperative to strengthen and adapt it to these new demands.[13]

It is not easy to pin down what Kawai means when he refers to Japanese spirit or Japanese culture. Is it a timeless inheritance of values and habits or an ideology employed and deployed in Japan? For Kawai, "Japanese spirit and culture" seems to serve as a general category for dispositions connected with what he calls the Japanese heart (*Nihon no kokoro*). The Japanese heart, historically, according to Kawai, has been a great, hidden source of energy for Japanese people. As he emphasized at this event and many others to follow, the Japanese heart of the past was in need of a change in order to function as the latent potential to meet the demands of the twenty-first century.[14] Kawai was quick to note that although Japanese culture remained intact across many difficult periods, the present time was perhaps the most difficult of all. The evidence for this, for Kawai, was the frightening behavior of the young. This behavior, as Kawai framed it, indicated a failure of moral transmission.

By the time of Kawai's next large public talk in Tokyo in the spring of 2001, he had articulated a clear image of how the Japanese heart and Japanese citizen would meet the demands of the new age.[15] *Independence, rather than dependence was the key, he said.* The Japanese version of the independent individual (*jiritsutekina kojin*) would be neither the ego-centered individuality of the West nor the past dependent (referencing Doi's *amae*) character of Japan. Kawai's depiction of the end of dependence and the rise of independence in Japan made the collective Japanese heart he often talked about seem a contradiction. For Kawai, there was a way to fuse individualism and collectivism, and that, as he said and wrote about frequently, was through traditional Japanese myths and their relevance for personal history.

As the opening epigraphs by Buscher and Tsing suggest, the frontier as imagined space and romanticized time has been an apt figure for capitalist expansionism. Translatable into various moments and conditions, in early twenty-first-century Japan, the frontier stood for a shift from embodied forms of training a homogeneous workforce in real time to an inner time of the individual heart, the limits of which were open and unknown. Kawai's substitution of myth for history was a well-chosen strategy for managing the conflicting meanings in his message and historical excess of the prewar and postwar past:

> When I was young, I read lots of stories because we were raised not to speak and to remain quiet. Japanese myths left a strong impression on me, because "myth is the same as history."[16]

To explain this equivalency, Kawai moved quickly from well-known Japanese folktales to his own personal history as a serious boy who didn't always believe what his teachers taught him. By the end of the talk, the fusing of these stories became a means of demonstrating how myth and history were, for him, one and the same.

In his youth, Kawai said, he was taught that the emperor was a god. He found this suspicious, he told the audience. "If you believe this," he said, "you think that Japan had undefeatable spiritual power, but then," he wondered later, "if this was so, how could Japan have been so miserably defeated?" During the postwar period, he became aware of the spirit of American science. It was then he decided, like so many of his age, to study a science. He chose mathematics. Kawai found that he wasn't good at math, but he needed a job following graduation, so he began to teach high school math. This is when he first became interested in counseling. Students came to him for advice. He wished to respond faithfully to their questions and began to look for books on psychology, finding that the study of clinical psychology did not exist in Japan. It was at this point that Kawai decided to change his life's course. He left science and applied for a Fulbright to study Jungian psychology in Switzerland.[17]

Kawai discovered through his own studies that, even though modern science had eliminated many diseases and found a way to objectively examine the psyche, the result of the research often went too far and focused exclusively on causes. "This is why," he suddenly noted, skipping over major historical periods, "if we continue to focus exclusively on causes in our contemporary situation in Japan, what we will be left with is nothing more than a circle of blame that goes from schools to homes to the Ministry of Education and local officials."[18]

To Kawai, the rational approach of the natural sciences did not solve problems with interpersonal relations (*ningen kankei*). Counseling is different, he told the audience. It's all about stories, not facts. There isn't a right and a wrong but many kinds of wisdom, and wisdom (*chie*) is not the same as knowledge (*chishiki*). Japanese schools have been caught up with teaching knowledge, rather than common wisdom, and that's why it hasn't been interesting for students.[19] Moreover, culture is all about common wisdom, and Japanese tradition is bursting with the energy of this wisdom and these stories.

"What we need to do," he said, "is look to our own stories." For Kawai, stories and myths are the same as history. He summed this up by saying, "If we continue to think in terms of cause and effect, nothing will come of it for us. For example, a student says, 'I can't get into college'; OK, but they can take responsibility for themselves and ask why they chose that path." In this way one can understand his or her own individuality and be satisfied that this is his or her life to live and his or her story. For Kawai, an individual's story is the sum of the choices that person makes, independently. *If an individual fails, that's that individual's story.* What is absent in Kawai's conscious conflating of fictional characters and the lives of recessionary Japanese is the very developmental time and trajectory of pre- and postwar national citizenship that Kawai and others sought to reenvision along the lines of neoliberal rationales—turning governance, like the movement of time itself, inward.

Kawai's role was not to indict, like MOE spokesman Terawaki. Kawai's role was to refigure the past into a new story for the present—a refiguration that repurposed associations of culture and spirit and made postwar and prewar pasts seem irrelevant. Kawai's psychologizing of problems of the present invented a present that seemed convincing to an audience looking for answers and certainty.

In this chapter, I investigate the claims of the reformers of education to relax education, allow people the "freedom" to choose their own way, while at the same time requiring the individual decision-maker to accept responsibility for his or her choices. *"It's your story"* (*jibun no monogatori), as Kawai says.* My examination of the reforms in this chapter reveals how psychologists of identity became centrally involved with the formation of education reform language and policy. I extend last chapter's examination of the MOE public announcements and the Youth A incident to a key governmental report and my ethnographic experience of the concern and confusion associated with the reduction in core curriculum. I also look at how a new course of study—comprehensive studies (*sōgōtekina gakushū*)—was implemented and how the schools were guided, or not, through this process. I show how these governmental programs were linked to the larger venture of replacing an unsustainable ideology of homogeneity and equality with an ideology of independence and inner potential.

The idea of creating a new citizen for a new century—an independent individual—has several intertwined aims. The creation of the independent citizen displaces the onus of responsibility for social troubles and individual futures onto the populace, in particular the family and home. The change creates a different narrative of cultural difference. This narrative diverges from and then seems to reconverge with the trajectory of psychological culturalisms of the past discussed in Chapter One. The focus of this chapter is the important differences between the national culturalisms of the past and the neoliberal individualization of the present—a transformation that began in education and leaned on the child problem.

Kawai pointed to an urgent need to fix the child by reengineering individual development as a "new frontier," a frontier that lies dormant within. This new language of education and psychology diverted attention from the effects of the long economic downturn at many levels.[20] Associated with myth, instead of history, the language of the individual seemed far removed from the arenas of industry and government. Yet it was precisely these realms that the meet up of education and psychology under the conditions of recession intended. The inner frontier was no less a subjectifying figuration than was 1950s "peace and prosperty's" income doubling and educational acceleration project or the 1980s "information society,"[21] with the notable exception that the forceful turn away from historical time and national space in a place like Japan so saturated with temporal and spatial difference has made this most recent figure difficult to oppose.

An important part of Kawai's role was reengineering national character. He explained that past discourses of Japaneseness are impediments to future growth. Kawai's message was for the recessionary citizen-subject. Japan must change by changing the Japanese people, one by one. The idea of creating people, *hitozukuri*, had been a key concept of the Meiji period's "civilization and enlightenment" project. A national education was the means, according to Meiji thinkers of the time like Masanao Nakamura, of developing a nation-identifying subject out of the regional diversity of alliances and allegiances that characterized Tokugawa society. The question that Japanese historians of education like Teruhisa Horio have asked of this past and the present is where the terms and imperatives for national identification will come from in the midst of neoliberalization. Will they be generated in a top-down fashion, as they have in previous modernity moments of reform, or from "below"[22] (meaning of and from the people)? And where will the locus of control and responsibility lie? Does the kind of freedom, independence, and notion of the individual circulated under the conditions of recession by the MOE and psychologists like Kawai mean support during economic crisis, natural and human-made disaster, or does "strength to live" and inner frontiers signal something different?

This was not the first time that Japan sought wide-reaching reforms of its educational and social spheres over the course of the postwar period. It is the opinion of many scholars that the present education changes are no more than a continuation, or perhaps a final realization of the Nakasone (late 1980s) reform project, often called the "third reform of education." My observations and investigations of public gatherings, central governmental reports, and school settings suggest otherwise. The education reforms of the twenty-first century went much beyond the Nakasone plan. The recessionary context and coming together of psychology and education are central to this difference.

It is not the purpose of this chapter to produce a full accounting of the government's efforts to adapt the educational establishment to the shifting economic and political needs of the state. I refer instead to critical moments and trajectories of thought that have served as precursors and precedents. The twenty-first-century reforms share similarities with earlier projects of what Michel Foucault referred to as the positive production of power. The newest shifts in control and consolidation of power are also quite different. The current reforms have worked from within existing and often conflictual discourses, institutions, programs, laws, and policies, turning them into problems, creating solutions for created problems, and obscuring past issues of temporality and value that might question the transformations and their relation to the recessionary context.

The Essence of Reforms

The project of rethinking education for the beginning of the twenty-first century resurfaced in earnest in the mid-1990s with the convening of the

Central Committee on Education (Chūō Kyōiku Shigikai) around the issue of the present state of education.[23] Although it was not stated as such in either of the two reports of this Central Committee, it was with a new and added urgency that the government reopened these discussions of the state of education in the mid-1990s. The push to reduce the government burden for education, in both financial and political senses, became more dramatic than anyone in the 1980s could have imagined. In the 1980s, the motivations of the Nakasone government were of a piece with the changing economic environment after the 1970s oil crisis and economic slowdowns.[24] Reducing the government's burden for education was part of the complex agenda of the MOE under Nakasone, as it became clear that the double-digit economic growth of the 1960s would not soon return, and the focus on income doubling and exam entrance had resulted in unprecedented levels of innerschool violence, suicides, school refusal, and bullying. By the mid-1980s, the narrative of homogeneity, supported by the equal access and funding for compulsory education throughout Japan, also seemed unsustainable.

Situating postwar projects within the historical frame of their combined ideological and economic conditions, Harry Harootunian uncovers the 1950s and 1980s efforts to overturn the progressive possibilities of the immediate postwar reforms of the constitution and of education, particularly the 1947 FLE.[25] In the late 1950s through the early 1960s, the MOE conceived of a new direction for education that diverged dramatically from the promises and protections of the FLE. Called the plan to produce the "ideal Japanese," it was created in tandem with former finance minister, turned prime minister, Hayato Ikeda and his high-growth economics. In the 1980s, as Japan's seemingly "miracle" economic growth began to slow, the national identification project shifted again. Reframed (in Japan) as a time beyond modernity, of culture and an information society, the rest of the world continued to view Japan as having its capitalist cake and eating it too, so to speak; a nation that had seemingly overcome or had a cultural solution to the natural and social ravages of late capitalism.[26]

From the mid-1990s, recession and its conditions of insecurity and uncertainty challenged previous narrative and ideological platforms of national identification. To manage the immanence of these conditions, reform proponents in the MOE returned to the Nakasone slogans of the deteriorating moral and social sensibilities of the young, while shifting their focus to the figurative force of the strange child, collapsing school and home, and the history of refiguring and reengineering. "Strength to live" (*ikiru chikara*) was the first example of new reform language. This newly articulated strength turned into one of the fastest-spreading, though nowhere clearly understood, buzzwords of the early 2000s. As MOE minister Takashi Kosugi wrote in his own personal account, before he was "let retire" from his position, the "strength to live" meant the need for a vast reorganization of the way that learning and manner training (*shitsuke*) are conceptualized and implemented.[27]

Along with conceptual changes came curricular and policy ones. Relaxed (*yutori*) education shortened the school week from six to five days. But issues arose around fitting the new comprehensive studies into this shorter week and how students, with a 30 percent reduction in core curriculum and a substantial reduction in teaching staff (because ostensibly if there is less time to teach not as many teachers are required) were to be prepared for the unchanging entrance exams, especially those who did or could not attend private cram schools.[28] Moreover, in place of the carefully explicated top-down instructions teachers had come to expect from the MOE, relaxed education and comprehensive studies came to the schools with little more than a set of guidelines that the schools were meant to figure out on their own, amidst plenty of parental anxiety and objection. One of the intentions of comprehensive studies was for the motivation and choice of subject to come from the students themselves, clearly not an easy task when there was a ratio of one (teacher) to (up to) forty students per class at the time.[29] How the staff at any given school was to turn these very general guidelines into reality was unknown and anxiety producing for many overworked homeroom schoolteachers who already shouldered much of the responsibility for their individual students, including the school refusers among them. Now they had much more.

Explaining the Reforms

The concern among parents at the elementary school in Kawasaki my two daughters attended was so great that members of the PTA asked the principal to convene a special explanation session. In the early period of the reforms, everyone was talking about the loss of core curriculum and what it meant for their children and families.[30] Principal Majima agreed to a two-hour morning session in the spring of 2001. A huge crowd turned out, although the timing prohibited the participation of most working parents, most of whom would have been fathers. In his characteristic openness, for which he was in the minority among the other school administrators I met in Tokyo and Kobe over the years, Principal Majima began the meeting by saying that many parents seemed confused about the reforms, and, frankly, so was he! He couldn't explain the situation perfectly, he said, because "there are parts of it that I don't really understand all that well myself" (*Jisai ni yoku wakarnai tokoro ga arimasu*).[31] He acknowledged everyone's unease by referring to the contents of a recent article in the *Asahi Newspaper* (one of hundreds at the time) that discussed the danger to the science curriculum and other core subjects of the loss of study hours in school. Still, principal Majima tried to make a good case for the need to foster presentation skills (*happyō suru noryoku*) and what he called a new sense of academic ability (*atarashii gakuryokukan*) promoted in the reforms. Although successful on some levels, his explanations failed to stem the spreading unease, punctuated as it was by his own uncertainty about how the schools were supposed to succeed without the benefit of specially trained or additional staff.[32] Each school was responsible for its own plan and schedule of implementation, though most of the requirements were set in advance.

Due to several ambitious young teachers at Imai, and the once heavy inflow of returnee children, which had earned the school an extra staff member, the school came up with an interim plan fairly quickly. It included a different theme for every two grades and a focus in the upper grades on finding out more about "different cultures." I was asked to participate in a demonstration that was meant to be an example of direct experience learning (*taiken gakushū*). The theme was "rice eating" in different countries around the world. Six of us, all mothers who had lived or originated in countries other than Japan, were to participate. We were asked to bring our favorite rice or rice dish and talk about how it is eaten in these other places of the world. Emphasis would be placed on the differences between these other places and Japan.

On arrival at the school, we were taken to a classroom, seated in formal fashion in front of the class, and given name tags adorned with the flags of the various countries we represented. My elder daughter, a sixth grader at the time, tried to tell her teachers that having lived in both Japan and the United States, she simply did not see difference in the way they continued to ask for it to be seen. As the program proceeded, her teacher, who was the event's organizer and the school's up-and-coming expert on international understanding, circulated among the students reminding them to take advantage of this important exposure to cultural difference. She then proceeded to go around the room, smelling the rice dishes and announcing how different they all were from Japanese rice. The students for their part seemed to be enjoying their time away from their studies, following which, in any case, approximately 60 percent of them would be heading off to after-school (private junior high) entrance exam cram schools (see Chapter 5).[33]

Imai Elementary was just one of the sites at which I witnessed the concerns and confusion that characterized the beginning of the new course of study supposed to generate strength and vitality in students. Tomuro Elementary, outside of Tokyo, was as different as it could be from the population surrounding the Imai Elementary environment of upper-end condominiums and single-owner homes. Tomuro was about an hour from our location in Kawasaki (about two hours from the center of Tokyo) in Atsugi City. I had spent several days in the spring of 2001 with students and teachers at Tomura, prior to the development of their own comprehensive studies, and was familiar with the types of challenges faced by a school that serves working-class and immigrant families, many of whom had been especially hard hit by recessionary restructuring and a shifting labor market. I heard much about the difficulties teachers at Tomuro faced on an everyday basis implementing the existing curriculum in their diverse and often disorderly classrooms .But none of us was prepared for the level of chaos that ensued when the students were escorted to the new computer facility, the pride and joy of Atsugi City, to begin their comprehensive studies. The computer room was beautifully organized; there was a brand-new desktop for every two students, and an instructional program loaded onto each one to guide the students through any search they wished to make. The teacher's computer was equipped with a monitoring device to make it possible to track the progress of all students. Teacher Naomi also had an assistant on hand for support.[34] For about half of the required fifty-minute period, most of the students found something to look up and followed the on-screen instructions. Things disintegrated after this. Students began spinning in their chairs in the center of the room, pulling each other's pants down, and generally making it impossible to do anything resembling the comprehensive studies' goal of "self-initiated" research. As the teacher commented to me afterward, the new comprehensive studies' curriculum seemed to have little understanding of the challenges faced by Tomuro students. They could have used extra work time in basic subjects, and perhaps a more interesting method of going about these, for which the teachers now had no time at all.

Producing Adults of Global Worth

During the early years of the twenty-first century, education reforms took on a new urgency as continued news of bad economic times was matched by reports of the loss of order in the schools and the failure of adult society. Just as emotional education was becoming an everyday term, a new series of juvenile crimes involving high school–aged students erupted onto the media scene. The media lost no time in reminding everyone that these were the contemporaries of the Kobe youth, who was fourteen at the time of his killing and wounding of elementary-aged children in 1997.

As the papers and television once more exploded with demands for answers to the frightening crisis among the youth, Prime Minister Mori Yoshirō convened a committee on the reforms called the "people's committee for education reform" (*kyōiku kaikaku kokumin kaigi*). Composed of everything but practicing teachers, with the exception of Ryōichi Kawakami, as a result of his best-selling *School Collapse*, the so-called people's committee made its report to Prime Minister Mori in the spring of 2001.

The committee's recommendations extended those of earlier reports on the reforms, with the important difference being the atmosphere surrounding the child, which seemed to hit another peak in the first part of the year 2000. The committee concluded its discussions with a list of seventeen proposals. The proposals included a set of concrete steps aimed to change the condition in the schools and with the young for the twenty-first century.[35] The committee resolved to create a means of "raising a moral Japanese person." The areas it targeted for doing so were the home, which the members of this committee unanimously agreed was "the origin of education"; the return of morals education to the schools; and a youth corps, called "service to the people" (*hōshi katsudo*), reminiscent of the forced labor (*kinrō hōshi*) of the prewar era, requiring all children of school age to participate in a service program of the state's origination from two weeks for the youngest up to one year for the older students. Coupled with this were recommendations for harsher steps against problem students in the schools, including suspensions and explusions where necessary.[36] For many the most significant people's committee recommendation had to do with the FLE. The members strongly advised making the law more "suitable" (*fusawashī*) to the current conditions of education and society in the twenty-first century, despite sixty years of teacher and parent opposition to any revision to this foundational postwar education law enacted in tandem with the postwar peace constitution. This final recommendation set off debates among teachers and intellectuals across the country that continued until the (first) Abe administration succeeded in pushing through revisions to the FLE in the winter of 2006.[37]

When the Battle Turns Royale

Ambiguous slogans and otherwise conflicting messages of the education reforms resulted in heightened social concern. For the most part, these were diffused by continued government insistence on an agenda that attended to the child problem. Challenges to this problematizing of the child were not totally absent, however. None posed the question more powerfully of whether "strength to live" sought to support and strengthen the position of the individual or to retract the state's responsibility and reinsert it in the guise of "latent potential" than the hugely graphic film *Battle Royale*, which opened in the spring of 2000.

Directed by master of filmic violence Kinji Fukusaku and starring Kitano (Beat) Takeshi, famous for his own share of disgruntled stylistics and bloody shoot-'em-ups, *Battle Royale* revolves around a fictional but eerily resonant version of the "new century education reform act" (BR Law, for short) and much worsened economic downturn of 15 percent unemployment. As social conditions deteriorate in the wake of disastrous financial conditions, the problem of the young is recast as an issue of life and death. According to the dictates of this BR Law, every year one junior high class out of 43,000 nationwide is to be randomly chosen to participate in a compulsory fight-to-the death survival game—a creepy inversion of the once equality-producing education system—out of which only one student is allowed to emerge alive. Teacher-turned-tormenter Takeshi, clad in khakis, reads his students the rules of the survival game. For not paying attention, Takeshi knives one student and decapitates another by way of a remote control titanium collar strapped to the students' necks. Teacher Takeshi then announces that the game be engaged in according to the new national rationale, "to wage battle in order to survive to be an adult of value to the nation" (*ikinokoru kachi no aru otona ni narimasho*).

Dramatic murders that characterize the *battle royale* take place by students equipped with an array of implements of survival (machine guns, knives, saws, grenades, poison, and so on).[38] Goriness is attenuated at moments by contrasting images of one student sacrificing for another, the choice of suicide over slaughter, and a closeness that grows between the two remaining students. The film's conclusion presents a strong contrast with the way it began—the roles of death, camraderie, and parody, suggesting the possibility of limits to state power.

Battle Royale takes up the issue of the management of the population when unities can no longer be imagined in the same way. In its unapologetic dramatization of how the genius of Japanese industrial innovation can be turned with surprising efficiency by the government (the ineptitude of which was faulted for the hardships faced after the 1995 Kobe earthquake) against its own people, and young people at that, the question is whether the present situation represents a problem of the child or a crisis of the nation itself. In both its poignancy and its melodrama, *Battle Royale* directs us to the specificity of Japan's struggles with the fashioning of a late modern national subjectivity in the era of neoliberal globalization.

Moreover, the anxiety and its representations of a crisis of order—the collapsed school and the altogether absent family—reveal a problem at the level of what has been presumed to be the unified common sense of Japanese culture. This transparent unity is put to the test by the exhibitions of the "transparent existence" of Kobe Youth A and other juvenile offenders, the tens of thousands of school refusers, the victims of bullying, and the 30 to 40 percent of young children whose time is spent laboring at education. These are the conditions of possibility for the extreme examples of repressive apparatus and the reductions of life to the status of a game controlled by the state in *Battle Royale*. In focusing national attention on the place from which culture is naturally expected to emerge—the child—social anxiety reinforces, rather than questions, the claims of culture to origin and continuity. In doing so, the child problem discourse dissuades attention from the absence at the level of the "real" management of the population, no longer as easily shorn up by the conflation of economics with culture, which obtained for much of the later twentieth century in Japan.

Kawai's "New Frontier"

By the time Hayao Kawai was appointed by Prime Minister Obuchi in 1999 to head up a special committee on "The Structure of Japan in the Twenty-First Century," he had already been a prominent member of every large committee or report on education and its reform during the critical years since 1996. Kawai had served on the Central Education Committee in 1996 and 1997. He was called on by education officials in Hyogo Prefecture in 1997, following the Kobe Youth A incident, to devise a means of explaining and containing the fallout effects of this unusual crime, which became the hallmark of emotional education. Kawai was included among the members chosen by Prime Minister Mori, who succeeded Obuchi when he fell ill, to serve on the fateful "People's Committee for Education Reform," the conclusions and recommendations of which were the most dramatic to date. However, prior to his participation on the "people's committee," Kawai was asked by Prime Minister Obuchi to lead the search for how Japan was to face the overall challenges facing it in the new century.

"The Structure of Japan in the Twenty-First Century," a special prime minister's committee, was comprised of thirty-three members from all areas of interest, who met together forty-four times over a period of ten months from March through December 1999. This committee's findings were compiled afterwards into a book, edited and written by Kawai, which opens with his own essay, "Japan's Frontier Is within Japan" (*Nihon no Furoteia wa Nihon no Naka ni aru*).[39] In this essay, the informal, almost grandfatherly tone that characterized much of Kawai's popular writing and public addresses was gone. Absent too were the more overt references to his counseling practice and the use of myth as a means of understanding history. Here we encounter a pragmatic and more openly neoliberal Kawai, laying out a stark vision of what he calls a new "governance" (*gabanansu*) and the role of the new independent individual in it.[40]

The sentiment of collapse and request from education officials for a new structure for a new century required replacing Doi's dependency theory.[41] Kawai's "new inner frontiers" represent more than an updating or amending of former categories of national characterizations. They resituated and transformed. They broke with the past even as they pulled on it. In the Japanese context, wrote Kawai, dependence and independence are not mutually exclusive.[42]

A New Governance

Reminiscent of many reports on the "decline" of the Japanese nation and culture from the late 1990s on, Kawai's report began with a warning of the dangers that lay ahead for Japan at what he calls this "critical turning point" (*judaina tenki*) in the nation's history.[43] This was the moment, he said, when Japan must prepare a "principle," an organization, and a desired Japanese figure that would be able to meet the challenges of the next several decades.

Since the Meiji era, wrote Kawai, Japan followed a policy of "catch up and overtake" the West, and "despite this harsh project still managed to hold onto a certain degree of its authentic Japaneseness."[44] We can be proud of these accomplishments, he wrote. In the coming century, however, in which the whole world will be in the throes of globalization, it is questionable whether the strong points of Japan, which have earned the nation its standing, would be up to the new tasks before it.[45] From now on, he insisted, it would be important for Japanese not to close themselves off in their difference but to open out onto the larger world: "Thus what we need now, instead of pausing to discuss the strengths of Japan, is to look toward the future of the world, devoting our whole selves to participating in it. Adopting this attitude," he maintains, "we will realize that Japan's frontier (*furonteia*) is within Japan (*Nihon no naka ni aru*) and proceed to design the nature of our own direction."[46]

Kawai proceeded from this introduction to outline his two major points: first, that Japan's future rested on the "latent strength" of its citizens; and, second, that to draw on this untapped potential, Japan required a new form of relationship between the government and its citizens, between authority and the individual, which he called a new governance.[47]

Since the beginning of the 1990s, he observed, the people of Japan have sensed with some fear that something has changed drastically. They have lived in fear "not of the economic bubble and what is associated with it, but the sense that the political and social systems, the value system and moral sense have been infested (*mushibande shimatta*) from within."⁴⁸ We should all remember, however, that this social organization and morality is something that was formed over the course of a long history in a difficult and demanding environment, and though it had not collapsed, it was in serious need of strengthening. "Moreover, as the country grew wealthier," he noted, "we found that we were lacking the model necessary for internationalism. And just as this was upon us we were thrown into globalization and the three society-shaking events of the Hanshin earthquake, Aum Shinrikyo, and Youth A."⁴⁹

Kawai argued that this is the point at which they discovered that Japan's successful model of "catch up and surpass" was unsuited for the challenges of the new age. It was also, he maintained, when they began to think that the solution lay within, "that within Japan lies a superior nature":

> This latent strength has been left to lie dormant. What we must do now is to reclaim this enormous frontier, by drawing out this latent strength. How are we going to go about this? We are going to change the way that the people and the State relate to each other. We are going to develop a vital and supple individual.⁵⁰

Kawai made clear that this direction demanded a new type of governance that was dependent on the establishment of the individual—something, he was careful to note, that had been inadequate up until that point in Japanese society. The Japanese were, he continued, "compelled to follow the world-wide tide of revolutionary change in which people, things, money, and information cross borders at a new rate, and change to fit the new world standard of a highly competitive era, by upping the power of the individual." At present, he argued, Japan faced a situation in which it takes time to make decisions and responsibility is ambiguous, and thus the task now was to create an individual who could make decisions at a new speed and would assume authority and clear responsibility.

Globalization, maintained Kawai, "is not shackled to older systems, customs, or other vested interests." Thus, Japan's plan needed to be to develop "global literacy," which would be based on access to the world and presentation ability. "Those countries with a low standard of global literacy will not be able to command a sophisticated work force, and those with a high standard (of global literacy) will become the gathering ground for the best and brightest from all over the world."[51] If the twentieth century was the century of the organization, claimed Kawai, then the twenty-first is the century of the individual.

Japanese people for a very long time have associated their existence with the household system where the freedom of the individual was limited. In the postwar era, under the strong pressure of the ideology of freedom, the traditional Japanese household system collapsed. In the midst of not knowing what to do, a proxy household system was created, the model for which was the company. Other kinds of stand-ins for the older system have emerged over the years, and these served as satisfactory places of attachment, but now there is a need for an individual who is independent and self-acting, who can take on risk, be intentional, assume responsibility, and not be tied to a place—a vital and supple individual:[52]

> With a new form of *governance* the latent strength of the individual will be easier to draw out, and our frontier will materialize before us. Many have asked how we are to reclaim this frontier. One of the key ways to cultivate this pioneering spirit in our education, and abolish the homogeneity and uniformity is to think of education in the broad sense. . . . There will two roles for the nation in education: one is obligatory enforced education [*gimu toshite kyōsei suru kyōiku*] and the other, a service education [*saabisu toshite no kyōiku*]. The first will provide a minimum standard, and the second will train those who are able to meet the demands of the marketplace. Right now these two kinds of education are intertwined, but in the future they will need to be separate. Along with this, we will need to reevaluate the role of the home, as one of the major bodies responsible for education, which isn't fulfilling its role at present.[53]

Neoliberalism and the Japanese Heart?

Chihiro, the Hayao Miyazaki heroine of *Spirited Away* (*Sen to Chihiro no Kamikakushi*) is the picture-girl of the latent strength that Kawai discusses. Miyazaki himself commented on how his young heroine seemed to represent the current problems and potential solution.[54] *Spirited Away* deals with a hopeless present, characterized by a mother and a father whose interests rest with their own immediate pleasures; in the middle of a massive feast they encounter in a deserted theme park (echoes of the construction boom and bust of the 1980s–1990s), they are turned into giant pigs. Chihiro, their ten-year-old daughter, who in the opening of the film is lackluster and bored, must overcome her weaknesses through tests of her inner strength and discovery of latent potential. Although she overcomes huge obstacles, they are arguably nothing like navigating the new requirements of life for members of recessionary generation (Chapter Six) whose parents are beset, unlike Chihiro's, by their own fears of restructuring and at a loss to know how to guide the young. As Miyazaki invests in the character of Chihiro, the future is one of discovering a new vitality, this time not by "overcoming the modern," but, as Hayao Kawai would have it, by reframing the terms and requirements of life such that the individual views the trajectory of his or her life as his or her own story, rather than situated in political and historical conditions—a story connected with the stories of others, but for which he or she alone is responsible for developing. In these stories, shorn of history and power, all life situations are potentially survival games.

This chapter has focused on the role of Hayao Kawai in the transformations that emerged from within education in the late twentieth and early twenty-first centuries. It has depicted the significance of education officials coming together with psychologists of identity to shift educational and cultural nationalist characterizations toward the independent heart and its inner frontiers. A unique figure in many ways, due to his background and prior marginalization in the Kansai area and as a Jungian among mostly Freudian-trained psychologists, Kawai's own strength was in his ability to reformulate his thinking to the particular conditions of the time. In this chapter I have also looked at the on-the-ground realities in schools, for teachers, and for parents of the effects of the new language and policies of education in the midst of a deepening recession.

In the next chapter, I turn to the topic of school and classroom "collapse," junior high history teacher Kawakami's depictions of the downfall of a prior form of order at the level of the body, the physical space of the school, and my observations in schools and classrooms.

Chapter Four

Collapsing Classrooms

In the 1950s and 1960s, human relations were simple. The child of this new era [1990s] doesn't understand what his teachers are all about. . . . The student movement and the inner-school violence of the 1980s were preferable to the 1990s strange child. We can't get through to these children; they're incomprehensible [*tsujinai; wakaranai*], and we don't have a clue what they're thinking.[1]

In his best-selling volume, *School Collapse* (*Gakkō Hōkai*, 1999), junior high history teacher Ryōichi Kawakami focused on the child problem and its relation to diminishing school authority and deteriorating discipline in the home. Kawakami and the private, all-male Professional Teachers' Association (Purokyōshi) had become famous in the mid-1990s for their writing on the strange child. These teachers insisted they were powerless in the face of the strange child—a child who was beyond their understanding of what and how a child should be.[2] In this new book on the school, Kawakami linked this strange child to problems of classroom management and shifting relations of respect between homes and schools. He claimed that the strange child was a sign of major changes in the adult population, particularly the weakened ability of adults to demonstrate resolve, fortitude, and other shared cultural traits to the young—traits that according to Kawakami and others were once embodied by all Japanese. According to Kawakami the stakes of school and classroom collapse were high. Declining respect for a once revered national institution—he referred to the school as "holy ground," because of its role in the inculcation of values and training of the body—was a serious problem for Japanese social order (*chitsujo*).

Kawakami described the shifting relation to the school as the violation of a social compact. For him and other members of the Professional Teachers' Association, social order was a result of a social compact based on common understandings of what it meant to be Japanese. This social compact symbolized Japanese national and cultural difference. The Purokyōshi wrote profusely about the decline of order in the schools, changing relations between homes and schools, and their distress about changes they said were undermining the cohesiveness and communication that had defined Japanese society in the prewar and postwar periods. The Purokyōshi met monthly. These meetings began with their objections to these changes and to the MOE's proposed solutions. But the discussions also ranged broadly over Japan's modern history, as they saw it, focusing on the role of modernity, Japanese education and the school's role in training the body as well as the mind.

Changes in their students and altered attitudes in the home vis-à-vis the school were attributed by the Purokyōshi to the past half-century of "imposed Western liberalism."[3] They did not often specify what they meant by Western liberalism, but when they did, it referred to the infiltration of individualism into what they described as a groupist, dependent society. Despite the fact that their members participated in the student movement of the 1960s, which among other things protested the rescinding of individual rights and the overextension of the Japanese prewar and postwar capitalist state into the private realm protected by the Fundamental Law of Education (FLE), Kawakami spoke of the strange child as a symptom of imposed Western values, he associated with the American Occupation of Japan (1945 through 1952).

The Purokyōshi did not think the MOE was on the right track. They did not take terms like *independent individual* seriously, even though they were central features of the MOE proposed solutions to the child problem. Perhaps because of the way MOE terms were first introduced in the context of recession, or because of discursively engrained notions of Japanese cultural difference, like Doi's dependency (Chapter One), Kawakami and the Purokyōshi were prevented from seeing that discursive constructs like individual, independent, self-development, and the like under the right conditions could do neoliberal work in Japan just as they had in Britain and the

United States. This was something that past Prime Minister Nakasone in the 1980s understood all too well. The term *neoliberal (shinjiyushugi)* did not begin to circulate widely prior to the late 2000s in Japan. Neither was there a lot of discussion about how neoliberal logics and language could transform the social and cultural environment, particularly the atmosphere of the young about whom Kawakami and his group were so troubled.

I was fortunate to have been included in a number of the Purokyōshi sessions; to have had the opportunity to talk with Kawakami at length, observe freely in his history classroom and all around Jonan junior high. This up-close long-term involvement was crucial to my understanding of how education and psychology had come together to create official and cultural discourse that was in the process of overturning the former focus on dependency and the body.

Kawakami and the Purokyōshi were the first to introduce the terms *strange* and *incomprehensible* into the discursive space of the early 1990s recessionary period. Unlike the government officials who appropriated recessionary uncertainty, Kawakami and his group sought to articulate the experience of this change. Their own subjectivities as members of the postwar dependency theory society were revealed in the process, which made their project so helpful for mine. Rather than dismiss the past as the MOE and its psychological experts were doing, Kawakami and the Purokyōshi were deeply concerned about its discarding. Listening to their group discussions and talking one on one with Kawakami about the strange child and school collapse served as continual reminders of the deep historicity of the national education system and the child as future citizen-subject of a nation for which the terms of modernity were neither simple nor taken for granted. Likewise, these conversations were important reminders of how the past is dismissed in the interests of a quickly changing present. Although Kawakami and his group did not include Japanese imperialism in their discussion of neglected history, it helped me to think about how their focus on the body was a remainder of this history, the part that had made it through the filter, censors, and renarrativizations of the 1950s and onwards.[4]

Born in the immediate postwar period and a public junior high school teacher from the mid-1970s, Kawakami had dedicated himself to Japanese public education. When I first met him at the end of the 1990s, he was at the height of his writing and speaking about the changes in the school and child. I told him that the focus of my study was the child problem, something he and his fellow Purokyōshi teachers considered a concrete reality. He facilitated my long-term observations in his classroom, arranged for me to accompany him to teachers' meetings, bimonthly Purokyōshi gatherings (discussed in detail in the following pages), and gave generously of his time in one-on-one interviews and conversations.

I learned a lot from Kawakami and his fellow teachers about their experiences in the Japanese education system and what they believed the school should be and could do. I also heard a lot from them about what they saw as unprecedented changes since the early 1990s. Kawakami did not talk about Kawai, even though he knew of him and met him at least once on the people's education reform committee convened in late 1999 (Chapter Three), out of which came the new language of "suitability" that was the first step in the combined efforts to revise the FLE that eventually took place in December 2006. Kawakami, as previously noted, downplayed the influence of psychologists like Kawai. For him, emotional education, attention to the independent heart, and the turn to patriotism from this individual, rather than from a collective, did not seem feasible. That was certainly the case during Kawakami's generation.

Kawakami often complained to me about the newly underway MOE education reform plan (*kyōiku kaikaku*) that had begun to affect school curricula and finances. He criticized the lack of teacher input into what needed reforming. But Kawakami, the Purokyōshi, other teachers, and education officials with whom I spoke in the early 2000s did not connect changed student behavior, juvenile violence, parent attitudes, and their own concerns about the present and the future with the recession and its wide-ranging effects. How and why they did not is one of the focuses of this chapter.

The Body and Language

Over the past ten years, the change in students is stunning. What parents don't know, but teachers do, is that the average ordinary kid is strange. Everyone criticizes the overregulation of kids, but are kids so pure and all teachers sadists? The school's role was to prepare kids for society; give them the ability to manage on their own [*ichininmae ni naru*] for which they need to absorb basic strengths. Lately kids have become weak. The lifestyle has changed, and so has the body. *Words are no longer absorbed by the body.* This is really a frightening thing.[5]

Within the environment of economic downturn and the changes that began to take place and affect each other in turn, Kawakami's notions of strangeness, incomprehensibility, and "words not absorbed by the body" are an important guide to the history of shared understandings that were being displaced and replaced by the MOE and its psychological experts. Set within the context of a country in deep recession, in which the meaning and structure of individual development was being transformed, government programs and ideologies of national and cultural difference that supported these changes had little to do with on-the-ground recessionary realities.

By the end of the 2000s, the recession was referred to as a world unto its own and palpably so. What was strange and incomprehensible, in fact, was a system being turned on its head. The strange child was one of the main forms this recessionary uncertainty took. The school had played a central role in producing the ideas and technologies of development, from the daily disciplinization of the minds and bodies of the young, to the inculcation of this disciplinization as culturally Japanese, which is to say somehow naturally occurring across the Japanese archipelago. Realizations about how the recession was transforming the role of the school were obscured by terms that focused on the problem with the child and solutions to this problem. These terms are part of what I call *the vocabulary of recession.*

Kawakami's concern for how words are not absorbed by student bodies suggests both recognition and misrecognition. Social divisions had begun to occur from the 1980s on in the Japanese population as a result of the very systems of development that were meant to produce common identification. The recession exacerbated these divisions, driving many parents to seek the privatized expertise of the supplementary school system at earlier ages for their children (Chapter Five). The Japanese government took advantage of the recessionary climate to shift away from the production of homogeneity, equality, and the notion of a homogenous national body, in which the schools had a central role. Homogeneity, like the FLE, no longer fit the world of recession and neoliberal transformation. Following education, the vocabulary of recession and new technologies of governance moved from education to the labor market for young workers (Chapter Six).

Ryu Murakami, well-known novelist, who among many others wrote and talked about the child problem and education, pointed out that what Kawakami lamented as waning authority was a sign of the breakdown of Japan's postwar system as a whole.[6] Murakami maintained that, in the absence of a new direction or value system to replace this failed system, there was nothing to show kids the way, to give them hope and vitality. According to Murakami, the aim of Japanese society during the 1960s through the 1980s high-growth society of his childhood was clear. Behind it was implicit or accepted authority, which he called "teachers' authority as a means to control." However, changes in the level of awareness and concern for education among parents has made this kind of control, which once included corporal punishment, inviolable. What is necessary at this point, maintained Murakami, is the creation of a new direction and a new system of governance.[7]

In this chapter, I explore the social anxiety surrounding the topic of classroom and school collapse in the late 1990s through mid-2000s. Along with the MOE program to relax education (*yutori kyōiku*), these educational changes were discussed and worried over continually by the national media, academics, and teacher's groups, including the Purokyōshi. The problem with schools and classrooms in recessionary Japan was part of the problem with the child. Kawakami considered them one and the same. As he repeated often in our conversations and as the Purokyōshi made the centerpiece of their many publications, there was a fundamental change taking place in their students. What they meant by the "incomprehensibility" to which they attributed the change and why it was such a significant problem at the time is the main concern of this chapter. In the early to mid-2000s, bookstores, newspapers, and electronic media (Internet was just becoming a major information source in Japan) were full of depictions of unmanageable classrooms. Classroom and school collapse was the subject of community meetings throughout Tokyo and of academic conferences. I attended many of them. The private school industry (cram schools or *juku*) joined in, deriding the national school system, championing their approach, and staging major add campaigns, parent information sessions, and "expos" of their educational products (Chapter Five).

In the following pages, I describe my observations and conversations at two public schools: Jonan Junior High School, Kawakami's school and the setting for his writing about school collapse and the incomprehensible child; and an elementary school near Kawasaki City that claimed to be collapse free. I discuss the effects at the local level of the nationwide discourse on collapse and how it affected all levels of social relationships: among parents, between teacher and parent, between teacher and student, and in the community at large. While critically exploring these viewpoints, I discuss the recessionary experience that defined everyday life at this time of economic change. I look at how claims of the breakdown of manner and moral training (*shitsuke*) in the homes dovetailed with discourses of school collapse, exposing both the school and the family to new forms of intervention by the state and private industry.

I show how the child problem also affected the ethnographic referents: children and adolescents. Problem discourses turned them into the necessary objects of intervention. They became the subjects of social anxiety and the objects of technologies of governance. These transformations have brought with them less equality, guidance, and conditions for collective identity and more so-called freedom to self-development, self-strengthen, and discover their latent potential on their own.

Exploring problem-making and social anxiety focused on the child does not suggest that I concur with many who have interpreted this anxiousness as overreaction and media hype. I take the problem discourses, social unease and their discursive forms, the child and school, seriously. They are effects of a particular history, intertwined and domestic of a non-Western and capitalist nation-state and national society at the end of the twentieth and beginning of the twenty-first centuries. These discourses in turn produced other effects on the lives of those who not of their choosing embody the representational force of, as Jacqueline Rose writes, "our symbolic investments in them."[8]

Defining Collapse

The term *collapse* associated with the school and the home first entered into regular use in the mid-1990s when elementary school teachers in different locations around Japan reported feeling that something significant was changing in the atmosphere of their classrooms. By 1998, "classroom collapse" (*gakkyū hōkai*) had become a catchword in the media. In 1999, it was rated one of the top ten new words of the year.[9] According to Naoki Oki, a prominent education critic and prolific writer on the danger associated with the child, the "new storminess" in the school is qualitatively different from problems of the past.[10] Much of the trouble in the decade of the 1980s was associated with secondary students. When it trickled down to the junior high it became known as "inner-school violence" (*kōnai bōryoku*).

The initial response of the MOE to 1980s inner-school violence was more direct disciplinization. This meant increased regulations, standardization, and regimentation of behavior, time schedules, and bodily comportment, a new stage but nonetheless part of the postwar project of dependency, homogenization, and credential society. In the latter part of the decade, extreme forms of these interventions led to the escalation of bullying, student-on-student and sometimes teacher-on-student violence. They also gave rise to a significant number of students who did not attend school due to rejection or phobia—the *futokō* or school refusers.[11] The end of the 1980s was also the beginning of a shift in the Nakasone government's response to challenges faced by the schools and to public outrage at increased regimentation. Nakasone's plans resonated with the already implemented rationales of governance of the Reagan and Thatcher governments, rolling back rather than ramping up direct intervention. The disturbances and responses of the 1980s, however, paled in comparison to those of the 1990s. The economic downturn threw the seeming security and certainty of national direction and individual futures into question, creating an environment of what some observers viewed fearfully as the lack of a stopgap and others saw as an opportunity to turn limitlessness into potential for which the individual would be newly responsible.

What Oki, Kawakami, and many others reported was perilously different about the turmoil of the 1990s through the 2000s was its spread through elementary schools nationwide and the seemingly unpredictable changes in behavior among "ordinary kids" described as a sudden loss of control (*kireru*).[12] Loss of control became so widely publicized during the first years of the twenty-first century that a nationwide survey attempting to identity its sources was conducted by the MOE. Fear about emotional outbreaks among the young gave rise to a large number of books and articles and large amounts of media coverage.

The elementary school in Japan has been celebrated by foreign observers of schooling, child rearing, and psychologically informed anthropology as one of Japan's brightest achievements. I uncover stark discrepancies between the reality on the ground in schools and homes, the way these national and social institutions have been written about in much of the anthropological and social scientific work to date and why I believe certain misconceptions were possible. Knowledge produced about the school and family in Japan has not been without its effects on the way that those at all levels of the system from teachers to policy makers view their system.

Although much of the writing on classroom collapse approaches the subject in broad terms, Oki, like Kawakami, deals in details. Oki devoted several volumes to creating a checklist of detection for the impending signs of collapse. According to Oki, a classroom is said to be in a state of collapse if and only if circumstances reach a point in which "lessons are unconductable" (*jugyō ga naritatanai*). This situation is evident, he maintained, when "kids get up at will and move around the room, sometimes even leaving it, engage in private conversation or other ego-centered behavior with little regard for the direction of the lesson or group activity, and lose their composure at a moment's notice."

Oki is careful to note that classroom clamor on its own does not constitute the breakdown of order necessary for a class to be considered collapsing. For things to reach these proportions, three factors need to be in place: "ordinary" kids begin to disturb; without warning, kids cannot restrain their emotions or suppress their own personal desires; kids become irritable with others for no reason and engage in violence as play. The fear that discipline, said to have been a key characteristic of the distinctiveness of Japanese corporate success, was declining among the young has made it a central point in the discourses on classroom and home breakdown.

Oki also notes an important difference between classroom collapse at different grade levels of the elementary school. Whereas the upper grades display signs resembling earlier phenomena in the junior high, it is among the lower grades that he finds the most dramatic changes. From the time of his survey of 2,000 schools in 1997, most of the teachers of the younger grades reported that their "first graders are strange." Among the things they cited were lack of social skills, inability to pay attention, physical lack of control or weakness, the absence of experience with basic everyday lifestyle skills, and a lack of training in managing their own things. Teachers in his survey reported that the task of introducing these children to the routines of the school has become enormous.

Compounding these various indications of the changes in the child is what writers like Oki and Kawakami refer to as a frightening erasure of boundaries between the categories of delinquent and ordinary.[13] These boundaries that delineated the ordinary stood for regularity, orderliness, and continuity of the center, something that, as I've discussed in previous chapters, was in the process of being transformed. Unmarked by the difference of race, class, or other kinds of social otherness, the ordinary child's seemingly unordinary, uncompliant comportment and articulations (in some cases of sympathy and identification with the claims of Youth A) challenged assumptions about this orderliness and continuity as central and naturally reproducible characteristics of Japanese society and culture.

Unlike in the 1980s, according to Kawakami and Oki, the changes in the child are not marked on the outside. The strange ordinary child is, in Kawakami's terms, walking in the streets looking like one thing, when he or she could at a moment's notice transform into another.[14] As I described in this book's Introduction, the end of the 1990s and first decade of the 2000s was indeed a time when the Japanese ordinary, and the ahistorical status it had been attributed by Japanese and foreigners alike, was being taken apart. What interested me was how this undoing was reframed, recoded, and turned into a problem for those most vulnerable, for whom the conditions of recession and insecurity are the only normal or ordinary they know.

The Decline of Manner Training (Shitsuke)

Depictions of the changes in the child and the seeming inability of the school and home to contend with these changes produced a great deal of unease among teachers and parents, many of whom were fearful that their own child could suddenly become a perpetrator of heinous acts like the infamous Youth A from Kobe.[15] Following the Kobe incident, violent youth incidents were turned into yardsticks of peril by the media, popular commentators, and government officials and exacerbated how classroom problems were viewed. In the face of these uncertainties and the acknowledged lack of understanding about how to deal with them, a new knowledge arose to explain and contain changes made into problems and to exonerate the ordinary.

The home, from the late 1990s on, became the object of a set of allegations that consolidated in the related phrase "home collapse." Criticism leveled at the home singled out the mother for both over- and underindulgence but also berated absent fathers, who spent all their time away from the family (never mind that this time was in overtime at their corporations). Fathers were blamed for the collapse of authority that their absence brought about just as many of them were working even longer hours trying to hold onto jobs, as we saw frightfully depicted by Kurosawa in *Tokyo Sonata*, they were in danger of losing. Mothers were faulted for obsession concern on the one hand and hands-off approaches to child rearing on the other.

The hands-off approach was characterized in the media by reports of mothers lacking experience, afraid to be alone with their young children, and generally fearful of the repercussions of raising a strange child. This unease divides again into two related figures of the mother: one who doesn't care about her kids and has become focused on her own desires, and one who is paralyzed by the immense responsibility of raising a child in the current atmosphere. On the other end of the spectrum was the image of the "education mama" (*kyoiku mama*). This mother-image first made its debut in the 1980s in discussions of the spiraling growth of the cram school industry and the singular devotion of these women to their children's educational success. Within the discursive environment of collapse, the once praised devotion to their children's academic competitiveness, was targeted as the reason for lacking social and human skills among the young, the first step it was alleged in the production of a strange child.[16] Hands-off or overdevoted, mothers, along with their so-called ineffectual workaholic fathers, were blamed for the sharp decline in harmony between home and school, the breakdown of community ties, and even the decline of the nation.

Teruyuki Hirota has devoted several books to overturning the view that education in the home suddenly deteriorated during the recessionary period. His research on the history of manner training in the homes and the role of mothers in Japan sheds helpful light on these far-ranging assumptions. Combining national surveys, media, and various other records on home education, Hirota argues that manner training has always occurred differently across regions and across social classes, "Children are treasures," despite common assumptions, is actually a very recent idea.[17] The idea that child rearing and manner training was done more enthusiastically in the past than the present seems to have been exclusive to the upper classes, according to Hirota, who adds the cautionary note that what in the past was called "manner training" might very well be called "abuse" (*gyakutai*) now.[18]

Hirota's histories of the home and the school are instructive for understanding the changes in symbolic status that the school has undergone over the postwar period. Hirota reports that from the immediate postwar through the 1960s income doubling era, the school was viewed as the source of preeminent knowledge about the child's education, and the local region depended on this knowledge to provide the skills and social training necessary for national rebuilding and high economic growth.[19] The 1950s and 1960s were a time, Hirota explains, in which the school was seen as a place of promise, or the place where promise was produced, which would better society and for which the family was thankful. Within this social climate, problems in education did not receive a great deal of media attention. When they did, they were treated as isolated events, regarded as unconnected to the larger concerns of the nation. Statistically speaking, there were far more dangerous children and youth-related incidents in the 1960s, but delinquency and other crimes of the youth, seriously violent ones included, appeared to occur within the lower classes and regional or minority populations and were therefore regarded as structural abnormalities. When they did occur, suggests Hirota, the school was not faulted.

By the mid-1970s, the situation had begun to shift. Hirota discusses the emergence of the "educative parent" as a major change; a parent whose attitude toward the school was no longer the kind of unquestioned reverence of which Kawakami speaks. This was also the period in which the school first came under scrutiny for the breakneck pace of school curriculum, "ability-centered" curriculum changes of the late 1950s, as well as its disciplinary methods. It was also in the mid-1970s, following the oil crisis of 1973, which had huge effects on Japanese economic growth, that the race for entrance to top universities ramped up and the exam preparation cram schools experienced their first huge peak in attendance. Teachers' complaints that parents are more concerned about their own child and class position than the nation is not so much sudden, writes Hirota, as it is more noticeable now.[20] As Hirota realized, a key feature of social unease was the sense that something had suddenly come apart; if so, it could possibly be remedied just as quickly.[21] The other part of this discursively produced picture of problem and solution created and perpetuated though in different ways and to different ends by Kawakami, Kawai and the MOE, was that if something was suddenly strange about the ordinary, it justified transformation.

Inside Schools and Homes

I was first invited to Jonan Junior High in Kawagoe City, Saitama Prefecture (approximately a two-hour commute from Kawasaki where I was based), in the fall of 2000 by Kawakami. Though our initial encounter was somewhat tense, filled with questions on both sides, mine about his writing and the history of the Professional Teachers' Association, and his about my background and why I had chosen the subject of the strange child for my research, by the end of the meeting we had arranged that I would observe at the monthly gatherings of the Purokyōshi and in his classroom.[22]

I began my observations at Jonan and at the Purokyōshi gatherings in January 2001. Over the course of the next several months, I accompanied teachers and students through their daily routines, from early morning meetings through cleanup, after-school activities, lunch, in the teacher's room, and in the health care and informal counseling facility.[23] Kawakami's motivation for arranging this unprecedented access for me had to do with his desire to provide me with a firsthand view of the collapse of the school and ordinary child about which he was writing at the time.[24] It was interesting that he did not attempt to structure my visits more closely, as I had heard would happen and as had happened with other observers. He believed that the atmosphere would speak for itself.

My discussion in this chapter of the position of the school and its relationship with the larger community focuses on the postwar period. Although thoroughly embedded within the history of the establishment of national schooling in the late nineteenth century, and the militarization of schooling in the prewar period, the postwar history of the school and its position within Japanese society involves a series of key shifts in regard and level of expectation of schooling. As a result, conditions of postwar schooling need to be situated within the international and domestic conditions of knowledge and power within which they emerge, develop, and are transformed. My approach differs from other English-language literature on schooling and the home in Japan, which has tended to separate schooling and family from the larger conditions of political and economic change, often unreflective of its own predispositions toward Japan as a necessary example of essentialized difference.

From conversations with parents at Jonan, I learned that the area around Kawagoe City had been hard hit by the economic downturn of the 1990s;

that many had experienced labor restructuring, either in the form of reduction of salary or full-on loss of employment. Everyone was tense about high
school entrance and confused about whether the changes being proposed by
the MOE were up to the task of fixing the problems in the news on the one
hand and of providing guidance for their children and family on the other. I
also learned that the previous year at Jonan had been full of physical destruction of school property and open fighting between students and teachers
reminiscent of the 1980s inner-school violence days. The important difference between then and now, according to these parents, was that the current
problems were not caused by a small group of troublesome kids but seemed
to erupt throughout the entire class. There seemed to be no mechanism in
place to stop things cascading out of control once they started.

The timing of my observations was chosen so as to view classrooms, and
the entire atmosphere of the school, at both the end of the year (in March),
when class groups are well integrated, and during the first term of the new
school year from April through June. I began my days in their morning
teacher's meeting, moving on to the homeroom meeting of one class group,
with which I stayed for most of the day, as their various subject teachers
switched off. Having read Kawakami's journal-like transcript of the chaos
Jonan had experienced the prior year, I was prepared for pandemonium. I
did not, however, encounter outright chaos. What I did find, albeit with a
significant difference among grade levels, class groups, and students themselves, was a drastic disconnect between the students and the subject matter
of the lessons. This gap between students and teachers resulted in a lot of
noise, sometimes startling kinds of rudeness between teacher and student,
and among students, and otherwise almost complete disinterest and apathy.
In every class, however, there was a small handful of students who attempted
to work diligently, despite the confusion that characterized the lessons.

Though this also differed from class to class, in general the reaction of
most teachers to the noise, rudeness, and blatant lack of interest was to proceed as if the disturbance did not exist. Most carried on as if all was in order,
writing on the board and speaking to the few students who seemed to be
listening. Depending on the day, most of the students got up and walked
around, slept, passed notes, threw small objects at each other, or drew comic
characters. When teachers did ask for participation, it was mainly to read
aloud from the textbook. It was apparent that some students had trouble
comprehending the reading, whereas others were reluctant to do so, and a

few again did well.[25] All of these students were aware but did not often talk about the fact that a major change was taking place in the labor market that would affect their futures in significant ways. No longer would a high school diploma guarantee secure employment, as it had during Japan's full employment generation of their parents. Many of their parents had not been to college, and others were, like the father of Youth A, junior high graduates. In an educational credential society that no longer supports full employment, either out of necessity or new attitudes toward the workforce on the part of corporations and government, those without access to a good college degree plus additional skills would soon be out of luck.

The overall student–teacher relationship seemed to be lacking in formality and authority, something that the older teachers in particular, had been accustomed to expect. Students' address to teachers was informal and many times even cloying. When students became used to my presence in the classroom, they began to approach me in much the same way they did their teachers, asking me freely about my life in the United States and in Japan and about my family. These were times when I learned a lot in turn about them, particularly their friends, hobbies, home lives, and attitudes toward school. I describe what I learned of the kids' interests and frustrations in the following.

Efforts were made by some teachers to quiet their classes but mostly to no avail. In a number of instances teachers attempted to stop students from leaving the room, hanging on the doors of the room, or starting a fight with another student in the hall. On their own, however, most teachers are no match for junior high students, especially male, when things turn physical, and students who engage in fights are unconcerned about the repercussions of their behavior. When I returned to the quieter atmosphere of the teacher's room following one of these hall incidents teachers involved echoed what Kawakami himself had told me many times: they feel they have little recourse to deal with these outbreaks of trouble. No longer allowed to engage in corporal punishment (*taibatsu*), their remaining option, contacting parents, is one they now consider mostly ineffective. Parents, they say, are uncooperative these days, either refusing to believe that their child could engage in such behavior or admitting that they are unable themselves to deal with their children (*te ni oienai*).[26]

When trouble occurred between students, as it often did, teachers were reluctant to become involved. I saw a number of instances of teasing, bordering on bullying; quarreling that seemed to go beyond the boundaries of normal roughhousing; ostracism; and other kinds of trouble. Talking to Kawakami and other teachers, I understood they felt they had nothing to gain by getting involved in the trouble, though I also came to see this as a way to deflect the problems away from themselves and onto the students. I will have much more to say in the following pages about problems between students and the issue of self and mutual policing in the classroom. Peer policing is employed by junior high and elementary school teachers alike to control classrooms in such a way that their orderliness has seemed to emerge naturally, as naturally as culture itself.[27]

There were several times and places during the day in which students took interest and found pleasure in learning: one of these was the *manga* drawing elective. What do the students find here, and why does their enjoyment in these areas serve as such a cause of alarm to teachers and parents?[28] The quiet and focused atmosphere of the drawing class was surprising at first. Unable to focus for more than a few minutes on the content of their other academic subjects, students seemed to have little problem with the precise and careful work that the comics they were creating required. The art teacher was eager to show me the products of last year's students, completed despite the tumultuousness of the school environment. She explained that the work done in this class is all student derived, from ideas through dialog. The teacher facilitates, advising, helping wherever needed with technique, structure, examples, and more, but otherwise students are allowed to proceed at their own pace and according to their own tastes, despite the fact that this included in many cases bizarre and violent depictions.

The relation of the manga to these young people's daily life is hardly cursory. Although print comics were a major attraction of the past generation in Japan (my husband and his friends report having waited anxiously for the next monthly issue of their favorite animated magazine), for 1990s kids in Japan comics, or manga, are their main source of "literature," with the exception of school textbooks (which are also increasingly drawn in comic figures). Local libraries have books to loan, and bookstores appear at first glance stocked with volumes, but a comparison of shelf space at both quickly reveals the obvious: that the manga sections exceed the book sections for children and youth by many times in size and variety. Kids draw manga constantly. (My own two did when we were in Japan; they watched anime on television and went over to their friends' to read their manga.)[29]

The key to the success of this class, professed the teacher, herself an artist, is that the students can express whatever is on their minds through these manga of their own making. There are no formal requirements or restrictions on the amount of time or content. Many of the manga are dark and eerie, and the characters are sharply angled and not always pleasant to view. But the teacher's expectations are not that these creations be projections of what she would like them to be.

When I brought up the student enjoyment and focus in art class to Kawakami and other teachers at the junior high, their reaction was nearly unanimous. They saw the pleasure derived from unstructured activities of this sort, along with the edginess of the creations, as further evidence for the incomprehensibility of students. For teachers, at issue was the decline of discipline and its relation to national allegiance. They connected this student enjoyment to the rising ranks of the *furītā*; young adults who cannot find or opt out of full-time employment, end up stuck with unstable part-time work, and as a result sometimes live longer at home with parents, putting off marriage and child rearing. Once a socially sanctioned dependence, particularly living at home until married, which stood in counterdistinction to the forced independence of youth in the United States, this lifestyle is increasingly labeled "weak" and "parasitical" in this era of economic downturn.

Fearful of the uncertainty all around them, parents and teachers often identified with Kawakami's view, that the source of the strangeness of the young was the democratic forms of social organization imposed on Japan during the postwar era. This modernity, as Kawakami often referred to it, had slowly destroyed the system of human relations in Japan from within, splitting the mind and the body (*atama to karada bunritsu suru*) and resulting in the emergence of these strange kids, whom he suggests are both monsters and victims.

The recessionary period in Japan has been a strange and incomprehensible time. Financial futures made insecure have resulted in a new uneasiness about shared understandings of the past and a whole set of requirements and expectations that have transformed the social and cultural environment so as to make it indeed unknown. What many teachers and parents seemed to miss, except perhaps the art teacher at Jonan, is that the young are the subjects and objects of recession, reform discourse, and neoliberal transformation. This time, their time, has become a time in which the life course, individual development, and the national developmental narrative have shifted.

Limits that do exist are being reworked and recoded, foisted onto the newly independent individual to individualize and figure out using his or her own potential. The MOE and its recruited psychologists' dismissal of the disciplines, ideologies, and problems of the past have been accompanied by the promotion of a seemingly freer self-development regime of the present. In this real-time survival game, freedom equals a liberalized job market's insecure employment, training one must now find on one's own, and the obligation to create an individual heart that loves the nation, even if this now means absorbing less support and more risk and responsibility.

"Our Minds Are a Product of the Postwar"

Kawakami's own views are a result of his studies with the Purokyōshi group.[30] Their meetings took place in Saitama Prefecture, in the bottom floor of a two-story building about twenty minutes from the Kawagoe station. The space they occupied was equipped with desktop computers; an area for printing and for compiling their weekly newsletter, *Objections (Igi Ari)*; a large meeting area with a long, low, flat table around which they gather during their meetings; and a small kitchen equipped with supplies for the relaxed, convivial after-meeting eating and drinking sessions. The many books they have published over the last ten years as a group and individually were on display at one side of the room.

I was escorted to the first meeting by Kawakami and entered to find seventeen men of varying ages seated on cushions around the long table in the center. Beginning at 3:30 in the afternoon on Saturdays, these gatherings frequently continued well into the night. My impression after that first night was one of startled amazement: Here was a group of elementary, junior high, and high school teachers engaged in a heated discussion about the Japanese historical predicament of modernity and their own conflicted subjectivities.[31] Our minds are a product of the borrowed postwar way of thinking, they say. The prewar thing is still within the body. It was their pronounced, though not highly publicized, purpose to find a way, their own way, to recapture what has been lost and reunite the mind and body.

Starting against a background of the 1966 *Anpō* (mutual security pact between Japan and the United States) and the 1968 student movement, the founders of the group, Tetsuji Suwa in particular, described that period as a time when democracy, equality, freedom, and the supremacy of the individual were in the air. The spokesman for the group, Kawakami, describes his as the first generation to absorb the full force of the impact these ideas had on society. They depict the tidal wave of this time as embodied in the phrases, "the Japanese of today are behind the times; Japan must change. Make it happen." Things, however, were not so simple. In their very denouncing of what they see as blind enthusiasm and disavowal, these men are nostalgic for the 1960s when, at least as they describe, there was more active energy among the young:

> However, the freedom and equality of students that everyone insisted on didn't work out well at all. We had classrooms of forty-five to fifty kids; when things got out of hand and we tried to restrain this freedom with force, we felt a contradiction. We ran up against this problem every day. Those raised in the prewar era would suppress their classes, and those classes seemed to be more full of vitality and livelier than ours.

Kawakami told me he had considered quitting during the violent 1980s. Here in Saitama, he explained, they decided to meet and talk about the position of the teacher. They came to the conclusion that things that others said were borrowed thoughts and decided to come up with their own way of thinking about education. They exchanged these views at their group meetings.[32]

According to the Purokyōshi, much academism in Japan has tried to write off student problems as unacademic and outside of disciplinary knowledge.[33] There are things that have been disallowed or disavowed from the public discourse. Kawakami and his group frequently criticize the famous scholar Maruyama Masao for the dissemination of these views in postwar society.[34] The Purokyōshi gather together to voice what they think privately and cannot say publicly. One of these things is *compulsion* (*kyōsei*) in relation to education. Under the present circumstances of a split mind and body, there can be no education without compulsion, they say. Of course, if things were made whole again, which is to say, mind and body were again joined, as they believe they were prior to the Occupation, this would of course be the prewar totalitarian state, there would not be a need for a debate about coercion after all.

Kawakami and the Purokyōshi members insist that others refuse to see this reality. Japanese, they say, try to adopt the position of subject, but can't: Their difference—one they no longer even recognize—stands in the way. The Purokyōshi point out that this split produces what they call an "impossibility," which results in an unsuccessful subject—the strange (*hen da*) child of the 1990s (and beyond) is its embodiment. This subject cannot speak its own inadequacy, as it would discover the impossible gap between knowing and doing, or mind and body, so it refuses to speak. This, they say among themselves, is the result of the postwar dispensation.[35]

On my way home from one of the meetings, I was accompanied by a young producer of children's programming at NHK (Japanese Public Television) who had also been invited to attend that evening's meeting. I learned how clearly the message of the Purokyōshi resonated for him. The work of academics in its purpose and plan is "all Western," my young interlocutor tole me. "The Purōkyoshi desire to get beyond this, to get beyond the Western mind and the borrowings from it. They want us to reach the level of the body, which because of our training is where the Japanese thing (*nihonteki na mono*) still exists. The split that we all have between mind and body is from the freedom and democracy of the postwar."[36] The Purokyōshi and those who attend their meetings often seemed caught between romanticizing the prewar and wartime sense of totality, total control, and collective body and, as 1960s student movement members, wishing to prevent the undoing of a fuller realization of rights, equality, and individual protections, just as the focus on the collective body was changing as a result of the Japanese inflection of neoliberal globalization,

The Purokyōshi were focused publicly on sending out a wake-up call, especially to parents, about the child they did not know. The school, they say, is unfairly held responsible for the lack of moral training among the young. No longer regarded as "sacred ground" by parents and the community, the school comes under fire for the problems and crimes perpetrated by kids both inside the school and beyond. They remember the school and teacher–student relationship of their youth as not only being focused on academic achievement but also inculcating a whole range of mental and physical comportments, the process of which often involved more physical contact than now, some of which was forceful. It was a comprehensive kind of communication and training, what they call an overall training ground in human relations. This relationship was at the base of the older system of order that those like Kawakami identify with their youth in the immediate postwar era. Now, however, mistrust and suspicion govern the relationships surrounding the school. The Purokyōshi call on parents and all members of the community to put their heads together; what took fifty years to create, they argue, will take another half century to undo.[37]

The Elementary School, Re-Viewed

Praised in the past as a model for developing the "whole child," Japan's elementary school system was once suggested as a model for the United States. Japanese elementary schools have also been credited with the formation of what has been referred to in educational and psychological literature as the Japanese personality and its relation to Japan's unique cultural inheritance. Particularly in its early stages, national schooling in Japan was given credit for a range of national and social successes, from worldwide excellence at mathematics to the low crime and divorce rates, techniques of power relativized as cultural difference—as in the different formation of the individual, different views of the child, different constructions of personality. Making Japanese culture the signifier of last resort conditioned the ways in which the elementary school, its practices, and the demands made of it by a postwar income-doubling nation-state were (or weren't) seen and written about by international observers.

Imai Elementary School, situated on several main train lines, claimed an exemplary absence from the conditions of collapse plaguing so many schools and neighborhoods. The area from which it draws its student population is split between the high-end Mitsubishi and other large firms' company housing, pockets of older well-established single-owner homes, and the rented apartments of self-employed families fairly hard hit by the decade-long recession. Besides servicing this local population, Imai in the mid-1980s was designated a "returnee" (*kikokushijo*) school. Though this program was a high priority of the MOE during the earlier decade as Japan expanded abroad, it was in the process of being drained of its resources.[38]

My relationship with Imai was extensive. My two daughters spent nearly two years at the school, joined its sports teams, and participated in the various events throughout the year. I joined the PTA to become acquainted with a range of parents: those who lived in the high-end company housing, some of whom had lived abroad, and families with husbands who were self-employed while the wives either worked part-time in local businesses or took in work from the outside.

My first days as observer throughout the school day at Imai Elementary took place during the third trimester of the year. Told repeatedly by the principal, with whom I had had several long conversations, that Imai's classrooms were stable, I went into my first full day of observation in a third grade class with a mixture of expectations.[39] Similar to my intensive observations at Jonan Junior High, and to the other elementary and junior high schools in which I observed for a shorter duration of time, I requested permission to be a regular part of the classroom and school routine and to continue this presence for an extended period of time.[40] I also asked to be able to communicate freely with the different members of staff at the school. I felt that only through this kind of unencumbered participation would I be able to get a good sense of the multitude of conditions that went into the kinds of situation that I had witnessed elsewhere.

My first day observing in classrooms and around the school was not uneventful. The third grade class with which I spent the first full day was incredibly loud.[41] At first, the teacher tried to ignore the noise, speaking over it as she passed out papers, and tried to talk about the plan for the day. This was after the class had been called to order by two students chosen for the week to be "class monitors."[42] Finding talking over the din to be impossible at one point, she began to chide the students with comments that ranged from "lots of talking today" and "It's really noisy in here" (*urusai no honto ni*). Not too long after this, two boys stood up in the middle of the class and refused to sit down. At this, the teacher, already unable to carry on lessons in any sort of regular fashion, lost her composure and started screaming, "What the (hell) are you doing?" By day's end, when she and I spoke about the class, she told me that to maintain enough order in the classroom to proceed with lessons, she regularly has to scream loudly and in much more deriding terms than she was ready to use in my presence. Was this a noncollapsing classroom or a different way of framing and managing the changes taking place given the better economic situation of most who attended the school?

There was a twenty-minute break midmorning. The teacher, having other things to do, left the room for the quiet (and warmth) of the teacher's room on the first floor, while the kids (and I) gathered around the only heater in the room by the teacher's desk.[43] Many of them (especially the girls) did not go outside to play during recess but tried to gather in one group or another to talk or play cards.

Although several subjects are taught by other teachers, including music and math, depending on the grade level, the homeroom teacher is solely responsible for the comportment and performance of his or her class, at both academic and the many extra-academic activities in which the classes engage.[44] Any creative divergence or supplement to the national curriculum (which was reduced by over 30 percent in the 1970s and has again, as part of the new series of reforms of 2002, been reduced by a similar amount) has to come from the homeroom teacher. When a teacher is struggling just to keep the noise level down, as this teacher was, lessons do not diverge in the slightest from standard worksheets and textbook lessons. Much of this seemed quite dry and uninteresting to the students.

As a result, students' attention is further diminished. Of course, Kawakami and others argue that part of schooling is learning how to pay attention, whether the material is to the student's own individual liking or not. This is the interesting weave of academics and discipline for which schools in Japan became well known from the early 1970s through the 1990s: learning math along with learning how to manage one's own desires. But this demand for self-maintenance turned out to be entirely unrealistic within the everyday reality of 1990s Japan, where kids were often left alone to entertain themselves with televisions, computers, video games, and cell phones that serve to accentuate and differentiate individual desire. Most kids no longer spent their after-school times with friends playing at self-created games. When they did get together, the chief activities, in urban settings at least, were often organized around acquisition: reading a friend's comics, going shopping (in the case of young girls), or (in the case of many young boys) choosing a playmate on the basis of the other's possession of the latest toy (something about which many children were well informed from the time of kindergarten).[45] Add to this the attractions and creativity of the supplementary education materials and after-school classes (Chapter Five) that over 80 percent of the Imai schoolchildren either received in the mail or attended, and under the conditions of the denial of the pervasiveness and significance of these realities, there was the recipe for a complex kind of classroom collapse.

During the course of my observations at Imai, I saw a great deal of difference in lesson style and classroom management. Overall, classes were unruly, but teachers seemed to handle this in different ways. In some cases, they resigned themselves to the inevitable and let the kids blow off steam (as one fifth grade teacher put it) until they were able to settle down. In some of the classes, kids were quiet during the tests, which were part of their everyday routine, though pandemonium would break out as soon as the faster students finished. According to public school teachers and supplementary school administrators, differences in academic ability skyrocketed over the course of the 2000s, as increasing numbers of kids attended after-school exam preparation classes or subscribed to supplementary materials for school study. The ambiance of the classes I observed at Imai Elementary was permeated by this difference, with some kids finishing within a very short time and not particularly respectful of others for whom the materials are challenging and for whom it takes almost twice the time to complete the same tests.

Without recourse to the parents or administration for help, homeroom teachers relied on a system they seemed to know was untenable but that kept some order in the classroom, albeit with the undesirable consequences of pitting one child or a group against another. This system is *peer policing*. In this system, students are put in a position of managing the classroom, doing everything from calling it to order to regulating their peers, even doling out punishments. It was not unusual for children to be told to stand in the back of the room for hours at a time or to be reprimanded by their peers without recourse to their own defense. From what I witnessed, the teacher did not take part in these events, leaving it to the kids. My daughters reported in their classrooms that this often deteriorated into a circle of taunting that passed among the kids but whose largest impact inevitably fell to the weakest or different in some way.[46]

My time in the upper grades at Imai was instructive as well.[47] Teachers in these grades were the direct recipients of the accumulation of problems from the earlier grades, compounded by the incredible schedules and lack of sleep many of the kids in the fifth and sixth grades experienced.[48] In a fifth grade class in which I observed, it seemed as if everyone was screaming at once, the teacher perhaps the loudest of all. Surprised at my own lack of tolerance under these conditions, I asked the teacher about this situation; he frankly replied that it had taken him a whole year to realize why his students were so loud, especially after the weekend. He reported finding that they had gotten less rest on the weekend than during the week. Many had extra school on the weekend, sometimes for the whole day, and those who did not attend cram school were often involved in sports teams, which required a great amount of devotion, strict discipline, and long hours. In any case, he had learned that Mondays, when I happened to sit in on his class for the first time, were lost days. His interim solution was to spend the day (a full day each week) catching up on little things and basically letting the class go.

He had developed a system during the year that he showed me for finding out about the temper of the students. He excused them from other homework to write short diaries about their weekends and after-schools. His use of this method of communication between teacher and student was not aimed at improving the students' writing abilities, though it did seem to have a positive effect in this area, but rather to try to gauge where the students were. He said that he wished that parents would consider that sending their kids to school in this exhausted state was not conducive to studying, managing their own things, books, pencils, and other things necessary for the classroom were being constantly forgotten or lost, and especially for getting along with others. The class also suffered from the huge discrepancies in ability between the kids, to the extent that the kids on the top were bored waiting through the regular lessons and often complained to the teacher and to their parents that they did not see why they should attend regular school at all.

When it came to organizing the sixth graders for their graduation ceremony, which was to take place in mid-March, the task was awesome. It took three weeks to teach them to walk quietly in single file and good posture to the gymnasium where the event was to take place. Graduation ceremonies or anything that involved outsiders in the school were conducted with the utmost formality, and thus a finishing ceremony like this was meant to come off well, despite all odds. I observed as the three sixth grade classes were prepared for this event by their teachers. The preparation involved endless hours of discussion, planning, and coordination among the homeroom teachers, the music instructor, and the principals who were to hand out the diplomas. All facets of the ceremony from initial procession to turning, sitting, coming up to receive diplomas, and of course the musical performance (practice for which began a full year in advance) were painstakingly rehearsed. What the parents were aware of was not the time spent away from studies that this endless rehearsal required, but the end result, which was a highly polished and (nearly) flawlessly executed ceremony.

Routine comportment—the ability of students in upper elementary grades to move smoothly through their everyday routines, including preparation for ceremonies of all kinds—was at a level commensurate with what others schools and other teachers outside of Imai referred to as "collapse." Imai's reputation, however, dictated that the teachers could and should handle whatever came up on their own. In some cases, this caused teachers to band together, trying to create solutions among the grade groups. In others, the long-standing rule of "homeroom teacher authority" continued to take precedence, often in difficult situations to the detriment of teacher and student.[49]

The other part of fifth and sixth grades that was strikingly evident were the problems that developed among the kids. One teacher, at a loss for what to do with her kids, did an informal survey of their feelings and found that all of the kids seemed to feel that they were potential victims, that they could be without friends at a moment's notice; they felt scared to be on their own. My older daughter reported this feeling on a regular basis in the classroom; having come from a school where friendships were much more fluid, she struggled with the complexity of relationships in the classroom. She also struggled with the difference in ability, wondering herself if she should attend cram school just to stay up with the others.[50]

Dependent Body to Independent Heart

Problems of individual students are increasingly dealt with through recourse to the new psychological frameworks adopted by the MOE. The implementation of this new knowledge about student ills was turned over at the time to the school nurse or other volunteers in the health care facility in each school. This newly introduced psychological approach to student problems dictated that students' individuality be the focus, unfortunately confining the problem in many cases to the private realm of individual phases and needs. Moreover, although the rhetoric of individual psychological care sounds progressive for a system bent so long on subsuming the needs of the individual within the larger requirements of group consolidation, in many cases this focus stopped at the level of the rhetoric, as there was neither the time nor the resources to handle each individual in all his or her individuality within the confines of the daily school routine. Where much of this excess ended up was in the health care room, with a health care worker who was, as Imai's school nurse related to me, completely unprepared to handle the kind of problems, the relation with parents about their children, as well as master the new psychological language all at once. She felt overwhelmed and many days did not want to show up at school herself. It was also her view that kids came more frequently to the health care room than before, asking for care for small things that she thought would have been ignored in order to continue playing. Part of what they came for was the quiet and the attention, she noted.

Parents, for their part, professed to being scared at not knowing the origin of problems. Many of my informants admitted to me in the course of our conversations that they felt as if they were not being adequately informed about their kids. In a conversation about recent juvenile crime and school collapse with a woman whom I had become close to through the PTA, she remarked that she thought her country had let her down. This highly educated woman, who had lived abroad several times during her life, now lived in fear in her own country about the current conditions among the young. She had, she said, a terrible unease about something that is not being made public about the recent series of juvenile crimes and school disturbances; she was fearful as well that the value system that she regarded as uniquely Japanese was no longer effectual. Her sole recourse, she increasingly felt, was to "protect her own family." Moreover, I found in my discussions with mothers that they were suspicious of each other and of each other's kids and worried about their own children, whose minds or psyches they now feel powerless to know or predict.

What Kawakami and others viewed as the unreflective attack on the school by the home, or the failure of the home and the community to support the school's authority, amounts on the ground to a palpable sense of mutual tension and suspicion between home and school, among parents, between students, and the increasing reliance on the school to deal with any and all problems that occur. What I came to understand as a further heightening of the competition (rather than the minimizing of it as the official rhetoric on its face would have it) includes various forms of confusion and fear that result in ostracism. Teachers with whom I spoke described this fear in varying forms as the constant concern over problems in communication between themselves and parents. They said that the protocols of communication, which they assumed to be appropriate, and the things that they felt could be implicitly understood in the past, no longer seemed to obtain in the same ways. Misunderstanding was rampant. The same words did not have the same meaning for parents, teachers, and students.[51]

Collapse as Recessionary Effect

My observations in schools claiming to be experiencing collapse, in those with a self-proclaimed absence of a lack of order, and from formal interviews and informal conversations with school staff and parents at both, have suggested to me that claims of collapsing classrooms and the home efface the heterogeneities of conditions in post-1990s schools and homes. This is not to deny the problem of order of which Kawakami spoke, but rather to recast the discussion in terms that take full account of the violences that the severe economic conditions have visited on an already troubled national narrative and the processes of identity formation that this narrative provided for the citizen-subjects of Japan. Small business failure; shrunken demand for the range of nonsalaried types of work; the need to absorb a larger number of (non-Japanese) "guest" workers and their families (who in the current conditions can no longer afford either to stay or go home); the heightened fears among salaried workers and their families over the loss of salary, position, and their children's future competitiveness—all the effects of the protracted economic recession—comprise the current conditions of uncertainty but are veiled in the more generalized anxiety over the child, decline of the school and the home. The absent-presence of these recessionary conditions in the discourse on collapse is important for an understanding of the tensions that exist for teachers, parents, and children but also for a recognition of how these differences become obscured in the changes in governance that have received strong impetus from the collapse discourses.

The Kobe serial wounding and killing of children incident proved pivotal in the narrative of school collapse and in the influx of psychologists purporting to deal with the problems of schools and homes. Writing on the child problem and the collapsing classroom gained new impetus after the Youth A incident in 1997.[52] To Kawakami, the Purokyōshi, and many others, the Youth A incident seemed to justify the need to do something about

Japanese childhood. Kawakami's focus on the body was an attempt to locate and ground the continuation of a shared disposition—in which the physical body absorbs and unites all Japanese bodies into one, similar to the prewar ideas of the *kyōdōtai* (national community) and *kokutai* (national polity or essence). For Kawakami and others who enter the discussion from the point of traditional physical training, the privileging of the body is linked to the diminished sense of morality. But it is this very focus on the physical body, as I have argued here, that has helped to strengthen the claims of the psychologists recruited by the MOE to shift responsibility for youth violence away from the education system and back on the family and individuals.

The problem associated with the young reflects larger struggles with the meaning of the mid- to late twentieth-century past and the direction of the national future. When articulated in the terms of the undisciplined bodies of the young, bodies that fail to produce the unique forms of social disposition and social bonds assumed to be tied to a kind of cultural repository, the more critical problem of a crisis of the national (narrative) itself is overlooked. Moreover, the spectacle of a child lacking any form of restraint is terrifying precisely because this child does not reproduce the values of an intact system. Strange children not only fail to reconfirm the intactness of society but also cannot serve as a latent source of value. They cannot adopt the subject position of a disciplined worker. They detach ideologically from the production of value from the state and replace it instead with timeless values.[53] In turn, the state's retracting and transforming while inserting an entirely new discursive vocabulary demonstrates not so much the collapse of an intact system by some outside force (Western liberal values, for example) but the undoing of a narrative of national unity, produced and reproduced over the course of the postwar period through the creation of a massive connectedness discourse between the cultural and the economic sides of Japanese society. The discourse and institutionalization of national uniqueness and unity emerged out of a long trajectory of local and global crossings of knowledge and power (Chapter One). In this chapter, I have shown how this trajectory of local and global crossings of knowledge is shifting at the site of the school and home.

In the next chapter, I turn to the exam preparation cram schools (*juku*) and the private education industry of which they are a large part. Talking to cram school managers; attending large parent expos of new educational products and private testing sessions; sitting in on cram school classes with students; talking to parents, students, and more, I ethnographically investigate how these private supplementary schools and educational services increasingly promoted themselves as substitutes, rather than supplements, to the public schools. Capitalizing on the discursive figures of the strange child, classroom and school collapse, and the new educational and psychological language of independence, their promotional campaigns, although promising certainty and support, further isolated and often added to the uncertainty of individual families and students. As Diane Negra and Yvonne Tasker, writing about media and recessionary conditions in the United States, explain, within discourses of privatization "there are no public or systematic problems, only individual troubles with no trace or connection to larger social forces."[54]

Chapter Five

The Cram School Industry in the Age of Recession

This era is one of choosing your school and global excellence. It is no longer sufficient to follow the old system; we have to look to the world's places of excellence and follow in their footsteps [photos of Stanford, MIT, Harvard, Cambridge, and Oxford appear on the enormous screen in back of the speaker]. From now on, we need to drop our reserve, forget about the idea of a standard level, and push our own abilities. This global excellence is entering Japan [the speaker shows data from industries]. Do you want to be left behind?[1]

Several months after our arrival in Tokyo and the registration of our two elementary school–aged daughters in a Japanese public school, we began to receive a wide range of advertisements for supplementary education. Most of these mailings included trial offers, ranging from home-use materials to sample no-cost lessons and free assessments of "academic strength." Without exception, these offers came packaged to impress and concern. Sparing little expense, these carefully crafted appeals to parental unease demonstrated their superior command of the information on the child's education, from declining academic ability (*gakuryoku teika*) and school collapse to the effects of the education reforms. They seemed to be saying, "This is your choice, but do you really have the right to turn your children into failures?" (or even worse). The paradox embedded in the idea of choice in an environment as anxiety ridden as that of the early twenty-first century in Japan was enunciated to me over and over again by parents and teachers. Their fears—summed up in the title of a best-selling book at the time by a supplementary school expert, *Only You Can Save Your Child*—named the child but focused on the larger uncertainties between national futures and personal ones.[2]

Jacques Donzelot has argued that no longer having the right to allow children to fail is an effect of the conflicting web of "psy" (or psychopedagogical) advice about the child that has penetrated and helped to define the modern (middle-class) liberal family since the mid-twentieth century.[3] Donzelot's approach to the family is one that takes it not as "a point of departure" but as a "moving resultant . . . an uncertain form, whose intelligibility can only come from studying the system of relations it maintains within the sociopolitical level."[4] In this chapter, I focus on the production of conflicted parental subjectivities and their relation to the supplementary education industry in Japan at the end of the twentieth and first decades of the twenty-first centuries. I am following the lead of Norma Field, Anne Allison, Merry White, and others. Field has used the notion of the "mother and child laboring team" to express the forms of everyday oppression that too often go unnoticed, or are blamed on those involved, because ostensibly it is their *choice* to become involved.[5] Allison has written about the postwar production of the "education mama" as a result of a gendered division of labor that instituted what she has called "nightwork"—the after-work company outings that have extended the workday into the night, separating the spheres of home and work.[6] Nightwork was also responsible for the prerecessionary assigning of responsibility for the middle-class home and success or failure of children in school to the stay-at-home mother.

The problem of choice came up frequently in my conversations with mothers and their children, suggesting the various restraints within which they felt compelled to choose. I found my own children's reactions to the offers with which we were inundated revealing. Despite coming from the United States, where advertising that targets, and many would say constructs, children's desires for a huge range of commodities is a multimillion dollar industry, my daughters were dazzled by the elaborate promises of free gifts (Game Boys, science games, attractive accessories) at a level to which they were unaccustomed. They also worried about falling behind others should they choose not to enroll in one of the schools or subscribe to one of the offers that came their way. By the time we began to receive these offers, my children had already become keenly aware that the majority of their school peers were enrolled in extra schooling or subscribed to supplementary study materials. My daughters repeatedly described their failed attempts to arrange to play with new friends after school due to all the different forms of supplementary schooling, and at the same time they were becoming aware of the stark divisions of ability produced by all this extra schooling—divisions that ultimately divided classrooms and split futures. In view of this, it is not at all surprising that the strongest motivation parents cite for enrolling their children in extra schooling is that the children "ask to go."[7]

In this chapter, I focus on how the child problem, educational discourses, and neoliberal transformations boosted the appeal of after-school schools and other private education services for recessionary-era parents, as the subjects of education problems and reforms loomed large and economic decline continued to bewilder and frighten. In assessing supplementary schooling industry gains, I examine how the private education industry emerged as the administrator of a substitute certainty—mediator and master of the changes in the child and the nation.[8]

I investigate how the cram schools and other private educational services contributed to the shift from dependence to independence. As the opening epigraph by a speaker at a large parent presentation session, organized by one of the largest cram school chains made clear, "It is no longer sufficient to follow the old system"; those who do will be left behind. The self-responsibility of the recessionary period came in the form of a choice but manifested as individual risk. It's "your story now," as Hayao Kawai in the role of psychological spokesperson for educational changes announced (Chapter Three), which is to say that within the transformations, including privatization of futures, individuals are responsible for their own progress or the lack of it. Inner frontiers and independent individuals are the new terms of human capital development; terms that neatly elide the domestic and global histories of value production, labor exploitation, and individual exposure to the booms and busts of capitalist economies. What the private education industry grasped early on was that this diverting of responsibility and risk to individual families meant a larger market share for them. The rolling back of financial support and responsibility on the part of the education ministry went hand in hand with the rolling out of an emotional education and a morals curriculum to develop an independent heart—a self-developing and nationally allegiant independence I've termed *neoliberal patriotism*. The requisite choices were something for which there was little preparation; hence the turn to a new class of educational experts for help.

The Supplementary School Industry, Explained

The supplementary education industry, or the education service industry (*kyōiku sābisu sangyō*), as the MOE has referred to it, is immense and varied in Japan. A large portion of this market is occupied by after-school schools (*juku*), which break down into the remedial-type schools (*hoshūjuku*) and exam preparation schools (*gakushū* or *shingakujuku*). The remedial schools, the oldest form of extra schooling, emerged during the accelerated curriculum of the high growth 1950s through the 1970s as an aid to children who could not keep up with the fast pace of studies and, as the saying at the time went, fell through the cracks (*ochikobore*). These after-school aid lessons focused on helping young students keep up with existing school homework. Exam preparation schools grew in number from the late 1970s on, as the economy slowed following the 1973 oil crisis, and the competition ramped up for entrance to top high schools and universities. They do not supplement existing schoolwork but rather exceed it. Similar to but yet different from the *Kumon method* with which many Americans are now familiar, exam preparation after-school schools employ different approaches and assignments than those of the public school curriculum. As I return to in the following discussion, they are not responsible for teaching nonacademic social skills and values. Their focus is gateway exams. Despite the significant role that compulsory education (*gimu kyōiku*) has played in students' national enculturation, students and parents I interviewed were beginning to see the exam schools as a substitute, rather than a supplement, for schooling. (It should be noted that after-school classes and activities such as music lessons, Japanese calligraphy, and English are sometimes included under the large catchword of *juku*. In the present context I focus principally on schools that provide exam preparation lessons).

Through extensive observation of after-school classes, prospective parent-directed events and interviews with managers and curriculum creators, I discovered how this private industry has carefully attuned itself to the new uncertainty about the child and the future. Promoting itself as specialist, the supplementary education industry has turned the conditions of recession to its advantage. In the following, I discuss how the industry's sophisticated sell was received, interpreted, and acted on by prospective consumers for whom the sense of uncertainty was closely linked to a sense of national and personal identity.

Though an overwhelming majority of Japanese students are enrolled in or subscribe to supplementary education, this rate differs by area (urban and rural), profession (salaried worker, self-employed, or contract worker), and views on education (often a product of the former two). Concerned that my supplementary schooling research ran the risk of being limited to "educationally ardent" (*kyōiku nesshin*) parents, my advisor at the University of Tokyo, Professor Teruyuki Hirota, encouraged me to seek out the unenrolled, uninvolved, and uninterested parents as well. Professor Hirota's advice in this area proved invaluable. I discovered how new social divisions of "the divided society" (*kakusa shakai*) are expressed and experienced in the realms of education, family, and later work (Chapter Six).

Within the altered economic environment of the late 1990s and the twenty-first century, one might suspect that there would be sharp declines in enrollment in supplementary schooling. Although it's clear that consumers of educational services and products scrutinize prices more than they did before the recession, the efforts of the private educational industry in addressing and capitalizing on the anxieties of parents have paid off.[9] Through huge investments in public advertising campaigns, including mass mailings, commuter train billboards, parent information sessions, and no-cost expositions of their products, these educational businesses distribute and promise the continuation of exhaustive data and personalized consultations on individual progress and how best to survive the self-responsibilities of recessionary life. This industry provides everything that the national school system seems increasingly unable, and unwilling, to supply—a seemingly unequivocal set of answers about how to best achieve success for the individual child and clear talk on "ending competition."[10]

It is important to note that while the government has been quick to criticize the harmful effects of attendance at exam preparation schools by over half of all Japanese children (another 30 percent of whom subscribe to monthly supplementary materials), the government's relationship to this private education industry continues to be less antagonistic than its spokespeople would have it appear. Established to support the income-doubling plan of the 1960s through a complex rhetoric of "equal opportunity" in education, the exam system has also served to sort and rank, thereby limiting the possibility of resistance to the system. The relationship between the government and the supplementary industry is thus in many ways a reciprocal one. Although the MOE publicly bemoans the "examination hell" so many Japanese children are compelled to endure, there are no immediate plans in the education reforms to dispense with the exam system, despite the languages and curricular changes of "relaxed (*yutori kyōiku*) education." Moreover, as several junior high school teachers pointed out to me, the exam system has served as one of the chief instruments of order over the past several decades.[11]

When responses are provided to questions about the exam system, the ministry's spokespeople speak in the newer terms of individual choice and responsibility (*sekinin*). As previously discussed, the increasingly unbridgeable gaps in ability—the effect of the participation by a majority of students in one form of supplementary education or another—have been an underacknowledged factor in classroom disruption by an education system shifting from an ideology of dependency and homogeneity to (neoliberal) independence and division—different values (and strategies for value production), as mothers I met at exam preparation events and schools put it. Within the environment of choice and responsibility, or responsibility as choice, the acceleration of this gap appears not unintended. Enter the supplementary schooling industry in its newly fashioned role as mediator of the enormous burdens placed on individual families of the neoliberal era. Tomiko Yoda, writing about shifts in mothering and gender, describes this burden as a process of the Japanese government's move to relinquish its direct control over, and hence responsibility for, the system of social management.[12]

In this chapter, I specify how the supplementary practices and terms of the private education industry specify the relationship between effects of recession and new forms of governance. Interviews and observations in this chapter highlight the shift away from the discursive conditions of homogeneity, collectivity, and an immutable core of culture at the same time that this immutability is reinscribed in the seemingly unlikely terms of an independent individual and a patriotism of the individualized heart.[13]

"You Need an Expert."

My daughter and I arrived at the Hiyoshi train station about 8:45 a.m. on a Sunday morning in the early summer of 2000 for a parent information session and a no-cost test of my third-grader's academic strength (*gakuryoku kenkō shindan*), sponsored by the largest nationwide junior high entrance exam preparation school, Nichinoken.[14] Making our way down to the Nichinoken headquarters, we were trailed by a steady stream of parents and kids.[15] The free test was being offered that day in two sessions, morning and afternoon.

The children were led to the fourth floor and directed to rooms of fifty each. Each child was assigned to a desk and instructed to fill in the cards in front of them with their Nichinoken number and their name and phone number. While waiting for all the children to quiet down, the staff discussed a "grand prix" quiz that was to take place. My younger daughter was noticeably nervous in this atmosphere. This was her first experience in a large and formal testing situation of this type. Not knowing what to expect, she was not eager for me to leave, though by this time all the other parents had vacated, hurrying to the parent information session on the subject of "2002: The Collapse of Academic Ability Report" (2002 *Nen Gakuryoku Hōkai Hōkoku*).[16]

After the parents were situated, our first speaker began his presentation by directing us to one of many glossy handouts that we had been given on entry that laid out in various statistical images how drastically the amount of time devoted to academic subjects in school was set to decrease in the new reforms. Explaining the meaning of these charts, graphs, and numbers for us, our speaker stated,

> There will be lots of kids who won't know the basics, not only because the school doesn't teach them, but because it doesn't teach the process. After 2002, all explanation of process will be gone.

He established early on that the MOE does not want or know the best thing for children, nor perhaps for the nation as a whole. "Bureaucrats are really something," he said in a tongue-in-cheek fashion, "'Minimum standard' is what they are aiming at."

We were asked to reflect on the latest "lesson participation day" at our own children's schools. Didn't we think the level was low? It should be higher, he said adamantly. "The new comprehensive studies (*sōgō-tekina gakushū*) time will leave a large gap between what parents learned and what kids will know; the rest will be left to the parents." (He directed us to a full two-page spread in the pamphlet entitled "what will happen" that laid out in clear detail what would not be taught after 2002.) "If you don't teach children, where do you think that this 'strength to live' will come from?" (Parents around me nodded their heads in agreement.)

The speaker went on to say that the ministry's position on classroom collapse was to drop the level of studies, because kids can't keep up. "This is ridiculous. First they tried to adjust to the middle level, now they're dropping even that." He illustrated this situation on the board by drawing a picture of two inverted triangles, placing one on top of the other. These triangles were intended to represent the future of Japanese education under the present reform program—a large top elite group, an even larger underclass, and a tiny middle. This is where things are going; he emphasized that there would be no middle at all. (This inverted triangle design translated the complicated language of Hayao Kawai about different courses, different stories into stark messages of new risk and responsibility for parents.) It had become the responsibility of the home (*katei*), shorthand for the private realm. Even though the total number of children was decreasing, entrance exams were on the rise.

About thirty minutes into the talk, one of the members of the teaching staff came up to the podium to update us on how our own children two floors down were doing. While our attention had been somewhere else, the staff had been monitoring our children's condition for us, and we should rest assured that all the children were doing well. This test, he said, was different from anything the children had faced at elementary school up until now; it was probably the first time they were seeing these kinds of problems. "Do you think you could do it?" we were asked half in jest, to which many parents shook their heads. Before returning to the test below, he gave us several tips on what to do and what to say when we picked up our children following the test. For instance, if your child said that the test was boring, you should answer, "That's 'natural'; tests are not fun." The point not to miss here, he said, is that many parents simply ignore their children's remarks of this kind, but we should use the situation as an opportunity to communicate a different message. Without scolding, or seeming uninterested in what they had been through, we should demonstrate our interest but also our resolve. Moreover, this was a lesson we should work hard to follow in everyday life as well. Too many parents just crush their children's "sense of curiosity." Rather, when our children ask us a question that has academic value, for instance about "value-added tax" or the like, we should be sure to give them a good answer.

As this teacher returned to the children and their test, our prior speaker returned invigorated, with a new forceful message:

> The year 2002 is a year of choice. What can your family do? Well, we all know that kids choose the easiest way out; for them play is the most natural thing. What they need is for someone to define for them a clear goal and show them how to reach it. We advise three points to build the child's desire and reach their goal: Spark their interest and curiosity, praise them, encourage them (most parents just scold or hit!). Tell them that they have the potential and just need to reach it.
>
> At elementary schools they just discourage kids; if you encourage them they will realize their own potential. So, you can scold them about making proper distinctions, but not about their studies. Please cooperate with this! *You need an expert.* Won't it be hard to achieve this at home in an easy to understand, tender way? There are plenty of things that kids don't know these days [for example, the traditional hearth]. These are things that parents take for granted. Parents' common sense is not kids'. Won't it be hard to fill in all of this at home? Even if you can awaken their interest, can you cover, do you know, everything they need to know?

Nichinoken promises to deliver a new thinking strength (*kangaeru chikara*), different from the ill-explained but everywhere publicized "strength to live" of the MOE. Several years ago, Nichinoken came to the conclusion that it was necessary to supplement for the schools at an even earlier age than before, and this is why they now advise parents to start their children at the third grade level for a full year of preparation and introduction:

> We found that children's concentration span was short, their study skills lacking, that there were more kids than before who had fallen behind. We found that we needed three years to nurture these things and to awaken their curiosity. For instance, I've been doing this work for thirty years now, and I've found that if you teach them something three times, there are those that miss three

times. Parents are naturally emotional about these things, and their reaction is to hit. [Everyone laughed, seeming to identify themselves with this comment].

Two weeks later, I was called in for a free personal interview to hear the results of my younger daughter's test. I was told that 14,000 third graders from Tokyo to Kyushu had taken the free test of academic strength sponsored by Nichinoken. It was explained to me that the child's strengths and weaknesses were evaluated from a range of viewpoints and that each problem was designed to measure a specific trait of the child's academic strength. This was not a test to discourage but rather to help me to understand where my daughter needed further strengthening.

I was provided with very specific suggestions for her. First, we should establish a study habit of thirty minutes a day. I should consider a private school, because the overall environment would be preferable to the public schools with their problems of bullying and breakdown of order. Personalizing the appeal further, my consultant said that Nichinoken would give our family their maximum effort; they would choose a school for my daughter that fit hers (and our) situation. Above all, they would try to seek a school that would fit her abilities. We would not be disappointed by their support, he said.

I could not help thinking how these sessions and follow-up meetings invoked the highly critical film of the 1980s, *Family Game* (*Kazoku Ge-mu*), now pushed to its limits, in which knowledge, data, and expertise totally encircle the family. Now the *juku* is the unchallenged specialist, not only about test taking but also about the organization of the domestic sphere and child rearing. Brought about by the unstated collusion between the government and the supplementary industry, a new intensification of the already diminutive family in Japan was taking place. In the *Anti-Oedipus: Capitalism and Schizophrenia*, Gilles Deleuze and Felix Guattari perform a caustic critique of the triangulation of the family that occurs from uses of Oedipus that are unattuned to complex formations of power through which modern subjects are produced. Borrowing from their illustration of "Mommy-Daddy-Me," or how the family is turned in on itself; drained of its confidence; and penetrated by a range of constraints, restraints, but also expert discourses, I would argue that the desire for expertise that is drawing an ever-larger section of the population in Japan to the supplementary industry might be captured through a slight revision of the Deleuze-Guattari image to one of "Mommy-*Juku*-Me."

In addition to these general information sessions, Nichinoken facilitates regular opportunities for parents to become more familiar with private junior high schools. This is done on a small-scale basis through "get-to-know" sessions at Nichinoken sites, as well as on a much grander scale through biannual expositions (expos) of products and schools. Once you are in the Nichinoken network, which is to say your child has taken one of the quarterly "free tests," you are placed in the pool of potential clients and receive constant mailings. At one such "get-to-know" session I attended, the head of school and other administrators from a well-established all-girls Catholic school came to introduce their school to prospective parents (all mothers). In addition to their ability to complete in five years (junior high and high school are combined) what it takes the public schools a full six to accomplish, this school promoted itself as a place where young women during the tumultuous years of adolescence would receive, in addition to academic ability, a strong sense of morality.[17] The aim of this meeting was clearly to project a sense of control and certainty with regard to the education of the female child. Not only is this school attuned to the importance of etiquette, and the larger concerns of social and moral education, but, given the homogeneous atmosphere among the girls, we were told that they are able to do this in a *truly* relaxed atmosphere in which children can freely "develop" (*nobiru*) their own interests.[18]

We were treated to a promotional video that began with a history of the school, founded in Meiji 23 (1891), followed by a montage of the spectacular architecture and religious symbols that adorn the school and give it a sense of tradition and morality. The focus then moved to the happy figures of girls studying, as the voice-over announced that the school attends to the individual growth of all the girls. As the film moved on to the school entrance ceremony, featuring music by Vivaldi in the background, we were treated to scenes of girls whose comportment and focus (no dyed hair or other material adornments here) reflected their internalized manners and also the type of "home" and the "values" of the home from which they had come.

From the girl's singing of a Latin hymn to the prayer that begins and concludes their day at the school, what struck me was how these markers of the foreign were presented as another unequivocal answer to the kinds of uncertainty that threaten the very moorings of middle-class belonging and its attendant connection to national-cultural identification in present-day Japan. These days, emphasized the principal, when it seems that kids have lost connection with any sense of values, Christianity has a lot to offer. After all, he reminded the mothers, it was you who gave birth to these children, got up with them in the middle of the night; the most important part of their growth after all is their "conscience" (*ryōshin*). A female staff member of the school came forward to address the concerns that closely parallel those of the moral deficiency of kids these days—the college entrance exams. She reminded us that there are many things to consider when choosing the right school for our children. For example, she said, how does the school keep you updated about your child's progress, and how much of the concern do they remove from the parent? At their school, once you enter, she promised, you can forget about the "standard deviation curve" (*hensachi*) entirely, and there will be no need for cram school until at least the senior year. The significance of the standard deviation curve and the "confidential report" (*naishinsho*) for parents of students attending a public junior high, and seeking entrance to a top public high school, is enormous. In Japan, the conclusion of obligatory education comes at the end of the junior high years (or after ninth grade). High school entrance is dependent on the results of the high school entrance exam, the student's place on the standard deviation curve, and the contents of the confidential student report. Although the overwhelming majority of students (over 95 percent) continue on to high school, there is a vast difference between the schools they enter in terms of academic level and the comportment of students.

On the way back on the train, I sat with the mother of one of my children's friends, who had also been at the meeting. Returning from abroad three years ago, she hadn't wanted to think about exam preparation schools. However, the unease about the child and schools had convinced her to look into private school entrance. It was not until her son was deeply involved in preparing for the junior high exams, however, that she realized how demanding this preparation was. He would return home at 10 p.m., and she was worried about his emotions and his confidence. Still, now that he had passed and was in a private school, she reported that there are lots of pluses to these schools. At private schools, she said, there is *real* homogeneity. Kids enter at the same academic level, so teachers don't have to be so careful. They don't have to take the high-school entrance exam and be worried about the confidential school report, and they come from families with "similar value systems." She suggested that I think seriously about enrolling my daughters in the exam preparation courses. When she took her daughter (now in fifth grade) to the individual consultation session at Nichinoken, they discussed various schools and her daughter's personality. The consultant described her daughter as a "good girl," but also energetic, and said that the schools she had not liked thus far probably would not suit her after all. At that, my acquaintance admitted to feeling relieved and impressed by the consultant's superior knowledge of schools and even of her daughter.

The Expo

On the advice of several of my informants, I went to see how this exposition of product and content comes off on a larger scale. Twice a year starting from the year 2000, Nichinoken has sponsored massive events to draw together large crowds of prospective parents to convention center settings, where one can experience firsthand, through documentary, discussion, and illustration, the path from uncertainty and lack of knowledge to the certainty of information and a school suited to the needs and desires of both parent and child. Yokohama International Convention Center, where one of two winter expos of 2001 were held, is an enormous place befitting a conference of global importance. Appropriately enough, at this enormous gathering of parents (90 percent of whom were women), it was precisely the issue of the global, and how families and individuals can prepare themselves for the future in the face of not only the receding of economic security, but the security of a national paradigm that went with it, that was the topic of the exposition.

These meetings are strategically scheduled to follow the results of the past year's exams, which are advertised in February every year. Entering the conference center and proceeding into the exposition halls, we were greeted by the smiling faces of Nichinoken staff distributing reams of gleaming packets of information. On the walls behind them, the numbers of successful entrants and the names of the schools they had successfully entered were juxtaposed to huge blowups of the faces of success and failure of Nichinoken students. Made into enormous murals, these numbers and faces represented the modern rite of passage into the disciplined (and up until now successful) society.

On our way into the lecture hall, we passed by rows and tables of books and goods that in all their newness and sophistication seemed to hold out the yet untapped promise of success and position that seemed more elusive than ever these days. Many of those attending seemed reluctant to leave, sensing some missed opportunity, but with an assurance that there would be plenty of time to browse after the talks, all of us made our way into the 10,000-person-capacity hall.

I sat down next to a couple who said they were interested in enrolling their third grade son in the starting course. We talked briefly about the situation in the schools, about which they professed to being worried, and about what part of the Nichinoken message they found most attractive. The presentation of the day started with a documentary film about the exam process. The motto of the film was "To the person who seeks a shining future: encouragement, not empty praise." This is precisely what these experienced staff can do that parents cannot. We saw evidence of this throughout the exam process displayed in the film. It is the staff who direct the child through his or her studies, advise and admonish (unemotionally) when needed. The staff, unlike the family, do not let emotion intercede. Possessing the most up-to-date information on the child, it is the staff who take him or her to the exam and prepares the child for what Nichinoken proudly announces is nothing short of the significance of the other major milestones in his or her life, such as a wedding and the births of his or her own children. On finding out the results of the exams, many children are overwhelmed by the enormousness of what they have done, relates the film. When they wake up the next morning, the first thing many do is turn to their parents and say, "Thank you."

At the end of the film, one of the heads of marketing appeared on the stage. This period is different from any of those before, he told us:

> This era is one of "choose your school" (*gakkō erabi*), and *global excellence*. It is no longer sufficient to follow the old system; we have to look to the world's places of excellence and follow in their footsteps [photos of Stanford, MIT, Harvard, Cambridge, and Oxford come on the enormous screen in back of him]. From now on, we need to drop our reserve, forget about the idea of a standard level, and push our own abilities. This global excellence is entering Japan [he presents some data from industries]; do you want to be left behind?

Now that the stage had been set, our next speaker came on with the message that everyone knows (but nevertheless) is implicit in this loftier idea of "global excellence," and the course that it necessary to take you there:

> The schools are in trouble. They have gone overboard with "rights" and "freedom" [*kenri; jiyū*] and can no longer impose rules when they need to. Parents have to change if they want their kids to change. Affection comes in many forms. There is too little of the kind of affection that requires enforcing rules these days. There are many kinds of affection; exams are one of these.

He gave us ten ways to "encourage" our kids, and admonished us to discipline our emotions against verbal and physical outbursts stemming from frustration at our children.

This expo, the private school introductions, the individual consultation, and the testing and information session: all seemed designed to demonstrate how Nichinoken is poised to supplement for what is now lacking in the school and the home and to remove parents from the terrible position of uncertainty and responsibility in which they are now placed.[19] At the individual meeting to which I was invited, I was offered the closest thing to what I imagined as "perfect information" about my child's academic ability (and how this reflected on the emotional and social parts of her personality) in comparison to children nationwide. In light of the conversations of parents whom I had overheard at the parent meeting and at my children's school up to that point, I was strongly aware of the high premium put on this knowledge for parents. As the speaker at the information session had stridently reminded us, the national schools' policy of discouragement has been misguided. It had, in his view, prevented individual abilities, from academic to athletic, from coming into view. The new policies of the MOE will not, according to this view, make up for the lacks in the child's education, just widen them. .

The Nichinoken approach, on the other hand, is not constrained by these failing policies or misguided motives. Ostensibly, neoliberal independence on the one hand and patriotism on the other create a sort of double-edged appeal for uncertainty reducing and take over some of the responsibility handed to the individual's private schooling industry. The view that Nichinoken project is of a government that is out of step with the new global reality of competition and competence, whereas their methods and approaches

are not based on outdated ideologies but in the sophisticated analysis of precise data. Moreover, they promise what the government seems more than
ever unable (or unwilling) to deliver: to take care of your needs. Their appeal
to parents works first to confirm (even enlarge on) the current sense of crisis
and uncertainty, second to demonstrate their superior knowledge of the crisis and what needs to be done to save one's own child and family from it, and
finally to promise to assume the responsibility for doing so.

In spite of all the energy put into this frontal campaign, the industry's
strongest appeal is in that which it leaves unsaid. Although their charts,
models, and detailed descriptions attest to the failure of the national schools'
approach and reforms, they neglect to address the difficult balancing act
with which the national school system has been handed, between creating
an aura of equality and homogeneity for which Japanese schools have been
so renowned, and producing a disciplined, competitive, individuated population to which end the exam system was instituted.

Over the past several decades, this conflicting set of demands placed on
the national schools has teetered dangerously out of balance at various moments, as social and economic conditions rendered this doubled role increasingly untenable. The imbalance spawned a series of peaks in enrollment and
the growth of exam preparation schools, whose mission increasingly exceeded their role of supplementation. Where the message comes through the
loudest for parents is in the insinuations that the present moment is unlike
any of those prior to it. The matter now is not one of a failed balancing act
or disingenuousness, but perhaps the collapse of them both. It is to say that
the late twentieth-century sense of security, which seemed to promise the
individual and family a future benefit, was based on an always tricky balance
of national ideology, a state-controlled school system and economic policy.
This sense of the secure future has been eroded by global economic changes
that have supplanted the nation-state as the authority of last resort over its
own economic determination.

Mothers and Managers

Kenji Hasegawa was the manager of the main branch of Nichinoken for
the Kawasaki/Yokohama region at the time that I made my initial contacts
in the capacity of researcher in May 2000 (Figure 5.1). I asked to conduct

Figure 5.1. Nichinoken (exam preparation school).
Photo by author.

observations during class time and interview him about how exam preparation schools for junior high entrance like his were adapting themselves to
the new economic and social concerns of the twenty-first century. I told him
that I was particularly interested in how these schools structure their relationship to the home.[20]

On the day of our first interview in the summer of 2000, Mr. Hasegawa
showed me into one of the rooms directly off the office used to counsel and
advise parents. He began by telling me that awareness of the junior high entrance exam among parents and students was high. There have been what he
termed several "booms" over the last several decades, and each in his opinion was connected to social and economic circumstances. In the early 1980s,
parents sought enrollment on the basis of "pride," he suggested. At that time,
those who enrolled their children weren't interested in lower-level schools.
After a tapering off later in the decade, in the early 1990s, parents sought
enrollment due to a continued sense of affluence and a strong memory of the
inner-school violence of the late 1980s. The boom of the first years of the
twenty-first century was different again, he said. Following the bursting of

the bubble of property values, and the negative economic outlook, parents became concerned for the future, their own and their children's. They were worried about the reduction of academic content in the new reforms and also about the many other problems among kids that plague the national schools. This was a boom of "school choice" he said, and his firm advised parents to look for a school that fit their child, not necessarily the highest-ranking one.

Parents were choosing this route for their children using the different criteria of a better environment, he continued,

> We run our program by constantly adjusting the classes and levels. There are tests four times a month to adjust level, but classes are changed just once a month. Following the fifth grade year, we introduce almost no new content. Rather than learn new things, the students review and strengthen what they have already. In the sixth grade year, the problems are mixed up, and the student's tools are tested against them.

Mr. Hasegawa described their third grade level as building study habits (*shūkan shisei zukkuri*), the fourth grade as the point where the mother would play the largest part in managing (the student's) time, and the fifth and sixth grades as a moment of making these studies their own. He emphasized that one of the big benefits of private schools that parents appreciate is that unlike in the public schools, which are not uniform, there was no need to go back over the same thing many times. At a private school, everyone proceeds at the same pace and can remain in this environment for six years. During this time, they finish the regular curriculum a whole year ahead of the public schools and then have a whole year for review and test preparation. He also emphasized that the private schools do a good job in the area of psychological care. At the public schools, those who can't do well tease the others who do, he said.

As far as his view of the parent's role, Mr. Hasegawa's explanation was illuminating:

> Parents soon look at the scores, and get nervous, but we counsel them to take it easy; otherwise they won't make it in the long run. We take each case differently. Communication is key. The mother's role is important; she has to watch her child and be very cooperative with us. She should be on hand, but

not teach, and definitely not time the child with a stopwatch. We warn mothers against this.

In other words, just the right amount of parental involvement, a very confined and well-defined parental subjectivity, is called into service. The junior high exam was indeed the combined "work of the parent and child," as Norma Field has argued, but, as Mr. Hasegawa made clear, the role of the parent was increasingly defined and delimited by the managers of these schools. Moreover, as a close acquaintance in Kobe, who had a sixth grader and fourth grader enrolled at Nichinoken, offered, mothers at the beginning of the twenty-first century were looking for a supplementary school that would look after their child (*mendō wo miru*).[21]

I talked to a number of mothers whose children were attending exam preparation schools at the time and who had children who had completed the process and entered private schools. Their counterconceptions of the relationship with the *juku* were helpful in rounding out the picture that management provided. Each year of the experience was different, I learned, and each was filled with its own kinds of tension and acceptance. During the intensive summer session in the critical sixth grade year, one of my respondents, who had begun to worry about her daughter's changed behavior around the house, told me,

> The *juku* is like a new religion [*shinshūkyō*]. You have to believe. The teacher at the *juku* wrote on my daughter's notes that, as a result of her studies this summer, her life would be transformed.[22]

Her daughter needed only four points to ascend into the higher class. The teachers had been prodding her to work harder, said the mother, so she had given up playing. "It's all in the way you present it to the kids," she said. "There is no room for doubt." Her daughter came unglued every night, she said; she didn't laugh except in her dreams.

"The cram school gives advice, but we still feel responsible," she said. She reported being troubled by her daughter's changed attitude. Her daughter cut off sentences suddenly, couldn't talk to her dad, and had no friends at the *juku*. The head teacher there told her that her daughter was stubborn because she complained about having to spend so much time on geography. This attitude had problems, the head teacher said. Despite everything that the teachers here said and did, mothers realized that not all kids absorbed the techniques or applied themselves in the same way; this difference was the point of all the anxiety. The cram school advised parents to work with and change their kids, but as my above informant said, this was her daughter's personality; she had lots of likes and dislikes.

The summer intensive program had started, and now only Sundays were free. Her daughter's friend had been told by her teacher at a different school that she would have to study until she dropped (*shinu hodo benkyō suru*) this summer. Her own daughter had been promoted to the higher class, but could she stay in it? If her relationship with her daughter was like this now, what would it be like when she was a teenager, the mother wondered. At this point in our conversation, my respondent suddenly added, "Japan feels dangerous. You don't always know what others will do."[23]

As several of the mothers with whom I interacted over an extended period related to me, the junior high exam is very different from the high school test. At age twelve, the children, young boys in particular, don't really know what they want. It is up to the parent to present it to them in the right way.[24] The junior high test in Japan is special, they said, because it sets the kids on a path and a process through which they are changed; this is a period of growth for them. Another mother described the idea of how to win kids over to the idea in the following way:

> Kids have a dream about going to a school, about being a certain person. That's why they are willing to give up so much vacation and playtime. It's important not to build the dream too high and not too low. This is hard! These are elementary-aged children after all, so the parent has to work hard to take them through it. This is not a problem of likes or dislikes. For the top levels, everything has to be sacrificed (*gisei suru*). Kids are pitiable when this happens, but that's the price to get them in (*soko made yaranai to hairanai*). They pretty much stop going to school and just go to the cram school. The regular school becomes superfluous. "Why do we have to go to school?" the kids ask. The end of the credential society (*gakureki shakai*) has meant the narrowing of chances (not the opposite).

Mothers were worried in other ways about the path they had chosen for their children. Several of them had read in the papers that the shocking crimes of the Kobe Youth A had to do with his failing the junior high entrance exam. They were all interested to know whether, as a result of my research in Kobe, I had found out anything that had not been revealed to the public about this heinous series of crimes by this junior high student in 1997. One mother in particular was suspicious of the government's role. As a citizen, she felt entitled to an explanation for the bizarre behavior among the youth recently. This sense that something was being hidden from the general public was fairly common among my informants. They were dubious about my offer of several good books to read on the Youth A incident. They no longer believed what they read about this shocking incident, as so very much had been written. None of it revealed the truth that they were longing to hear, however, about how a boy from an ordinary family could harbor such deep resentment and commit such a series of crimes.

The Everyday of the Juku

The summer session for sixth graders begins in late July, just a week after school lets out, and continues to the end of August and the start of the second term of school. There is a break for the Obon holidays of five days in the middle; otherwise, with the exception of Sundays, many of the children enrolled in exam schools go to school throughout their summer vacation. My first observation session of lessons and the school atmosphere at Nichinoken began in late July following the first test of the summer to adjust rank and ensure class homogeneity. The students are distinctly aware of the meanings of these scores, as they not only dictate the class they will be in but their seat within the class and ultimately the junior high for which they can try. During the minimal breaks between lessons (about ten minutes), many of the kids can be found checking their ranks and comparing them to the overall scores.

The weather on the first day I attended was hot and very humid, typical of Tokyo summers. As I boarded the train for the several-station ride to the school, there were already a number of kids on the train talking cheerfully to their friends, seemingly unaffected by the heat. They were easily identifiable by their school bags with the Nichinoken insignia (an "N" with an inverted fountain pen through the middle) on them. In the shape of an old-fashioned book bag, they lay horizontally on the back (rather than vertically like backpacks and the typical national school bags), in order to fit flat against the chairs in what turned out to be quite crowded classrooms. They were efficiently designed with ample space to hold all the books and notebooks that the child carries, sometimes over long distances by train, as well as other necessities like an umbrella for bad weather and, of course, a cell phone holder, now fairly ubiquitous among older students and elementary children attending *juku*.

When we arrived, Mr. Hasegawa was at the entrance calling out in a loud voice for all the kids gathered and cavorting around to get to their classrooms. The general atmosphere of the school on that day was boisterous and loud. In between classes, the kids gathered in the small foyer space with several vending machines and a couple of tables. With the exception of before and after class, these in-between breaks are of short duration, and the students' break for dinner (about twenty minutes) was the only time they had to converse with their friends.

The bell rang shortly thereafter, and the teacher entered the room. The students in this class quieted down without any warning. He wrote a quick assignment on the board and then left the room. The students began to work quietly in their workbooks. This was the sixth grade top or crown (*eikan*) class, and I was observing their math lesson. This class had thirty students in all: one-third girls and two-thirds boys. (I was later to learn that this is not a big class at this school). The only sounds in the class for the first ten minutes while the teacher was absent were those of erasers, sniffing, and some fidgeting in chairs. Otherwise it was absolutely quiet.

The teacher, who had on a short-sleeved shirt, tie, and Nichinoken tie clip, stood and watched as the class worked. The classrooms were sparse, to say the least. The teacher stood most of the time, having no desk to speak of. There were no windows in the room, which made it seem more like office space than a classroom. The temperature was kept comfortable by an industrial-size air-conditioner (also with heating capabilities) in the back of the room (an item conspicuously absent from regular schools, where endurance to heat and cold has been considered an important element of bodily training). Still, these rooms were sparse, plain, and in the lower levels cramped compared to the many regular schoolrooms in which I had observed.

The schedule for that first day and for the whole week was a consecutive six hours of study (from 2:30 to 8:30 p.m.). Breaks were few and far between. On this day, this class, with whom I stayed for the duration of the afternoon and evening, had two math and two social studies classes back to back.

It should be noted that the cram school sees this summer as crucial to the preparation for the test, and failure to participate fully is communicated to both parents and children as unacceptable.

When the teacher finally spoke, the students listened closely. This was Nichinoken's cream of the crop, and they were slated for the top schools. They have devoted what many outside the system would perhaps see as a maniacal amount of time and energy, as well as money for extra supplements and extra counseling to this course. The teacher talked to them about what to expect on the test (still a full six months away) and how they were all in this together. Expect surprises, he said. Their parents and Nichinoken have given them the highest level of preparation. He then got down to the specifics of the test problems they would face.

This teacher, like many of the others that I saw (in particular at the top levels) went through the analysis and breakdown of the problems as the professional that he was. (I was reminded of my brief experience many years earlier teaching top-level foreign university students the TOEFL ["Teaching of English as a Foreign Language"]). He showed them ways of solving the problems, pointing to problem spots and moving at an altogether brisk clip. Forty minutes later, the class was still completely quiet, though a couple of kids had started to look around. The teacher's reliance on the blackboard to diagram and explain, and the expectation that the students will get everything down in their notebooks, stood in sharp contrast to my observations of regular school classes, where in some cases the board was hardly ever used and the students copied very little in their notebooks. The teacher's address to this class befitted the level of the students' achievement.

Unlike the other levels I visited on following days, these teachers were addressed as if they deserved this respect and position. When the bell rang, the teacher was still making his final points. The kids waited for him to finish and then jumped up and congregated in the back to play a game using their rulers and erasers (other classes that I sat in used pencils or whatever was available) to create a shuffleboard sort of game.

At successive observations during this summer session and over the course of the year, the difference in the treatment of classes according to their level and the comportment of students in these levels was in stark contrast to this "crown" class. Lower levels had greater numbers of students (up to forty-five in some classes) and a very different level of attentiveness. Whereas the teachers at the highest level did not seem enthusiastic about my presence, the lower-level teachers were clearly annoyed to have me in their classrooms. They had to spend a good part of their time quieting students who got bored after thirty to forty minutes of study. They needed to explain more and go back over explanations several times for those who did not pick it up the first time.

Whereas the relationship between teacher and student seemed relaxed in the upper levels, at the lower levels it often fluctuated between antagonistic and cloying—the teacher needing to alternately scold and coax students, many of whom did not seem to want to spend this many extra hours at study. It became starkly evident to me that not every child who attends a school like Nichinoken is devoted to the same degree nor expected by the school to achieve the same level. There was none of the pretense here about all being equal or the same, but, on the other hand, there was no need to second-guess where one was in the rankings. As a child's test scores improved he or she not only changed classes but moved up through the seats, in what seemed reminiscent of organizations like symphonies, with their first and second chairs. But we would be ill advised to accept these performance resonances too easily, without considering that the population involved are not all acknowledged prodigies, even, as Norma Field has poignantly argued, the process in which they are involved should be seen as one of prodigization.

Norma Field discusses the generalizing of the model of a child prodigy to the larger population of ordinary children in what she calls the "mother–child laboring and consuming team." Although her observations about this process of prodigization are as apt today as they were at the end of the 1980s and early 1990s, it is important to emphasize that the changed perceptions that have resulted from economic and social uncertainties have caused the cram schools to refashion their approach to assume a larger portion of the families' (read "mostly mothers") role. They have become the professed experts, specialists in a market that is driven by the desire for certainty, and this informs their changes in approach and growing appeal. It also has altered the figure and idea of the infamous "education mama," and many of those with whom I conversed seemed uncomfortable with this image.

The routines of those who participate in this process, as I witnessed firsthand among several families with whom I stayed during my trips to Kobe, and from my many conversations in and around Tokyo, can be completely submerged in the atmosphere necessary for concentration and devotion. At one of the homes in which I stayed, the late-night routines of the older children (fourth and sixth graders) made morning risings in time for regular school an oppressive task, and morning meals almost nonexistent. (When the older boy did eat in the morning, he clearly had no appetite, and no time, for a sit-down healthy breakfast of rice, soup, and vegetables, and most often requested a piece of frozen pizza or other fast-food type of treat).

There was little time for play after school, as there was homework and snacks and dinners to prepare to take to the *juku*. The younger of the two boys had been promoted to the special "Nada" class, which required longer hours and more and harder homework even than his brother in his final year. The mother, who was a full-time homemaker, professed to feeling harried all the time. Though she had plenty of time during the day to herself, she said, the routine and the concerns she had about this process kept her in a constant state of agitation. She had heard from several of her friends about other *juku* that did a better job than Nichinoken in easing these concerns of mothers, taking more individual time with students. It was not advisable to change in the middle, but she was considering, she said, having a look at what they had to offer. I spoke at length to her husband as well about the exam process and his feelings about what was happening to their family routine.

They had been a family that, due to the husband's position as a dentist, had been able to take off and spend time together on the weekends in the past. Now that was impossible. All their time together was now spent preparing late-night snacks or solving homework problems into the night. Though he, like his wife, did not seem to fit the mold of "education crazy" that has been so publicized in the press both in Japan and worldwide, the father said that now that they were well into this process, he and his wife both regretted the time that they had spent "playing," when they could have had their children enrolled in preexam lessons, such as Kumon and the like. He acknowledged feeling torn by these feelings of regret but could not help but wonder whether their earlier more free and easy lifestyle had made it harder for his children to succeed in the process before them.

Consuming Alternatives

As a member of the PTA at my children's school, and as a result of my children's participation on sports teams in the area, I met and conversed with several groups of parents, who felt either unable financially, unwilling in terms of the time commitment, or simply opposed on the basis of their own educational philosophy, to enroll their children in several years of nonstop extra schooling. Of course, it needs to be said that prior to entering schools for entrance exam preparation, many children attend lessons that target the preschool, kindergarten, and early elementary year student. So, it would be more correct to say that the road to the junior high exam is one that begins in kindergarten with studies at Kumon, the program that specializes in training younger children and professes that there is no limit to what they can achieve at this age.[25] Thus, the bifurcation of the student population happens early on in most major urban centers in Japan, with a large portion of the population beginning their children in some form of extra schooling from the beginning of their formal schooling and for some even earlier.

There are a number of other options for supplementing regular schooling that have emerged to provide an alternative to the full-scale exam preparation route at the junior high level.[26] In these harsh economic times, there are increasing numbers of parents who have turned to one of these alternatives; for their part, these companies are looking to advance their market share against the exam schools. Positioning themselves as an aid to schoolwork, for those who either have trouble with their studies or want to stay slightly ahead of other children, the Benesee company's "Challenge" materials have doubled their subscriber pool at the elementary level. The popularity of this home-use brand of supplementary materials had grown substantially outside the urban centers, and among the sector of the population who do not want to subject their children (or themselves) to the exam process. This does not mean, however, that this group, whose parents have for the most part graduated from "good" colleges, and hold mostly salaried jobs, were unconcerned about the situation in the schools. What it did mean was that they were seeking a way to ensure that their children would stay just ahead of the curriculum of the schools: To service this desire a special niche in the supplementary market has emerged (to the tune of US$50 to US$60 a month).

The challenge of those in charge of curriculum and marketing at "Challenge" is to hold children's interest, such that they will look forward to receiving the materials every month, and thus complete the exercises on their own, while supplying parents with the kind of information about their children's growth and education at which the big exam schools specialize. The head of the marketing division for elementary school curriculum at "Challenge" told me that his parent population is more cost conscious than those who send their children along the junior high exam preparation path. Parents often complain about the cost of the materials and request that they cut costs by providing fewer gifts and other rewards with the materials. However, the children, he said, look forward to these rewards; in the case of home-use materials, if the children are not interested, they will not do the exercises, which in the long run translates into their parents discontinuing their subscriptions.[27]

In our case, my daughters' choice of sports and playtime over supplementary work put us in close contact with families whose children were neither enrolled in a form of cram school nor subscribed to home-use materials but nevertheless sought to recoup some part of the academics-plus-endurance experience that the *juku* provide. One of these ways, as we were to discover, parents sought for their children was through participation on a sports team. Describing in requisite detail the world of children's sports in Japan goes well beyond the limitations of the present chapter. However, the position and reactions of several of the mothers of elementary-aged children on my younger daughter's all-girls dodgeball team proved instructive of the extents that become imaginable once futures seem no longer sure, let alone guaranteed.

Our experience with this team was, on the one hand, of a group of welcoming girls and mothers, and on the other, its coach, whose method of training included explicitly disciplinary tactics that all too often bordered on violence. The portion of this experience that I want to highlight here has to do with the parents' reactions to my dismay and protests about the coach's style. Though it was clear to the other parents as well that his approach frightened the girls and often proved a hindrance to their participation in the sport, they stopped short of confronting him about it.[28] When, in one instance, I refused to let my daughter participate until the coach got his emotions under control, a great deal of embarrassment was caused to all, and the other mothers seemed perplexed by my behavior. Speaking to several of them about the coach's actions and my reactions sometime later, I discovered that although other mothers professed dislike for his violent manner, they admitted to appreciating the toughness this kind of experience would provide their daughters.[29] Besides, they did not believe that he would go so far as to seriously injure the girls. If the girls could manage under a monster (*oni*) like this, as they put it, they could certainly overcome future obstacles much more easily.

The sensibility that these mothers evidenced was again different from that of a group of women, whose husbands were nonsalaried workers and who took in side work. I became well acquainted with one such family and their larger community of friends as a result of our daughters finding themselves in the same class and neither of them attending cram school. Although these women seemed uninterested in competing over educational rewards, or in gaining their children endurance in the realm of sports, they were not unaffected by the need to participate in activities that gave them a sense of belonging to the larger middle class, even if through the process of consuming as an alternative.

While the labor and anxiety of the exam-preparation mothers were a source of humor to these nonsalaried workers' wives, they took very seriously the procurement of the latest toy for their sons, for which they were willing to stand in lines for hours, and the cutest accessories for their daughters, for which they looked forward to shopping. For most of these women, concern for the future was an immediate and palpable reality. Many were unable, due to the failures of small companies in the area, to cover the monthly automatic withdrawals from their bank accounts for school lunches and materials. Nonetheless, they found in the comfort of consumption a means of confirming their family's belonging, however tenuous, to the remaining aura of social stability built on the idea of a homogeneous society of middle-class membership.

National and Personal Futures

The sense of possibilities narrowing rather than expanding is not lost on a large group of parents, for whom the course of the nation does not seem to guarantee their children's future, as it once did their own. The supplementary education industry has benefited from these newfound uncertainties and the retreat of the public schools. The family, in turn, has furthered its reliance on these extra services, which have shorn it up in return for intervening further into and changing from within any remaining realms of private difference. Those who do not or cannot partake of these supplements are not exempted from their influence, nor can parents escape the realization that they have become increasingly placed in a position of making the choice, nevertheless.

In the final chapter, I turn to the recessionary generation, the young born at the end of the 1980s or early 1990s, peers of Youth A, who became the subjects and objects of the child problem and its discursive solutions. For this generation, recessionary effects, the discursive figure of the strange child, the new language of responsibility, risk, inner frontiers, and the independent individual composed the vocabulary of their lives. They knew no other, as many of them told me. By the time they reached adulthood, the college entrance process and job search requirements had changed in ways that their parents' generation did not understand. Skills, abilities, self-development, a part-time labor force, and a new group of terms and conditions for independence had emerged, as my discussion of the film *Tokyo Sonata* in Chapter One depicted in frightening scenes of what failure looks like and how slim the chances of success are. In this last chapter, I discuss my interactions with recessionary young people in the midst of big life decisions, the ways in which they understand the past and its relation to the present, and how they are negotiating and in some cases remaking the temporalities and spaces of their lives.

Chapter Six

The Recessionary Generation
Times and Spaces

I don't want the same anguish as my parents. They lived within the confines of
the system [*onaji rairu no naka*]. I want to find a different track. We weren't born
into the postwar system. We were born into recession. This is an age when the
older are not the knowledgeable ones; the younger are. We have to find our
own way.[1]

This chapter focuses on young people in their twenties, who came of age
following the bursting of the financial bubble of the early 1990s, who grew
up in the midst of recessionary conditions, discourses, and effects.[2] Unlike
the older generations for whom the time of recession has been a strange and
unfamiliar one, young people attest to knowing only this time of economic
downturn and social instability. "It's all depression," one college-aged student offered in a recent interview, referring to the economic and social situation in Japan.[3]

In this chapter, I focus on this generation's experiences and expressions of the time of their lives. Those I talked to and spent time with in,
around, and outside urban areas described the recessionary period as an inverted time in which they are the subjects of change and often the objects of
blame. The terms they use to describe their lives suggest a kind of temporal
shift, though not necessarily a linear one. Forward and backward as spatial–
temporal directionalities and hierarchies have been altered by neoliberal

forms and vocabularies of governance and by members of this generation into ideas of turning and remaking. Although forcefully populated by notions of individuation, separation, and disillusion, the discursive field of the second decade of the twenty-first century also includes notions of possibility and mutuality—even as these possibilities and mutualities are born of the impossibilities of former urban credential society lives.

It is a time in which former discursive measurements of social and national reproduction that provided an often clear, albeit often dangerous, direction for their parents, and grandparents, have fallen by the wayside.[4] Those former measurements included the inculcations of the prewar imperial education system and its figurations of family-state and national body, and their replacement by an educationally managed credential society and totalized focus on catch-up economic development for which Japanese culture became the reason for shared identification and sacrifice.

The youths in two of Kiyoshi Kurusawa's well-known films, *Tokyo Sonata* and *Bright Future*,[5] live lives and make life decisions that seem to take little from the system of their parents' generation, as if they live in a completely different time, one severed from postwar and prewar unifying frames. It is the time of the game, the epitome of neoliberal governance according to Jacques Donzelot, a game of life seemingly unaffected by history, in which there are constantly winners and losers. The independent individual, an entrepreneur of the self, has been handed the responsibility, formerly of government, for self-work. There are no set rules for how this is to be done, which is why the MOE's "self-strengthening" and Hayao Kawai's "frontiers within" are apt identity prerogatives for this time. In the two Kurosawa films, the past, which the neoliberal present repudiates, serves as little guide. The everyday of dead-end part-time labor (*Bright Future*) or the slow disintegration of the family as a result of corporate restructuring (*Tokyo Sonata*) demonstrate what the discursive overturnings of a liberalizing economy and society look like.

Self-responsible and self-developing, the young take on the position of knowledge. Positioned as the knowing subjects—the knowledgeable ones—the subjectivities of the recessionary generation are formed through the effects, language, and discursive substitutions of the late 1990s and first decade of the 2000s. From the mid-2000s, terms of individual development—independent individual, the heart, latent frontiers, self-development, and responsibility—created by the coming together of education and psychology became keywords not only in education but of the critical posteducation phase of life this generation entered on its own. Self-responsible for their own human capital development in a highly speculative system, within which limits are unknown, employers, like the government, have shifted responsibility for training and workforce investment to the independent individual. As responsibility for self-development has shifted so too has the category of childhood itself, defined by a hierarchy of time away from an imagined original point through the temporal stages of inculcation and acquisition of linguistic, social, and cultural knowledge that we call subjectivity. When the young man in the opening epigraph speaks of "a different track," of "finding [his] own way," of existing in his own time, he expresses the shifting of developmental frameworks, of systems of reproduction, of the ironies of the independent heart in recessionary Japan. This neoliberalization of time—an erasure of the past for an enclosed present of the game and the entrepreneur of the self-player—separates and isolates but also creates the possibility of other times and spaces.

In prior chapters, I portrayed the discourses, forms, and other reactions set off by the 1990s recession as a set of linked effects. In this chapter, I extend this analysis by taking account of those in the process of fashioning their identities in the midst of the recessionary environment. I begin with recessionary changes: of confusion and uncertainty articulated as strangeness and incomprehensibility, the displacing of former cultural categories, and the reversal of positions of knowledge as this reversal upsets the temporal difference between child and adult. In this recessionary time, the adult no longer represents a full or completed time of development. The representation of the adult as the instructor has disappeared. The past, the so-called track (*rairu*) of development that had signified national, cultural, and historical continuity and commonality, has shifted with the new discursive constructs of independence and the heart.

The recession has pried apart something greater than what we regularly refer to as a generation gap. Developmental predictabilities of a temporally managed credential acquisition society have been superseded, if not completely replaced, by what Takehiko Kariya has called the "learning competency society" and with them cultural and political inversions and conversions of the postwar system.[6] The postwar system was predicated on a standardization of the life cycle. Managed by various forms of government—from education to industry—and narrated by cultural discourses of dependency and homogeneity, the postwar system seemed to promise the continuation of middle-class membership, stable employment, and some safeguard from the often devastating social and economic unheavals and uncertainties experienced by Western capitalist societies during the late twentieth century.[7]

Iwama Natsuki, writing of the changing attitudes toward work of the young in Japan has argued that the pre-1990s sense of shared purpose and middle-class identification had more to do with managed consensus than statistical reality.[8] Less than a third of the Japanese population had stable middle-class incomes during the heyday of double-digit growth (10 percent and above) from the late 1950s through the 1970s and the subsequent period of medium economic growth (4 to 5 percent) of the late 1970s through the 1980s. Iwama shifts the focus of awareness away from the child problem and the so-called strange, inadequate, psychosocial development of the youth. Opening her book with a short discussion of what is now known in Japan as the divided society (*kakusa shakai*), Iwama suggests that readers look beyond the idea of a sudden collapse of morals and middle-class society to the arrangements and mechanisms that persuaded the Japanese people to self-identify as mostly middle-class during the period prior to the bubble's bursting. In other words, instead of obscuring the postwar past, for the seemingly progressive present of the neoliberal individual, Iwama seeks to open it up to an exploration of identification, sacrifice, and exploitation to better understand the temporal and spatial obfuscations of the past and the present.

Divided society suggests a new kind of division of the population. Iwama describes this division as a shift away from the expectation of things improving, personally and nationally—a kind of implicit benefit (*onkei*) open to all who worked hard—to the absence or severing of this promise. Rather than unproblematically faulting those who do not or cannot be the embodiment of idealized national reproduction, Iwama recognizes and describes this change in the youth. "The young," she writes, "facing the prospects of hard work without the same anticipation of improvement or benefit, have decided they do not want or need the consciousness and identifications of the past generations."[9] Through the end of the 1980s, the postwar system produced a sense of security within Japanese society: a developmental narrative or time that seemed to guarantee the continuity of national economic success. The plummeting stock market and property values of the early 1990s, followed by neoliberal rationalities of governance, inverted and then converted this system of benefits and identifications.

For the generation of recession, the recessionary discourses make up the vocabulary of their lives. This is particularly evident when the terms invert and twist the old. These terms undermine former meanings rather than build on them. In saying, as many I spoke to do, that they were born into recession and not the postwar system, some of my interviewees said they identified with the discourses and symbols of the recession and felt as if they, themselves, were the problem. Being cast in the role of the offender, rather than the victim, is an effect of the child problem and its accompanying remedies and solutions. What I mean by this is not just that young people raised within the period of economic downturn need to accustom themselves to economic conditions very different than those of their parents' youth, which they do. The altered *quality* and specificity of conditions this generation now lives are often overlooked.

My discussion in this chapter extends earlier chapters' focus on problem discourses, solutions, effects on schooling and the home, and the shift from dependent body to independent heart by adding in the voices, strategies, and in some cases alternatives of the young people of the recessionary generation. These young people are the subjects and the objects of this discursive environment. They are the subjects because recessionary discourses have transformed the expectations—and subjective requirements of their lives—independence, self-development, self-responsibility, inner frontiers. These discursive constructs distance the recessionary generation from the postwar generation in personal and national ways. The vocabulary of recession has inverted former discursive terms of identity and development, replacing and displacing the postwar period and its social and cultural associations. This history has been written off, domestically and internationally, with very little attention to the effects on individuals and national narratives of this making and unmaking, writing on and writing off. The replacements of the neoliberal moment are also displacements of human and environmental forms of sacrifice and exploitation of the homogeneous dependent bodies and now independent hearts.

My discussion reframes notions of transition, trade-offs, and "lost decade(s)" as effects of neoliberal conditions and reformulations of life that have been overlooked.[10] I investigate how the subject and object status of the recessionary generation has thrust these young people into a different kind of time. My strategy is to reveal what this time looks like and requires, while revealing where openings have emerged for the young people of recession. The recessionary period constitutes life conditions full of frightening responsibilities for personal success and failure with little transferred from the past to serve as a guideline. As a result of the very conditions of the inverting and converting of developmental time and its narratives of difference and predictability, the status of the present and future are changed in the process. Impossibilities abound, but possibilities also emerge.[11]

Yoshitaka Mori, Gabriella Lukacs, Anne Allison, Mark Driscoll, and others have written about progressive projects of the recessionary generation. Mori, focusing on "creativity of the age of the *furītā* [part-time labor force]," writes about art as political practice that brings attention to the plight of those who have lost their livelihoods and homes in the midst of the recession.[12] Anne Allison depicts the emergence of new spaces of belonging "in an era of self-responsibility." Gabriella Lukacs explores the motivations of young people who write novels on their cell phones in search of meaning and to help others confront a present that presents itself in the naturalized terms of global progress.[13]

Alongside the heady requirements of the recessionary generations' conditions for life-making in an uncharted time, this chapter describes forms and spaces of life, spaces of possibility that challenge the often contradictory discourses and policies of the present, that suggest spaces and times beyond the specific confines from dependence to independence.

The Vocabulary of Their Lives

In the winter of 2009, I began interviewing Japanese sophomore and junior college-aged students about their education, work expectations, and the recessionary representations that had been a media mainstay since their elementary school years. In an earlier article I have discussed how the FLE revisions at the end of 2006 capitalized on the idea of something terribly wrong with Japanese children and youth that required fixing. The first Abe government (2004–2006) targeted this heightened state of concern by promoting FLE revision as a way to fix the "hearts" of young Japanese. Their so-called lost identification with the Japanese nation could best be remedied, according to government reformers, by promoting a "love of country" (*kuni wo ai suru*) through patriotic education. Japanese academics, notably Taka-hashi Tetsuya, Hirota Teruyuki, Kariya Takehiko, and Fujita Hidenori, voiced strong opposition. They questioned what kind of patriotism could emerge from the language of self-risk, responsibility and independence.

My exploration of how the effects of recession have affected the way young Japanese think about themselves and their generation began in a serendipitous way following an "Anthropology of Japan" class at the University of Washington. Several Japanese exchange students approached me after class and asked to talk further about an article of mine on the figure of the strange child.[14] They seemed glad we were reading and talking about this topic in class. They said they wanted me to know they grew up hearing there was something strange about Japanese kids—their generation. They described what it felt like to grow up in a discursive environment saturated with a language of problems focused on their generation.

On their return to Japan, these students faced a frozen job market and a discursive environment of self-development that turned their parent's knowl-edge of cultural identity on its head.[15] As young adults, they told me about their concern for their futures, in particular the demands of the workplace in the era of restructuring, labor reforms, changes in education, and the gap between their generation and that of their parents.[16] I followed up these conversations with a series of meetings and interviews in Japan from 2009 through 2013. In conversations and interviews with young adults in Japan, I began with their concerns and preoccupations, including the job search pro-cess, which was undergoing significant changes of its own at the time.

The job search, or job hunting as it is referred to, has remained a highly structured time of life. Japanese companies continue to prefer recent gradu-ates for their full-time entry-level positions. Landing a job is a singular mo-ment for young Japanese, a chance at the middle-class security their par-ents' generation took mostly for granted. Job search success for young adults since the late 1990s has decreased dramatically in Japan, so too following the 2008–2009 recession for young people elsewhere. Young Japanese must prepare themselves in radically new ways for a job market that has "slimmed down" and stayed slim, reducing the number of secure positions for new graduates by over 50 percent. One telling sign of this much changed state of employment is the change in private advice and preparation literature. Bookstores in Tokyo, Osaka, and other large cities, which for several decades have had large sections addressed to parents and students on high school and college exam preparation, now have equally large areas devoted to job preparation and directed solely to the young applicant. In addition to strong college credentials, from the mid-2000s the job search began to require a range of new psychosocial skills and training: self-analysis (*jiko bunseki*) and the management of enormous amounts of incoming information and preparation of online applications.[17] Third-year college students in the midst of their job hunt have explained that you can tell when someone has begun job applications by his or her cell phone and changed behavior. Information and requests pour in and require immediate response. One of the reasons this process has become such a focus of social concern and debate is that it encapsulates the altered sense of individual and national time.

Uncertainty on the personal level dovetails with the retreat of various institutional means of preparation for the entry into adult life. Prior to the onset of the economic downturn, preparation had been in the hands of the education system and large companies. The young as well as their parents are now left to their own devices, which has meant increased business for supplementary services (Chapter Five). Private industry has taken the place of public services and seriously disadvantaged lower-income parents, who relied on the public school to prepare their children for the future. Preparation is now left to the young adult, who by the end of the sophomore year in college understands that it is up to him- or herself to get information about the new employment information sessions, learn how to fill out all the online applications, learn how to prepare for multiple interviews (for any one position), and become accustomed to hiring guidelines—born of the neoliberal environment of reforms and restructuring from the late 1990s on. Individual preparation, successful articulation of distinctive strengths and abilities, and the ongoing development of potential have become compulsory. The time spent on preparation led several of my interviewees to harshly criticize their own higher education. They wondered why these institutions were not in tune with the changes they face and devoted to helping them prepare for them.

The bursting of the financial bubble in the early 1990s and prolonged financial crisis have meant not only fewer opportunities for stable work but an entire set of expectations without guarantees and with recriminations that had not existed before. The "work hard and things will get better" narrative that informed the past generations' middle-class and national identification is no longer part of these young people's lives. A new language of recession—*restructuring, bankruptcy, part-time labor, divided society*—falls from these young people's lips, just as *lifetime employment* and *homogeneous society* once did from their parents' generation.[18]

With shrinking numbers of stable, full-time positions available, the highly structured job search process has become an increasingly anxious time. Several Japanese students talked to me about what would have been previously considered unusual or extreme services and technologies of which prospective applicants avail themselves: job search cram schools, plastic surgery, and in extreme cases—but also in increasing numbers—ending their lives in the face of the odds of failure. Interviewees in Tokyo, Yokohama, and Kobe described the shift from a credential society to the independent individual as a *mental change*: from the seeming certainties of the long process of exams and college entrance, to the requirements of an independent self, that can articulate strengths and weaknesses, gain qualifications, and demonstrate in discrete terms their value to a company.[19]

As these young people enunciated these changes, and their own responses to them, they enact their own conversion. As one of the students put it, "We need latent ability; we need to develop our own communication skills and mental strength." Although this expression suggests how national discourses about youth and value production are materializing, it also points to international shifts of human capital development being experienced worldwide under governments adopting neoliberal rationales of governance. What is clear is that there are important deviations from the focus on homogeneous dependent bodies for which the state is responsible to the new disciplinary effects of the present.

My interviewees often explained that responsibility for their own development absolved them of responsibility beyond themselves: "I don't expect to stay with one company, because things can collapse with any of them in the future, so my goal is to improve myself."[20] Others echoed this statement through their answers to what they were looking for in a company and what they would consider success. Several who had just started a new job noted, "We see our work to save money, not necessarily for the future of Japan. . . . We want our own time." They acknowledged that, in a tough working environment, they may have to work until the "final train of the night," an expression that signifies the after-hours overtime system of corporate Japan. But, unlike their parents, if they do not like the working environment, they will change jobs. They talked frequently about "their own time."

For the immediate future, this time would be subordinated to the demands of recessionary employment, and they realized they are more replaceable and exchangeable then their parent's generation had been. But working until the last train leaves the station for these young people is less about the common sense of the older generations and more about what needs to be endured for now. They do not envision one job being a career but merely a stop along the way.

This shifting sense of work, labor potential, and individualization was evident in interviews I conducted in late 2010 with a group of students in Yokohama:

> I'm looking for the kind of place I want to work. . . This includes a sense of atmosphere, a place where I can be myself, a place where I can grow. I'm not interested in a competitive atmosphere between workers; I want a place I can relax.[21]

This is the generation that has been required to prepare for life by themselves. Some have embraced the requirements of the independent individual to an extent that goes beyond the government-sponsored language of independence, inner strength, and frontiers within. Taking on the project of discovering and developing their own potential, these members of the recessionary generation convert the demands for self-responsibility into the self-appreciation of their own value in the marketplace for themselves: "[I want] my own way of living, my own freedom."

This attitude to employment has often been disdainfully attributed to the young workers of the part-time labor force. Recessionary-era part-time laborers have had to settle for equal amounts of work for less pay and little to no job security. However, in the case quoted here, the articulations of "my own freedom" were that of a young man and his girlfriend who had just graduated from top universities and landed full-time jobs. What is new to their generation is that they do not view their positions as permanent. The young woman said she worked hard to become fluent in English to find a job with an online company. She knows she may have to follow company demands and move from place to place for several years, but eventually she plans to join a smaller company with more flexibility. The young man went on to explain that satisfaction is a key factor for him in a job, "[I] don't want the same anguish as my parents."[22]

Michael Feher frames these requirements and articulations of self-development as a form of what he refers to as self-appreciation or "betting on certain behaviors, sentiments, and lifestyles": [23]

> In the neo-liberal world of globalized and unregulated financial markets, corporate governance is concerned less with optimizing returns on investment over time than with growth or appreciation . . . the investor in his or her human capital is concerned with appreciating, or increasing the capital to which he or she is identified . . . not so much to profit from our accumulated potential as to constantly value or appreciate ourselves or at least to prevent our own depreciation.[24]

Feher investigates the overlooked question of "the type of subjectivity simultaneously presupposed and targeted by neoliberal policies . . . the type of subject that is constituted by the regime of human capital appreciation and tasked with upholding it."[25] What is particularly important for my discussion here is Feher's explanation of the speculative nature of the relation between the governing of this self-appreciating subject and human capital. Feher writes, "The conditions under which neoliberal subjects come to appreciate themselves is especially difficult to predict because the future marketability of [a] conduct or sentiment cannot be easily anticipated and correlation between financial and psychological forms of self-appreciation cannot be homogeneously established."[26] Feher calls this "playing the capital market." The type of subjectivity being simultaneously presupposed and targeted, "subjects whose life becomes a strategy aimed as self-appreciation," resonates with how members of the recessionary generation in Japan encounter, understand, and negotiate the demands for productivity, expectations of potential, changing institutions of the workplace, and its relation to their lives.[27]

The Time of Development

Just as the child problem and education reform deliberations were dominating the media from the end of the 1990s on, the film *Battle Royale* (*Batoru Rowaiaru*, 2000, Kinji Fukasaku) hit the national screens. Unlike the abrupt elimination of a lifetime employee's career and the silent terror this change triggers in the opening of *Tokyo Sonata* in 2008, *Battle Royale* begins with loud, visceral, and unending chaos. A teacher gets knifed, students run wild in the halls, and the military abounds—supposedly in a Japan with a well-entrenched standing army.[28] With helicopters circling overhead, the lone victor of a survival game mandated by the newly promulgated BR Law (Battle Royale, *BR Hō*), appears in a military jeep, clutching a doll drenched in blood.[29] "It's a young girl, and she's smiling!," chant scores of reporters witnessing the scene. Wearing her school uniform and the blood of her peers on her face and body, this female child-survivor seems the antithesis of Miyazaki Hayao's beloved young female heroines of prerecessionary times.[30] Survivors of the neoliberal present are no longer confined, it would appear, to the disciplined male body. The transference of risk and responsibility onto all individuals is played out on the physical battlefield of survival in *Battle Royale*: "Life is a game, battle to become adults of worth!" (*Jinsei wa ga-mu desu. Tatakatte, Kachi ni aru otona ni narimasho!*) The teacher broadcasts these words to his electronically monitored class. As he does, and as the students begin to battle for their lives, the brutality of capitalist competition in the twenty-first century is staged in its stark and immediate form. *Battle Royale* seems a staging ground for poignancy and parody. As a result of the pre-1990s equally financed education system, the developmental system of education to job guidance, and its culture of dependence, most Japanese were not confronted with forms of capitalist violence, like the mass lay-offs experienced in the United States. From *Battle Royale* (2000) to *Bright Future* (2003) and *Tokyo Sonata* (2008), however, we see expressions of what the changed environment of personal risk in Japan looks like—from openly brutal to the dangers of a quietly troubling new normal.[31]

Bright Future (*Akarui Mirai*, 2003) focuses on two young part-time workers at a small urban hand-towel factory, for whom life outside the factory seems no more meaningful than their repetitive low-paid work. The one thing that unites the young men and disrupts their surrounding urban *ennui* is their interest in a jellyfish that one of them keeps as a "pet." Over the course of the film, the title's "bright" and "future" seem more a reference to the shiny (though poisonous) illumination and measured movements of the jellyfish than the progression of events, including committing murder and undergoing imprisonment, by one of the young men. The one deviation to an otherwise bleak film, in both color and tone, is a temporary relationship that emerges between the imprisoned young man's estranged father, who owns a small recycling shop, and the friend now left on his own, who goes to work for the father. A future, perhaps, but of a flattened quality and temporality that suggests and portends individual peril at worst and lack of disconnection at best.

Tokyo Sonata turns to the domestic space of the ordinary family, depicting the terror of an ordinary time on its way out and the havoc of a family drained of its ability to reproduce its own future. The film opens as the authority of the family and the family's relationship to the outside world of work and education is being overturned. In the world of recession, a new "normal" has emerged, one that has no use for the hard-earned postwar arrangement and system of past prosperity and homogeneous identification. The father's carefully groomed male subjectivity is of little value in the global market of exchange. Instead, well-groomed, Japanese-speaking, and much less expensive Chinese labor can translate bodily worth into skills and contributions in ways that the Japanese postwar generation was never expected or trained to do.

Unfolding in sacrificial movements, like the sonata in its title, the stability and authority maintained silently by adults deteriorates on the screen before our eyes, and the children and youths realize they have to figure things out on their own. The world of recession is one in which these mostly silent sacrifices of adults and children—women as mothers, men as workers and fathers, and children as educational laborers—no longer add up to the lifetimes of the past.

What is this "normal" depicted in *Tokyo Sonata*? What has happened in the shift from the developmental time of economic prosperity? What about all those lives lived, sacrifices made to the representations of sublime bodies and a non-Western nation that had finally overcome the modern? What are the effects of this aftermath on the subjects of recession?

Uncertainty has been addressed by the Japanese government by problem-making and remedy-producing forms of representation and policy. But what the public has been looking for instead is a set of guidelines, something to help them adapt to the loss of the predictability of the developmental narrative, the structures, and the ideologies of dependence. As *Tokyo Sonata* director Kurosawa depicts, the language of recession is not a language anyone can rely on. When characters in *Tokyo Sonata* call out for help, there is no one around to respond, as if language itself has lost its ability to represent and connect.

Credentials to Learning Capital

Significant crossovers exist between concerns over the child and schools and the generation of youth and work, in particular that of diagnosing what has changed and the types of remedies proposed. Notable is the media and private industry discussion of the changes in the education to work transition, including the uncertainty surrounding how to best prepare one's child for the future when the low birthrate has mostly ensured that anyone can get into college. College is no longer enough. Only those with top academic pedigrees and added skills—international experience, English, law licenses, self-presentation skills, and more—will land full-time job. Takehiko Kariya explains the dynamics of the shift as follows:

> Responsibility for human capital accumulation has shifted to the workers themselves. Self-development [*jiko-kaihatsu*] and self-education [*jiko-keihatsu*] are today commonly used words to capture this shift of responsibility to the individuals for their own working lives.[32]

The class divisions or cleavages that result from this economic upheaval are what concerns educational sociologists. Japan is in the midst of a shift, according to Kariya, from a credential society to what he has called a "learning-capital society." Japanese schools and companies can no longer be counted on as the sources of training. As Kariya explains, companies' expectations of "broader and more flexible competencies" or "the abilities to learn, adapt, and improve constantly by recognizing and exploiting disparate resources," occur at the same time overall employment stability is decreasing with the cuts in labor costs and the increase in the number of part-time jobs.[33] Workers must arrive on the market with the knowledge and skills *to be* trained as well as with demonstrable competency for innovative and self-directed abilities to contribute to the rapidly changing knowledge economy.[34]

Kariya and others are concerned that this environment is dividing Japanese society and disadvantaging many of its members; those who do not have the facility to gain and manage these responsibilities and risks on their own. The young Japanese adults whom I interviewed voice strong opinions regarding Kariya's notion of "learning capital." They say that they are expected to have top credentials and extra abilities and competencies. A friend's son who graduated from a middle-level college and is now in the midst of his job search told me that a friend of his proved this by filling out two kinds of "entry sheets"—the first level of job applications. On the first, his friend put his true middle-level college credential; on the other, the University of Tokyo. His friend got no response to the former and an immediate response to the latter. Top credentials, the young say, are still necessary, but just to get your so-called foot in the electronic door of this much elongated, complex, and for some mostly impossible job search.

Kariya inquires further into the effects of this shift on society and the young. By way of a response, I return to Michael Feher's notion of self-appreciation and my own notion of neoliberal time and patriotism. Neo-liberal rationales of national and corporate governance create conditions in which young people of the recessionary generation in Japan (and elsewhere) must learn to become "producers" and "investors" in themselves—their lives are ongoing projects geared toward the constant appreciation or increase of their own market value.[35] What is particular about the conditions facing the recessionary generation in Japan is the sudden and tremendous temporal and symbolic chasm between their parents' generation and their own. As notions of individual development have been upturned, along with the discursive environment of their production, the young have become the focus of uncertainty and insecurity.

The dramatic and traumatic nature of these changes is underplayed and obscured by way of what I have called a neoliberal discursive twist. The vocabulary of the self—*individual, independence, freedom, strength,* and *frontiers*—has been constructed discursively by the MOE, postrecessionary psychologists of identity, and most recently by the second Abe administration, as a necessary next step beyond modernization to globalization and its seemingly desirable brand of liberalism. This liberalism is not the liberalism of rights, however, but a *liberalization* of risks, and the vocabulary of recession is circulating in a distinctive and combined context of "rollback and rollout" (Chapter One) neoliberalism. A seeming lack in Japan of liberal subjectivity and vocabulary of the individual was often praised when postwar group-identifying dependent selves were viewed as integral to economic success. But this same seeming lack has been derided at different historical moments as the discursively produced version(s) of this national-cultural difference produced the less seemly results of early twentieth-century imperialism and 1990s protracted recession.

Increased instability and government withdrawal from guidance and training accompany the shifts in schooling of the education reform and its increased emphasis on patriotism and national identification. Pulling back from social services, while intervening in personal ones, is a characteristic of "forceful liberalism" everywhere, in the words of Jacques Donzelot.[36] Recessionary Japan's distinguishing expressions of this new liberalism are neoliberal independence and patriotism.

Despite the structural changes of the recessionary period and its effects on everything from self-preparation to human capital appreciation strategies, adult commentary has alternated between diagnosing the problematic psychological disposition of the youth and faulting the young for being ill suited to the demands of the contemporary workplace, all the while unaware of just how onerous managing and navigating the up-to-the-minute requirements of personal development are. *Tokyo Sonata* tells the story of this contradiction by turning the problem back on the older generation.

Policy and private business experts' mid-2000's focus on the lack of will and work ethic among the recessionary generation mimics the late-1990s eruption of concern over the Japanese child and education that became known at the child problem. High-level governmental committees, recruited experts, and their produced knowledge created second-order effects. One of the more influential of these discussed earlier was the notion of an inner frontier of latent potential. The late Hayao Kawai in his 2002 report for a special prime minister's committee titled "The Structure of Japan in the Twenty-First Century" (*Nijuiseki Nihon no Kōzō: Nihon no Furontiea ha Nihon no Naka ni aru*) raised the stakes of the requirements on the young. Kawai's idea was to turn the development process over to and back on the individual. Reimagining the time of the child's development as a site of "latent (*senzaiteki*) potential," Kawai proclaimed that each individual should think of him- or herself, to borrow a term from Anna Tsing, as a "resource frontier."[37] Resource frontiers are seemingly endless sources of value creation, which according to Kawai each individual was in charge of discovering and developing for him- or herself. In the midst of frozen job prospects, uncertain futures, and declining fortunes, this was an effective and strategic choice of terms to be sure. *Latent* suggests something not yet evident, but inherent, a capacity or potential available but hidden beneath the surface, not yet ready to emerge. *Latency* is also a term used within psychological discourse (at varying levels of complexity) to refer to the individual and his or her subject(ive) development. These terms and shifts to the individual might seem unusual and even ineffective in a place like Japan, a nation, until recently, assumed to be less focused on individual psychology than, for instance, the United States. Yet, it was precisely during the period of the 1990s, as the Japanese public began to experience the waning of economic success, and the loss of economic growth that social concern and media coverage turned vehemently to a/the *problem* with the young. It was within these conditions of possibility in the 1990s that the psychological explanations provided by Kawai and others, which focused on the problem with the individual, began to gain public acceptance.[38]

Moreover, potential and latency are both notions associated with childhood, and it is precisely the young who have been singled out as representative and reservoir of this frontier of potential or the future yet-to-be.[39] One senses a tension between the notions of frontier and latency—a tension that is resolvable if we consider the very conditions and concerns about national and individual futures and social and cultural reproduction present during the period of economic decline. Although latent potential suggests something known and knowable, something that is not yet visible but a future probability, the inner frontier becomes a powerful signifier of the unknown or that which lies beyond the known. The inner frontier is valuable precisely for this reason because it is yet to be discovered. It is an apt analogy of capitalist development, which combines risk and possibility to produce value while occluding the cost and affected populations who become the temporal and spatial objects of frontier creation and its mechanisms of extraction.

Anna Tsing describes frontiers as imaginative projects. Tsing's notion of project inserts history and historicity into this discussion: the history of the imagining and reimagining of human bodies as having potential for value creation or, in the case of Tsing's focus, the remaking of natural systems into what she calls "resource frontiers." Projects are not just discovered; to return to Karatani Kojin's discussion (Chapter 1) of the discovery of the child, projects are made. Tsing adds to Karatani by focusing on what she calls "the complex processes of taming and exclusion," necessary to create frontiers both within and without.[40]

Childhood and youth are not naturally but rather culturally imagined sites of potential. These life stages are transformed and transposed in the historical and social imaginaries of nation-states as arenas of useable value and representations of national developmental time. But the frontier, as

Tsing cogently writes, is always an effect of a conversion, of something wild and diverse, something that resists being placed in a box or defined into a knowable, exploitable resource. There are costs associated with these conversions (Introduction and Chapters One and Three). From postwar modernization theory, to late twentieth-century neoliberal discourses of human capital development, the furtive efforts on the part of the Japanese government to manage and produce its own recessionary changes and the history of the symbolic investments they reveal, conflicts, contradictions, and costs are incurred. Those who have been made the subjects and objects of the independent and frontier language of neoliberal extraction have also begun to respond to the neoliberal moment by reversing, recovering, and returning to other spaces and other possible futures.

Alternative Spaces

In 1999, when I first arrived in Japan for long-term fieldwork, the city of Kobe was in difficult shape. Small to medium-size companies had been hit hard by the economic downturn of the early 1990s. The city was still recovering from the Hanshin earthquake of 1995; this slow recovery has since been recognized as an early sign of inefficient governmental response to emergencies. In 1997, Kobe was thrown again into the national spotlight following the Youth A killings. Most of my time in Kobe was spent tracking the relationship between the Youth A incident, the discourse of the child problem, and how it became a focus of national debate and concern about education and middle-class futures. It was precisely these futures of the "fiercely committed company men" (*moretsu shaiin*) (and families) of the 1980s, who stayed from dawn to beyond dusk at their companies, instead of heading home that had been so taken for granted during the high economic growth period.

Classrooms were supposedly collapsing due to the so-called changing psychology of the child. The focus on psychological change seemed to obscure the class divisions that were beginning to widen between those families who could afford extra supplementary schooling at earlier and earlier ages and those who could not. During this time, the Japanese government's slogans shifted from national guidance to individual responsibility. The promise of long-term benefits for staying the course switched to information about bankruptcies and restructuring. As a result, it was not a huge surprise when, at the end of 2006, the Abe government was able to push through the revisions to a sixty-year-old postwar education law. The government lavished words and gifts on public school children—*notes for their hearts*—that articulated a collectivity borne out of individuals "raising themselves." Indeed, the government seemed to cultivate a certain sort of nationalism needed by the neoliberal state. In the words of Hayao Kawai, everyone would be encouraged or "free" to discover his or her own frontiers within. Just as Japan discovered its own identity, an all-too-smooth parallel appeared. Full-time and even lifetime security had been replaced by unstable and uncertain work alongside a plethora of terms for precarious labor.[41]

Even though economic forecasts had worsened due to the global recession after 2008—what is known in Japan as the *Lehman shock*—and the tension surrounding college entrance and the job search threatened to take over the entirety of the undergraduate experience,[42] my Kobe friends were beginning in the summer of 2012 to focus on something other than their recessionary anxieties. As they put it that summer, "New things are not necessarily the best."

My friend's husband has worked independently for the last ten years. Formerly a white-collar employee of a large clothing company in Kobe, he retired in 2000 when he saw the writing on the wall regarding corporate downsizing. He said he felt sorry for today's youth in Japan. Society had become much more complicated, and there was so much information. He spoke, in particular, of all the uncertainty present in young people's lives, from education to the job search process. Like many of the baby boomer generation (*dankai no sedai*), he shared a nostalgia for the sacrifices of the postwar era of prosperity. However, he understood that it was precisely the aggressiveness of the past's developmentalism and its social, representational, and natural violence that were to blame for the present situation. With this in mind, he told me, even though he had been focused on importing clothing in China, he was now shifting from the new to restoring the beauty and usefulness of the old. One of his new business ventures, he explained, was not development, in the sense of destruction and construction, but restoration (*saisei suru*).

His family had left him a small 1950s-era apartment building on the outskirts of Kobe, which in the past would have been a prime site for gentrification. He realized that, if he upgraded his property in this way, it would price people out of the neighborhood and break up a community. So, as he and his wife explained and later showed me, they were in the process of refurbishing this 1950s-era local building. The husband and wife team were in the process of fixing up the rooms for rent, designing a meeting, events, and gathering area on the top floor, and fashioning a community garden out back. His wife called this "restoring the old and applying to the new" (*furui mono wo ikashite*).

I asked about the business sense of this project, and although he mentioned inheritance taxes and the like, what they emphasized was their desire to become part of the diverse communities and create ways of life, livelihood, and spaces on the outskirts of urban and rural areas. Only five years earlier, this entrepreneur friend of mine had talked about the "digital" age, the necessity to put feelers out in every direction for the next opportunity, and his always needing to stay ahead of the business curve with all its uncertainties. Although products of the era of the aggressive company employee (*moretsu shaiin*), he, his wife, and others were becoming ardently anti-*moretsu*.[43]

From that first to the most recent conversation during my visit in 2014, everything seemed to revolve around restoring the old and forming community as a result. The idea that the *new* is not necessarily better meant taking part in something that brought people together with others, across differences of income and ethnicity, and this process was altering the sense of individual and national development.

The many books and magazines the old and young were reading further articulated this change. Focused on lifestyle, many dealt with where to find old objects and how to refurbish materials one already owned. These resources appealed to the readers' desire for alternative spaces and times. Detailed stories of young people in their late twenties to early thirties who have moved or reverse migrated (*ijū*) emphasized the determination of the younger generation for a drastic change in lifestyle. Snapshots of some of the spaces the young are creating go hand in hand with their own expressions that challenge the recessionary lexicon: making a place for people to gather, raising their own food, and taking time to do things by hand. After the March 2011 Fukushima disasters, young reverse migrants talked about resizing their lives, of raising children in a space of their own making away far away from the urban centers:

> Living in Okinawa is great. I have more time with my kids—before we came here they were in nursery school, and I was at work. Being apart most of the

day was natural. Now our family, from the time we wake up to the time we go to bed, are all together. Okinawa has a rich natural environment. There is a river right in front of the house, and the kids play energetically in the environment. There is a big increase in the number of children in Okinawa, too, and our kids get along well with the local children. Is it completely safe here? No, this is an era of no absolute safety or certainty. For the future, Okinawa does not have nuclear power stations, but it does have American bases and their problems. Nuclear power stations and the American base problem are related; anywhere you go, what you think about is peace.[44]

The urban baby boomers in their sixties—as well as the 1980s generation who grew up believing Japan was number one—witnessed the collapse of an entire structure of miracle effects and practices and the bursting of the economic bubble. For the past generations, restoring and reverse migration have different meanings and uses than they do for those born into economic downturn, who as of 2014 were in their early to late twenties. As many of them have told me, they have never known anything but recession, critiques of the child problem, and neoliberal individuating rationales. It is to several of these young reverse migrants and their alternative spaces and senses of time I turn to now.

Spaces and Times of Reciprocity

For the many young people making the choice to move out of populous Japanese cities, the context of these choices is critical to gaining an understanding of why some of the young are leaving and what they are creating when they resettle. Learning how to turn their lives into projects of never-ending self-enhancement is what young adults of this recessionary generation in Japan face regularly in all aspects of their lives, from school to work and gender roles. There are occasions when the difficulty of these requirements is suddenly voiced and out in the open. This was the case in a recent class session of mine on generational change in Japan, South Korea, and the United States, a course I have taught since 2009. An American student suddenly raised his hand to ask, "How do you do that self-development stuff?" The class became very quiet. Even the neck-tied and seeming self-assured

UW business students, who often seemed unsympathetic to the recessionary realities in Japan, seemed tongue tied.

In the midst of a developmental shift in Japanese society, young people are experimenting with their lives in ways that recall Japanese reverse migration movements of the 1920s, 1960s, and 1970s. Spontaneous and retemporalizing, the projects of these young people suggest a reaction to the environment of held-up opportunities and requirements, to ideas of development that had only one destructive direction—"reigning disaster triumphant."[45]

Set in the recessionary context that has made it impossible to make a life as scripted by the prebubble idealized developmental narrative, of good home, gendered division of labor, good school, and secure job, the young people in the two back-to-the land locations I visited between 2012–2014 describe what they are doing as finding a way to make a life, when work in Tokyo, Osaka, and other major cities no longer pays more than the rent. The spaces these young people have created they describe as "a means of expression" (*hyōgen dekiru basho*) and "spaces of reciprocity" (*kōkan*). Just as the words and world of Takeo Doi's dependence theory have been replaced with the recessionary language of the strong independent individual, and the need to find one's own latent frontier within, these young migrants' response is to come together and create spaces of life "where you can get along without a lot of money."

This is about making lives in the midst of a long recession that has transformed previously taken-for-granted ideas of temporality and spatiality; upended deeply entrenched certitudes of economic, social, and cultural life; and opened up questions about the histories of modern progress and growth. These responses are projects of recessionary youth, their spaces, and the spatiotemporalities of their movement. How are these young people converting the requirements of self-development and focusing the recessionary lexicon away from the young as a problem? In what ways does this early twenty-first-century migration movement resonate with the counterculturalists of the 1960s and 1970s?

CHIKAKO'S CONTAINER CAFÉ

Chikako Usunaga is a young woman from the outskirts of Kobe, in the Kansai region southwest of Tokyo. I was introduced to Chikako in the summer of 2012 by my friends who are refurbishing their apartment building.

In their search for secondhand things they came across Chikako's café, which, I was told, is not easy to find. There are no signs, and Chikako does not advertise widely, so potential customers have to hear about it by word of mouth.

The café is located in the outer limits of Kobe's border with Akashi City. Chikako calls the space she has worked to create over the last ten years Kokage (the shade of a tree). As Chikako explains, she went the regular route from school to work but always thought it was not for her. She saved her money in hopes of doing something on her own. In 2002, she decided to learn to make things on her own and began creating a range of desserts, growing her own vegetables, and learning to make many of the other items necessary for the small café she was planning. As she put it, "Making things has a meaning."

Behind these decisions was her desire to do something to preserve the area and to bring local people together, many of them older. The site that Chikako chose is adjacent to her family's 200-year-old farmhouse, a thatched-roof home. Beautifully kept up by her mother and father, it is in need of young people to stay and help, so creating Kokage is also about preserving her family home. Her father and mother, however, were opposed to her project from the start, saying that a young woman like Chikako should continue to look for a husband to support her. She has won them over a little at a time, and there is a story to that as well. It was her father's idea to use a vegetable container to sell things from the farm. So, she started to build it from the inside out, little by little—in the first stage there were no windows. With her father's help, as he saw her persistence and enjoyment, they turned her imagination into reality.

Kokage is a result of slow and very deliberate work to create a space for the community. The furniture, accessories, and decorations are all secondhand or handmade in some way. Kokage expresses what words cannot. But, for Chikako, the expression is not directly about her; it is an articulation of a different kind of work, time, and sensibility:

> In the world today, things are very convenient, and if you have money you
> can get anything you want. But, I think that in this way people don't get any
> relief. . . . Out of the inconvenient, starting from scratch, little by little, taking
> time, making by hand, things, thoughts, and a sense of happiness is felt.

Figure 6.1. Chikako's Container Café.
Photo by author.

Figure 6.2. Chikako's Container Café.
Photo by author.

Figure 6.3. Chikako's Container Café.
Photo by author.

Making things, I see the smiling faces of the people who encounter them afterwards and a kind of natural warmth. This encounter, this warmth, is important to me, so I insist on making everything I can by hand. . . . I use things from our garden, plants and vegetables for display and cooking. Expression is a matter of balance.

When I started things for Kokage ten years ago, I was determined not to give up on it, and this determination was communicated, I think, to my parents. To get them onboard, something important to me, I tried to show and explain what I wanted to create until they finally said, "We think we have a sense of what you want to do." I understand why they have been opposed. They still haven't said they agree, but they seem happy to see the growth of Kokage, and they have even become encouraging. I don't have plans to enlarge it because I still want to do it by myself and want it to rely on the vegetables we grow and what I can make.[46]

Places like Chikako's do not exist anywhere else, my friends inform me: a place to commune and relax with neighbors, amid rice fields, millet, all sorts of wild plants. Chikako works hard to communicate this feeling. There is an originality to what she is doing and, above all, a relaxed sense of time passing (*yutari to jikan ga nagareru to*). Also special is Chikako's desire to preserve and protect her 200-year-old family home. For my Kobe friends, there is no other place like Chikako's. At Chikako's, they say, there is a relaxed sense of time passing, a sense of preservation and protection of her surroundings and a sincerity to everything she does.

Chikako has begun to work the early morning shift at a local sweets factory so as not to feel pressured to change the way she is doing things in her own space. She knows, she says, that places like hers are fashionable lately, but she's not interested in this and insists on not advertising or using social media. She invites her mostly elderly neighbors for lunch and tea. News of what she is doing has spread by word of mouth too, but there are few signs. Each year as Chikako says she learns new things. It gives her a sense of the direction in which she wants to go. She says she feels secure in this space of her own making. She's not sure how it will turn out. My friend calls her sensitive and very smart. Rather than not doing, she does with what she has, they say.

A THIRD TIME

In the older part of Kochi city, in Kochi Prefecture on the southern coast of the island of Shikoku, next to a number of rusted-out buildings and in a structure formerly used to sell rice, is a nondescript small gathering place with an unusual name for its surroundings, Terzo Tempo. The name comes from the Italian, meaning a third time. Kochi city was, as of 2013, one of the poorest prefectures in Japan. But in the nineteenth and early twentieth centuries it became famous as the birthplace of the Freedom and People's Rights Movement (*Jiyū Minken Undō*). As thoughtfully discussed by Teruhisa Horio, the Freedom and People's Rights movement was a group during the mid- to late Meiji period who fought for educational rights, or what Horio has called "enlightenment from below," as opposed to the "enlightenment from above" system that won out and supported the Meiji emperor and colonization of East Asia.[47]

Sano and his wife, the owners and operators of Terzo Tempo, moved to Kochi in 2008. They moved away from Tokyo, where they had both studied and intended to stay, to create a life in Kochi. Sano searched for a place that he could make his own and explains that he likes old things: "They are easier to get used to." In fact, everything in the small store, café, and meeting place is old, used, reused, or repurposed. Each item has a story—a local story—because that is part of what Terzo Tempo is about: using local materials from wood for the tables, food they and others grow, and the labor of all those who gather there. They did not have a model, he told me; they just set up the place a little at a time through trial and error.

The name Terzo Tempo means many things to Sano, and the idea for the name just came to him one day, when he remembered reading about a soccer team in Italy by the same name. He explained that everyone has a first time and a second time—a time for work and for family—but there is also a *third* time. The third time can influence the first and second, making them fuller and better. The Sanos have plenty of their own meanings, too, as do the group of friends, who gather daily after work to chat at Terzo Tempo. Most are recent migrants to Kochi, who originally came to visit, met the Sanos, and decided to stay and do something on their own. The group numbers

Figure 6.4. Terzo Tempo.
Photo by author.

about ten to fifteen on any given day. Besides talking, they plan events, music mostly, in a place they all worked to restore. They also plot how to help others make a life. People from the surrounding area are always dropping by Terzo Tempo to leave off their handmade items and name cards, about which the Sanos and the others help to spread the word. Because the café is in an older and low-cost area, it was interesting to see how long-time locals drop in and sit among the young people. The Sanos treat them with a lot of respect, give discounts when needed, and take things and services in trade.

One of the young women who came by when I was there has her own place called Rusk, a small store selling used and new clothing. I asked her why she moved to Kochi:

> I wanted to open my own store . . . but where to do it, I thought. There are lots of little stores in Osaka. By coincidence, I came on a trip to Kochi and met the Sanos. They accept anyone right away, so I decided to give it a try here. And I found that it was easy through them to just become part of the group, [which is] unthinkable in Osaka.

She then told me not to miss the special foods of Kochi. She also directed my friend and I to another member of the group, Ma-san do. Ma-san do is a well-known member of this community, along with the Sanos, and is aware of all of the events going on, she said.

So, I sought out Ma-san do, who came by a few hours later on his bike, also his store. Originally from Okinawa, where his parents were in the business of selling sake, he lived there until the age of fifteen and then moved to Osaka for two years. It was only later, and not from him, I realized that Ma-san do is not this young man's real name but the name of his very small business. *Ma-san do* is Okinawan for "it's delicious." Ma-san do has a shop on wheels, selling and trading his Okinawan doughnuts (*sata andagi*) daily and at the Sunday organic market. He told me the Kochi market is the biggest outdoor organic market in all of Japan. "The vegetables are cheap," he said, "so you can get along without a lot of money. We depend on each other and share [*otagai ni suru*]." He and his own young family run a small guesthouse. It is very cheap, he told me. I could stay with them next time I'm in Kochi, if I'm okay without a bath because they don't have one. He also related to me how the group of young people who congregate after work at Terzo Tempo

Figure 6.5. Terzo Tempo. Ma-san do's bike.
Photo by author.

are already doing in Kochi all the things that the media make such a big deal about these days in other places: community design, transition town, urban permaculture, and the like. The key, he emphasized, is that it is hard to build a life on your own. (I noticed afterwards that few of these young migrants use words like *credential society* or *life-time employment*.)

As Ma-san do and I talked, young people came and went from the café. They sell their music here, too, and all perform together. Together they remodeled a storage area where they put on big events. Ma-san do seemed to know everyone. Although Mr. Sano might be the better educated, he is also more reserved; Ma-san do is gregarious and talked to everyone easily. His phone was always ringing, and he seemed a natural arranger.

The next day, I made a trip to the famous Katsurahama and the tourist site that Kochi is well known for these days, the Ryōma Sakamoto memorial. On the way back, I asked the taxi driver about the recent fandom for

Sakamoto. The driver was silent a minute, then turned to me and said very deliberately, "Japanese want guidance. They want someone to tell them what to do in these uncertain times."

There Is a History to Alternatives

With the beginnings of the Japanese modernization project in the late 1800s, forced and often violent consolidations of different locales into a national framework became an integral part of the Meiji "civilization and enlighten-ment" campaign. The 1930s brought economic depression but also the farm co-op movement and Tachibana Kozaburo's Kyodaimura.[48] Mitsuru Hashi-moto, in his "*Chihou*: Yanagita Kunio's Japan," explains how the upheavals of the nation building project of the late nineteenth century changed life in the regions forever. As Marilyn Ivy insightfully explains, with marginaliza-tion came loss and longing; what had been made superfluous by progressive time—the countryside—was also rendered essential. The marginal became the all-important traditional, which could be used to reconstruct *a* past. Not *the* past that was full of regional and cultural difference from Aomori and Hokkaido in the north to Kyushu and Okinawa in the south, but *a* sense of a unified, homogeneous past that could represent, demonstrate, and explain the time of progress in Japan from the 1860s through the 1940s.[49]

Following the period of the income-doubling campaign of the late 1950s through the early 1970s and the shift from double-digit to lower economic growth, the countryside was once again made to occupy a double role, imag-ined nationally (and commercially) as both the outside or other of the mod-ern and the seemingly unchanging traditional: a process that Ivy refers to as the "appropriated marginal."[50] As Ivy shows, advertising companies in the 1970s and 1980s produced images of domestic travel destinations that despite massive energy-hungry dam construction projects, environmental accidents, and depopulation of rural spaces during this period, seemed to promise the Japanese urban traveler, often (or because) gendered female, a space in which to "discover" Japan and themselves as subjects of a supposed continuity of time and space, other than the Japan of the fiercely competitive lifestyle and its developmental timeframe.[51]

As the world coined the phrase "the Japanese miracle," not only were human resources flooding the cities from the countryside, but thousands of young men were streamed into science and engineering, as the patriotic thing to do. Postwar modernization and internationally envied rates of economic growth came along with chemicals dumped, dams built that would submerge villages, and resource frontiers mobilized. Within what seemed like a dream of capitalist expansion came the voices of the "tribe"—individuals who did not fit the high-growth mold, who left Japan for India, Tibet, and elsewhere in the East to seek quiet. When they returned, they found like-minded Americans seeking their own way out of normative social and economic disciplinary frameworks and their exploitation of human and natural resources. Gary Snyder, the well-known American poet, essayist, and naturalist, arrived in Japan in the late 1960s to study Buddhism. He met up with young Japanese back from their travels and formed the commune or ashram on Suwanose-jima in the middle of the Ryukyus (Okinawa).

In 1969, Snyder wrote:

> We use the term Tribe because it suggests the type of new society now emerging within the industrial nations. In America of course the word has associations with the American Indians which we like. This new subculture is, in fact, more similar to that ancient and successful tribe, the European Gypsies—a group without nation or territory which maintains its own values, its language and religion, no matter what country it may be in. The Tribe proposes a totally different style: based on community houses, villages and ashrams; tribe-run farms or workshops or companies; large open families; pilgrimages and wanderings from center to center.[52]

The mid- to late twentieth century was the time of "the tribe" and those associated with a similar counterculture sensibility, who were living in a world quite different than that of today. Though this ashram has disappeared, there are still individuals living out their lives in a less pronounced but no less dramatically different way. Andy Couturier, a writer who came to Japan in the 1990s to teach English, met up with these individuals and documented the unique lives they lead in his *A Different Kind of Luxury*.[53] Their counter-sensibility was born of a clear distaste for the destruction of life they witnessed all around them.

Despite this history, contemporary reverse migration for twenty-first-century young migrants is neither natural or simple. Advancement and achievement of the credential society since the 1970s for young people from the regional cities and the countryside have been coded to mean migrating to Tokyo, not away from or back to a rural area—directions that are often seen not only in reverse but *as* reverse or backwards. I found out about Terzo Tempo from a story in the first issue of *Turns*,[54] a new magazine devoted to domestic migration or what young people call "U-turn" (as in *you* turn), I-turn, or as the name of the magazine goes a turning around.[55] Though friends who had shared this magazine with me seemed unsure if it was widely read, when I arrived in Kochi, the Sanos did not seem surprised to see me. The *Turns* story about their café had produced lots of visitors. What had the others come to see? Were they interested in what it is like to find or create a way of life in Kochi? What the magazine story overlooked, or perhaps underplayed, was the recessionary context of un- and underemployment, responsibility and risk shifted onto the individual, and the decentralization and deregulation that have made places like Tokyo and Osaka no longer liveable for young people trying to make it on much less than before, no matter how much self-development they do.

This is what attracted me to Ma-san do. He, the Sanos, and others proudly explain that in most other settings, Ma-san do's educational level would condemn him to lower-level service, construction, or a highly insecure job and future. But in this small community of friends, all of whom trying to make it together and enjoying themselves in the process, Man-san do is doing what he is not only good at but what is also highly valued: connecting people, spreading information, listening, and learning quickly. "Ask Ma-san do," they say, "he knows everyone and everything."

Decentralization and deregulation, according to Takehiko Kariya, are making things even more difficult for prefectures and cities like Kochi, where young people are moving to make a life. School subsidies, which up to the early 2000s had been figured on a progressive scale—the poorest areas got more—are ending.[56] Yet effects of decentralization and deregulation are what brought people together around this small café, and it is what is creating a community that embraces the local space, the local people, and the many young people moving here from across a long history of regional differences, united perhaps more now by their shared experience of being in the same generation. As a friend of mine in Kobe suggested to me after I returned from my trip to Kochi, these other spaces and times of life are a trend with many different tributaries like a river.

A number of recent books about sustainability in Japan fault the government for being two-faced, touting Japanese society and culture as tied to nature on the one hand and destroying it on the other. The state and Japanese corporations come up with all sorts of names for sustainable projects that sound good, but they do not follow through. Other observers fall into all-too-familiar patterns of reducing this contradiction to culture or national character, as if there is no history to either of these and other national ideologies are less complex and contradictory. But for these I- and U-turners young and old, becoming sustainable is part and parcel of their rethinking the way they use time and space; taking time and making the time, on their own, in their own way, with others.

The effects of recession have left many Japanese on their own in a world that discredits the standardized postwar past of homogeneous identification and replaces it with independence and endless self-development. This time without direction or guidance, a time where each individual is responsible for him- or herself, has created a sense that the future does not exist, as in the fictional, but nevertheless fearful, battles of *Battle Royale*, *Bright Future*, the Sasaki family in *Tokyo Sonata*, and the legions of real-life young part-time or temporary workers. But, neoliberal time is also producing, often out of necessity, a small consciousness revolution. When income no longer covers more than the rent in the major cities, a young person must turn elsewhere. The change I saw taking place represents a movement away from more than just physical space. Members of the recessionary generation seem to be rethinking notions of convenience and remaking the ideas of reciprocity and mutuality to create lives in and for the present and not in a race for the future. There is a sense of possibility in the spaces these young people are creating, in their making lives within a difficult set of conditions. These are important stories of this moment in Japan, and many more still waiting to be told.

Conclusion

This book has ethnographically followed the making of a problem and the pedagogical, psychological, and neoliberal "solutions" created to address it. I have argued that this problem and the solution making were linked to effects of anthropological knowledge and national-cultural fashioning. Prominent among these were postwar "writing on and off" of Japan and global rationales of governance that "rolled back" social support and reintervened to manage the effects of this retracting of government. I have argued that the process of problematizing affected the subjectification and identification of those growing up in the times and spaces of the 1990s economic downturn. Problematizing and remedying technologies diverted attention from a deepening financial crisis that altered individual and national economic futures as well as naturalized ideas of nation, culture, and modern temporality in Japan. Obscured in this process has been the transformation of governance, starting within the education system, and moving to the family and world of work.

Ethnographically following the emergence of the child problem meant understanding what this discursive form did and how it did it. This work has involved investigating the historicity of the child, its connection with other forms of modern knowledge and power, and exploring the sites and spaces of the child's appearance. Working in both of these ways brought me into contact with the means by which ideologies of dependency and homogeneity were being displaced and replaced by transposed notions of independence and self-development. Framed as inevitable, rather than as a project of global and domestic governing, this shift turned the population into self-responsible risk-bearing entrepreneurs of themselves, "little bits of human capital" encased in a game (theory) that is no longer confined to the halls of academia.[1]

Equally an ethnography of education and schooling and its coming together with psychology under the conditions of recession, this book tells the story of the effects of recessionary discourses of panic and neoliberal language of transformation on public schooling and the coincident development of the private education industry from the late 1990s through the first and second decades of the 2000s. Long-term participant observation allowed me to witness micro and macro changes implemented during this time and how they affected children, families, teachers, and young adults. As education became the site of contestation and transformation, its tight linkages with work and labor shifted too, overturning expectations of social stability. The credential society of exam preparation, university reputation, and lifetime employment underwent a desecuritizing at this time. Restructuring of existing employee jobs and "flexibilitizing" or "liberalizing" of entry-level employment has been the cause of newfound uncertainty that resonated much beyond employment. The consequent recourse to private services and educational and posteducational human capital development has accentuated social class divisions between those who are financially able to access these extras and those who are not. Income differences are not necessarily new, as Natsuki Iwama (Chapter Six) reminds us, but the decreasing provision of public guidance, support, and ideologies of inclusion and exclusion that subordinated these differences are.

Within this context of long-term recession, problemitization, liberalization, and Japan's triple disaster of 2011, the Japanese prime minister's address at the end of April 2015 to a joint session of the U.S. Congress was noteworthy. "Come see the new Japan," Abe entreated the senators, members of Congress, and American public. Which new Japan is this, I wondered; not irradiated Fukushima, the unquestioned cover-up of past nuclear plant accidents, and the ruination of so much land and so many lives. Nor did PM Abe refer to the full "liberalization" of the labor market, his so-called third arrow that even his surrogates have referred to as "drilling into (social) bedrock." What does a completely liberalized, in the sense of deprived of protection and support, Japanese society look like? Prime Minister Abe was also certainly not referring to the dramatic rise in rates of depression (*utsubyō* or *utsu*, as now commonly known) and medicalization among the young and old due to job-related pressures and employment failure. So, perhaps Mr. Abe was referring to the "cool Japan" brand and all the new construction for the Olympics. Will they address the division of society into winners and losers, or the castigating of the young for being products of a recessionary environment, and the postwar and prewar legacies they did not create?

Abe could have mapped out the challenges shared by young people in Japan, the United States, and elsewhere around the world. He could have explained that while no one has the solution to the human and natural extractive forms of twenty-first-century global capitalism, there are Japanese, young and old, seeking alternatives. They are protesting the global reach of the neoliberal project's infiltration and decimation of key conditions of livelihood, environment, and culture by creating their own alternative spaces of democratic possibility. The time of young Japanese hasn't been so much "lost," as many have suggested, as it has been transformed by new rationales of governance that operate from within long-held social and cultural ideologies and terminologies. Within this context, Mr. Abe could have courageously outlined the ongoing problems of the American base-ification of Okinawa and his own government's refusal to teach young Japanese about Japan's twentieth-century imperial project, the violences inflicted on East Asian neighbors, and the tremendous loss of life and livelihood of ordinary Japanese in the name of the colonial pursuit of territory, resources, and power. Does keeping their own history from the young turn them into so-called monsters or make them "dislike" themselves or their own country as some members of Abe's generation have alleged? Is this the reason young Japanese already burdened with the individuating technologies of neoliberal subjectivity must also be required to develop "hearts that love their country"? If "history is indeed hard," it does not become easier by keeping its complexities from those who encounter them daily in the present.

These were missed opportunities but perhaps not unintentionally so. Being courageous would open up domestic questions about the forms of power I have tried to uncover throughout this book within my discussion of the child problem, recessionary language, notion of neoliberal patriotism, and more. Because of this lack of prime ministerial or top level will, some Japanese friends of mine shrug and say, "Democracy is not in our blood."

Genetics or essentialized culture continue to operate as fallback explanations despite vastly altered conditions of recessionary life. How then have the Japanese people opposed the revision of the antiaggression clause Article 9 of the postwar Constitution, despite repeated attempts since the early 1950s by Japanese leaders and outside pressure for revision? Current conditions of neoliberalization from education to labor are what places democracy in jeopardy everywhere as Wendy Brown has forcefully argued. Not an inevitable result, foregone conclusion, or natural product anywhere, explains Brown; democratic ideas, vocabularies, and possibilities must be taught, nurtured, imagined, and fought for everywhere.[2]

Notes

INTRODUCTION

1. Jacqueline Rose, *The Case of Peter Pan or the Impossibility of Children's Fiction*, xvii.

2. Peter Miller and Nikolas Rose, *Governing the Present*.

3. Hirokazu Miyazaki, "The Temporality of No Hope," 243.

4. The Japanese for *world of recession* is *fukeiki no yo*. *Unease* is my rendering of the Japanese *fuan*.

5. The Japanese term *mondai*, or problem, has been used in similar ways in other critical contexts, as Ken C. Kawashima shows in his analysis of "the Korean problem" (*chōsenjin mondai*) and history of Korean workers in interwar Japan. See Ken C. Kawashimam, *The Proletarian Gamble*. The "Okinawa *mondai*" is another example. As Rose and Miller state in the opening quotation, problems become visible by being rendered problematic.

6. Benedict Anderson, *Imagined Communities*, 22.

7. Miyoshi's essay, "Japan Is Not Interesting," ends as Japan slides into long-term recession and Western interest moves to China and later South Korea. See Ann Anagnost, "Introduction: Life-Making in Neoliberal Times." In the area of education, the comparisons have drastically shifted from Japan to China and South Korea. See Nancy Abelmann, Jung-Ah Choi, and So Jin Park, *No Alternative?*; Se-Woong Koo, "How South Korea Enslaves Its Students"; and Helen Gao, "China's Education Gap."

8. In the following I discuss at more length the position that the notion of dependent identity occupied in a vast genre of writing about Japanese character and personality in the 1970s and 1980s known as *Nihonjinron* (discussions about Japaneseness by Japanese writers).

9. Takatoshi Ito, "Retrospective on the Bubble Period and Its Relationship to Development in the 1990s."

10. Japan was the single largest bankroller of U.S. debt at the time.

11. In Chapter Two, I also describe my interviews with Youth A's defense lawyer. As Mr. Noguchi explained to me, the media did not take the time to understand the individual and local conditions surrounding the fourteen-year-old killer. If they had, Noguchi said, it would not have been as easy to nationalize ("all kids are strange"), minimize, and ultimately neglect the highly specific nature of Youth A's delusionary world. For an insightful analysis of the media coverage of school shootings in the United States, see Ansel Herz, "Does Media Coverage of School Shootings Lead to More School Shootings?"

12. The English word *strange* comes from the Latin *extraneus*, or external. It refers to the unusual, surprising, the difficult to understand or explain, the unfamiliar or alien. One of the examples for *strange* in the *Oxford English Dictionary* (OED) is "children have strange ideas." (Right!) The Japanese term for *strange*, *hen* or *hen da*, includes the idea of change or transformation, something I return to successive chapters.

13. Claudia Casteneda, *Figurations*.

14. From a set of personal interviews with Ryōichi Kawakami in 1999 and 2000 and from my observations in his classroom.

15. Jamie Peck and Adam Tickell, "Neoliberalizing Space," 380–404. I return in the latter part of this Introduction to Peck and Tickell's ideas of "roll back and roll out" neoliberalization.

16. Later in this Introduction I also discuss the connections between the first Abe government and the current one. See the cover story, "Abe's Master Plan," in *The Economist*, May 18, 2013.

17. Leo Ching, Yoshikuni Igarashi, and others have discussed how an all-consuming focus on national character and its relation to human capital development in the mid- to late twentieth century in Japan served to dismiss the multiethnic imperial past, as well as obscure forms of human and environmental extraction necessary for accelerated economic growth. In the next chapter, I show how discourses of national character and identity shifted in the postwar period as a result of the culture and personality approach in American cultural anthropology and its relation to the child category in Japan.

18. Tomiko Yoda, "A Roadmap to Millennial Japan," 43.

19. Also see Teruhisa Horio, *Educational Thought and Ideology in Modern Japan*; and Andrea G. Arai, "Notes to the Heart."

20. Michael Latham, "Introduction."

21. See Yoshikuni Igarashi, *Bodies of Memory*.

22. For an excellent discussion of the problem with posing group and individual as absolute dichotomies in workplace organization, see Knuth Dohse, Ulrich Jurgens, and Thomas Malsch, *From "Fordism" to "Toyotism"?* See also Marilyn Ivy, "Benedict's Shame," and her "Critical Texts, Mass Artifacts."

23. Ezra F. Vogel, *Japan as Number One*.

24. See Anne Allison's *Permitted and Prohibited Desires*, particularly the two chapters "Producing Mothers" and "Obento as Ideological State Apparatus."

25. Anne Allison, *Permitted and Prohibited Desires*.

26. Michel Foucault, "The Subject and Power." See also Michel Foucault, *Discipline and Punish*. For the relevance of Foucault's notion of productive power for contemporary neoliberal discourse and policy, see Andrew Barry, Thomas Osborne, and Nikolas Rose, *Foucault and Political Reason*. Additionally, for Foucault's genealogical method and its relation to modern forms of power, see his "Nietzche, Genealogy, History," in Michel Foucault, Donald F. Bouchard, and Sherry Simon, *Language, Counter-Memory, Practice*.

27. Here I would also add Tetsuya Takahashi who, although not strictly an educationalist, has written of the role of the state in education in Japan and the influence of psychological language and identity discourse on the new direction of education. I note his contributions to my work throughout and have written about his insightful *"Heart" and War ("Kokoro" to Sensō)* in my "Notes to the Heart."

28. See especially Teruhisa Horio's *Educational Thought and Ideology in Modern Japan*, chapters 13–14; and Takehiko Kariya, "From 'Credential' Society to 'Learning Capital' Society," 87–113.

29. I discuss my ethnographic experience of what led up to this historic revision in Chapter Two and have written about it extensively in A. Arai, "Notes to the Heart."

30. Some of the ethnographies of Japan that have most informed and inspired me in researching and writing my own are Marilyn Ivy's *Discourses of the Vanishing*; Chris Nelson's *Dancing with the Dead*; Memory, Performance and Everyday Life in Postwar Okinawa; Gabriella Lukacs's *Scripted Affects Branded Selves*; Junko Kitanaka's *Depression in Japan*; and Takashi Fujitani's historical ethnography of the emperor system, *Splendid Monarchy*.

31. Gilles Deleuze, "Forward," ix–xvii.

32. A final comment on contribution is necessary. Conceptually, historically, and ethnographically, this book owes much to the insight and daring of Marilyn Ivy's *Discourses of the Vanishing*. Ivy was the first to bring the specificities of capitalist modernity's appropriations, displacements, and separations to bear ethnographically on notions of cultural unity and national commonality at the end of the 1980s, a time when Japan's economic success was unquestionably linked to its unique cultural character. Additionally, for thinking about recessionary times, discursive figures of crisis, and the reforms that emerge out of them, my thinking has been guided by recent ethnographies of women's language in the workplace by Miyako Inoue, television dramas and their "reconciling of the irreconcilable" neoliberal discourse by Gabriella Lukacs, Hirokazu Miyazaki's work on neoliberalism and finance, and Junko Kitanaka's on psychology and depression.

33. Robert Stolz, *Bad Water.* Stolz applies Marx's notion of "subsumption" to the relationship between environmental accidents and abuses of the prewar modernity project and postwar high-growth modernization.

34. See Michiko Ishimure, *Lake of Heaven* (Bruce Allen, trans.); and Lea Stenson and Asao Sarukawa Aroldi, eds., *Reverberations from Fukushima.*

35. Hayao Kawai, "The Structure of Japan in the 21st Century."

36. Private education industries are of course not exclusive to Japan. South Korea's cram school industry easily rivals the Japanese one in intensity, as does China's. The United States has, over the last two decades, beginning from the "learn from Japan" phase of the 1980s, seen our own private schooling services intensify with chains like Kumon in most major cities. Sylvan Learning Centers and test preparation schools for SAT and ACT college entrance exams are nearly unavoidable for aspiring high school juniors and seniors. Chapter Four discusses what happens when the supplement becomes a substitute.

37. Marilyn Ivy, *Discourses of the Vanishing*, 25.

CHAPTER ONE

1. Stefan Tanaka, *New Times in Modern Japan*, 27.

2. David Ambaras, *Bad Youth.*

3. Karatani Kojin, *The Origins of Modern Japanese Literature*, 115.

4. Ruth Benedict and Margaret Mead, eds., *An Anthropologist at Work.*

5. Ruth Benedict, *Patterns of Culture.*

6. In the work of two of Franz Boas's principal students, Ruth Benedict and Margaret Mead, what George Stocking argues were the tensions in Boas's thought were forgotten in the drive to forge a science out of the yet vague idea of the personality of a culture.

7. For Boas, "on the one hand culture was an accidental accretion of individual elements, on the other (culture) was an integrated spiritual totality which somehow conditioned the form of its elements." George Stocking traces this duality and the latter focus on "whole cultures and their psychological meaning in the "geniuses" of "peoples" to the German intellectual heritage in which Boas received his first training and from which he never completely dissociated his thought.

8. William C. Manson, "Abram Kardiner and the NeoFreudian Alternative in Culture and Personality," 87.

9. Ruth Benedict, *The Chrysanthemum and the Sword*, 252.

10. Ibid., 254.

11. Sonia Ryang, *Japan and National Anthropology*, 47: "*Chrysanthemum* . . . supplied the Japanese with an appropriate discursive tool and conceptual constructs to explain themselves to Westerners." In a contingent twist of fate, as Ryang explains, although "*Chrysanthemum* did rescue Japan from U.S. racist propaganda and fanatic demonization . . . it did other things too, occluding Japan's wartime and co-

lonial responsibilities over its Asian subordinates and failing to explain Japan's historical position with reference to international political economy . . ." (Ibid., 65).

12. Doi has repeatedly argued that the lack of a single lexical equivalent in English for *amae* represents a linguistic uniqueness symbolic of the uniqueness of Japanese cultural values as a whole.

13. Benedict Anderson, *Imagined Communities*, 10.

14. Key works in this area are the well-known studies by Gorer, Embree, and Benedict. Other examples from the late 1970s through the 1990s that informed by Doi's *The Anatomy of Dependence* are Takie Lebra, *Japanese Patterns of Behavior, Becoming Japanese*; Joy Hendry, *Merry White, in The Japanese Educational Challenge*; Millie Creighton, "The Shifting Image of Childhood among Consumer Affluence"; Hideo Kojima, "Childrearing Concepts as a Belief-Value System of the Society and the Individual"; Catherine Lewis, *Educating Hearts and Minds*; Edward Beauchamp, "What Can We Learn from Japan? A Postscript on Japanese Education"; Gail Benjamin, *Japanese Lessons*; Nancy Rosenberger, ed., *The Japanese Sense of Self*; and a long list of others.

15. Michael E. Latham, "Introduction"; and Victor Koschmann, "Modernization and Democratic Values."

16. Michael E. Latham, "Introduction," 5.

17. Yoshino Kosaku, *Cultural Nationalism in Contemporary Japan*, 19.

18. Tessa Morris-Suzuki, *Beyond Computopia*; and Yoneji Masuda, *The Information Society as Post-Industrial Society*.

19. See Chapter Six here and chapter 4 in Mary Brinton's *Lost in Transition*.

20. Takehiko Kariya, "From Credential Society to 'Learning Capital' Society."

21. Jennifer Robertson, Julie Higashi, Takahashi Tetsuya (and others) have discussed the multifacetedness of *kokoro*. As Higashi notes, *kokoro* has been rendered in English as feelings, mind, heart, spirit, emotions, and thoughts. For my purposes here, I employ the often-used rendering of *kokoro* as "heart." I do so to do justice to the multivocality of this term and the application of its range of meanings to the effects of psychology of identity discourse on education discourse during the recessionary period of the late 1990s to the present.

22. From a public lecture entitled "Nihon Bunka no Yukue" (The Direction of Japanese Culture) given by Hayao Kawai, renowned Jungian clinical psychologist, advisor to the Ministry of Education, and former director of the International Center for the Study of Japanese Culture.

23. Takashi Fujitani, *Splendid Monarchy*. Also see Kimberly Brandt's *Kingdom of Beauty: Mingei and the Politics of Folk Art in Imperial Japan*.

24. Andrea G. Arai, "Notes to the Heart."

25. As Kawakami often complained, there were no teachers on the reform committees. The ideological and political differences between Kawakami and Kawai are important for understanding the context of the transformations that emerged

from education in the 1990s and 2000s. I discuss these in more detail in Chapters Three and Four.

26. See Chapter Two here and my "Notes to the Heart" for a discussion of the new moral education textbook.

27. One also might think of films such as Kon Ichikawa's *Manin Densha* (Crowded Streetcar) about the precarity of the employment system at earlier times in Japan's postwar growth period. (I would like to thank Michael Fisch for telling me about this film).

28. *Tōkyō saonata* [*Tokyo Sonata*] directed by Kiyoshi Kurosawa, 2008. The Japanese phrase is, "*Kyūmei bo-to ichattan da yo. . . .*"

29. Ibid. The Japanese here is, "*Sasaki-san mo taihen desu ne?*"

30. Christopher P. Hood, "The Third Great Reform of the Japanese Education System."

31. Takehiko Kariya, "The End of Egalitarian Education in Japan."

32. Takehiko Kariya, "The End of Egalitarian Education in Japan"; Horio Teruhisa, *Educational Thought and Ideology in Modern Japan*; Hirota Teruyuki, personal communication with the author; and Hirota Teruyuki, *Nihonjin no shitsuke wa suitaishita ka* [*Has Japanese Manner Training Really Declined?*].

33. Adam Peck and Jamie Tickell, "Neoliberalizing Space," 380–404.

34. Ibid.

35. Yves Tiberghien,"Thirty Years of Neo-Liberal Reforms in Japan."

36. Of these expectations aimed at the young in contemporary Japan, several Japanese exchange students in my University of Washington anthropology classes over the last several years have exclaimed, "It's harsh to expect us to be what we have never been trained for and our parents don't understand."

37. Jacques Donzelot, "Michel Foucault and Liberal Intelligence," 130.

38. "Abe's Master Plan." *The Economist*, May 18, 2013: 13.

39. Interview in Kobe with women's group, March and July, 2009.

40. Ibid.

41. In using the outmoded terms here I am gesturing to two earlier moments of representational shifts in the 1860s through the 1890s and the immediate postwar period of the American Occupation of Japan (1945 through 1952). During both of these times a crisis of representation occurred, such that words no longer represented social reality as they had before.

42. See Hirokazu Miyazaki's article, "The Temporality of No Hope."

43. Ann Anagnost, Andrea Arai, and Hai Ren, *Global Futures in East Asia*, 15.

44. This example parallels the opening examples in the Introduction to *Global Futures in East Asia*, in which a busload of Japanese part-time, flexible young workers are misrecognized as Chinese.

45. *Ii kaisha ni haitemo, tōsan suru kara.* A "freeter," romanized as *furītā* in Japanese, is a member of the new underemployed part-time workforce in Japan. *Furītā* is a neologism made up of the German *arbeiter* and the English *free*. These workers

are anything but free, however, except in the neoliberal sense of shouldering more responsibility and risk. Interview in Seattle, Washington, 2010.

46. Ibid.

47. Michel Foucault, *Lectures on the Will to Know.*

CHAPTER TWO

1. From the NHK television series on school problems and Ken Terawaki, *Toward Education Change in the Twenty-First Century,* 40. *Inner self* is my rendering of the Japanese term *naimen,* a term that began to be used regularly in the media by psychologists and other commentators on the problem with the child from the late 1990s on. As explained in Chapter One (see especially note 21), I have chosen to render the Japanese *kokoro* as heart.

2. Manabu Sato, "Imagining Neo-Liberalism and the Hidden Realities of the Politics of Reform," 226, 236.

3. This series was aired on NHK (Japan's national public broadcasting network) over a period of two weeks from the end of May through early June of 2001.

4. In his book that preceded this series on educational changes in the twenty-first century, Terawaki skirts issues such as the public's demands for smaller class size (no more than thirty students). The implication is that this sort of change will be up to the public to fund.

5. Shōnen A (Youth A) is the official designation given to the teenager from Kobe who was responsible for the decapitation of a sixth grade student and fatal stabbing of another elementary school student in 1997. Japanese juvenile justice law mandates the anonymity of juvenile offenders in the media, thereby protecting their identity.

6. Ken Terawaki, *Nijuiseki he Kyōiku wa Kawaru* [Toward twenty-first century educational change], 17. The Japanese for "don't amount to anything" is *jibun wa yaku ni tatanai.*

7. From the NHK television series on school problems and Ken Terawaki, *Nijuiseki he Kyōiku wa Kawaru,* 40.

8. Teruhisa Horio, *Educational Thought and Ideology in Modern Japan.*

9. Terawaki argues that not only technological knowledge, but also farming, agriculture, culture, and the heart will be important in the twenty-first century in Japan.

10. *Shōgai kyōiku* (lifelong learning) is a term that Terawaki uses to refer to the idea promoted strongly by the MOE for education to be continuous throughout life. Ken Terawaki, *Nijuiseki he Kyōiku wa Kawaru.*

11. I discuss school refusal and other schooling problems that became large issues of the 1980s in Chapter Four.

12. Manabu Sato, "Imagining Neo-Liberalism and the Hidden Realities of the Politics of Reform," 229.

13. Ibid., 227.

14. Quoted in Sato, "Imagining Neo-Liberalism and the Hidden Realities of the Politics of Reform."

15. Roger Goodman, "The Why, What and How of Educational Reform in Japan."

16. Keita Takeyama, "Reconceptualizing the Politics of Japanese Education, Reimagining Comparative Studies of Japanese Education," 256.

17. Ibid., 257.

18. Andrea G. Arai, "The Wild Child of 1990s Japan."

19. For more on the youth's articulation of revenge, see Marilyn Ivy, "Revenge and Recapitation in Recessionary Japan."

20. See Adrienne Carey Hurley, *Revolutionary Suicide and Other Desperate Measures.*

21. See Andrea Arai, "Notes to the Heart," for a fuller explanation of the kinds of knowledge and respect that these school and psychological reformers had in mind.

22. For the notion of "troubled subjectivity," see Yumiko Iida's excellent discussion in her "Between the Technique of Living an Endless Routine and the Madness of Absolute Degree Zero," 423–464.

23. Ibid., 446.

24. Ibid., 448.

25. The heads of the neighborhood and community associations were anxious to show me the fruits of their combined labors prior to the 1997 event and the disaster and crime prevention center that they erected shortly after the event in an effort to salvage any bit of the value of their neighborhood and property, which became among the least desirable in the city following this event.

26. Entrance exams are mandatory for entrance to public high school and college in Japan but not to public junior high. A longer discussion of the exam system and cram school changes in the age of recession in Chapter Five.

27. Yoshikuni Noguchi, *Soredemo Shōnen wo Batsushimasuka?* [Under the circumstances will you still punish the youth?].

28. AERA put out a special issue on "Kodomo ga Abunai" [Danger of/to the Child], November 11, 1997, which focused almost entirely on the frightening sense that it is now impossible to know what goes on with the child.

29. As a result of these interests and his many writings on "the Japanese heart," Kawai was elected to the directorship of the International Center for the Study of Japanese Culture (Nichibunken) in 1999.

30. *Kokoro no kyōiku no jujitsu ni mukete.*

31. *Kodomo yori fukaku wakaru Tame ni* [Toward a deeper understanding of the child]. (1) The child has an internal world all his or her own. (2) Children are an existence in the process of developing. (3) Adolescence is a period in which the ego goes from its basis to its final construction. (4) At the base of children's way of life

are interpersonal relations. (5) Children incorporate their values and viewpoints into their way of life.

32. An education that promotes thinking about the importance of life and death, an education that promotes the home as the basic instiller of life skills and ethics, an education that reacts to the influence of the information society. *Yōjiki kara no kokoro no kyōiku no arikatta ni tsuite* [The form of emotional education from the time of childhood].

33. The program now takes place throughout Hyogo Prefecture in two separate weeks; half of the second-year students participate in February and half in June.

34. Due to the logistical difficulties involved in finding enough locations to which to assign this many students in one week, the program is divided into a week in June and a week in February.

35. I spent the second week of June with the students and teachers of three schools in areas with different socioeconomic levels. During this time, I conversed with school staff about the arrangements involved and time spent in the setup of the program each year, particular constraints that they faced, and the advantages and disadvantages of this program from the perspective of school staff. Observing on-site with the students, I discussed the program with them and the community members, in various business and services with which they were meant to interact during this time. My unhampered observation of this program in action at various schools and sites was arranged by Toru Sasai at the Kobe education authority. I am grateful to Mr. Sasai for his time spent conversing with me and for the various introductions he made on my behalf.

36. Katsuyoshi Sōri, "Hyogo Trial Week and Children," *Sekai* June, 2001.

CHAPTER THREE

1. Bram Büscher, *Transforming the Frontier*, 9–10.

2. Anna Tsing, "How to Make Resources in Order to Destroy Them (and Then Save Them?) on the Salvage Frontier."

3. T. Lemke, "The Birth of Bio-Politics," 201.

4. This was the first of two annual public gatherings with Kawai Hayao that I attended during my fieldwork. At both of these gatherings, Kawai discussed his latest publication, which was not yet out in print but was available for advance sale.

5. In addition to these more popularly written volumes, there is an academic collection (*zenshū*) of Kawai's writings that focuses predominantly on his unique contribution—the introduction of Jungian thought to Japan and the application of this thought to the study of Japanese history and tradition. There is also a twelve-volume series on Kawai's counseling and discussions of Japanese culture.

6. Hayao Kawai passed away in 2007.

7. Takeo Doi achieved fame early through his publication of *The Structure of Dependency*. Kawai, on the other hand, without an original theory, remained a much smaller influence in the discourses on the Japanese, until the late 1990s after his appointment as director of the International Center for the Study of Japanese Culture (*Nichibunken*).

8. As Professor Teruyuki Hirota cogently explained to me, Kawai's fame would eventually subside, but the effects of his involvement in the government's education reforms would remain long after he was gone from the scene.

9. Frontier (*furonteia*) is the central image of a report by the special prime minister's committee (headed by Kawai) on "The Structure of Japan in the Twenty-First Century," published in 2000 and authored by Kawai. I discuss this image of the frontier and its various resonances here, as I examine the concept of governance (*gabanansu*) with which the reforms were associated.

10. Maruyama Masao was a leading Japanese political theorist of the prewar and postwar eras. For a very interesting discussion of Maruyama's participation in the postwar conferences on modernization in Japan, see Victor Koschmann, "Modernization and Democratic Values."

11. Public Speech, "The Condition of Japanese Culture: Education in a New Age." Introduction made for Kawai Hayao, Tokyo, June 2001.

12. Kawai Hayao, public talk in Tokyo June 2001.

13. Ibid.

14. The Japanese terms Kawai uses are *senzaitekina chikara*.

15. Kawai's second talk in 2001 was entitled "The Wisdom of Stories" (*Ohanashi no Chie*), for which a new book by the same name was available, hot off the presses, as well.

16. Kawai noted that his favorite Japanese myths, the ones in which one could identify a source for independence, were "Momotarō" (The peach boy), "Urashima Tarō" (The fisher lad) and "Issun Boshi" (One-inch boy). In each of these stories the hero sets off as a result of his own initiative on an adventure and is uncertain as to what the outcome might be. In two of the cases, the outcome is good, and the hero returns triumphant (against all odds in the case of "Issun Boshi"), but though the ending is not a clearly happy one in all of the three, the hero makes do with his lot. The parallel that Kawai wanted to create here was between these mythic characters making do with what happened to them, and twenty-first-century citizens taking responsibility for their fates as independent individuals. The recessionary context hardly ever made it into these discussions of the linkages between myth and history!

17. Kawai's writings on his experience with the psychology of Carl Jung and Kawai's introduction of Jung's thought to Japan are fascinating studies in and of themselves. For my purposes here, however, I would like to note a few of the more striking differences between Jung and Freud that have been discussed in the following works: Edward Glover's *Freud or Jung* (1950); Jacqueline Rose's *The Case of*

Peter Pan; and Andrew Samuels's *Jung and the Post-Jungians*. Glover, a renowned Freudian psychoanalyst and writer, launched a diatribe-like attack against what he viewed as the destructive and even dangerous tendencies of Jung's thought; Glover devotes an entire section to Jung's pronouncements of Hitler's role as a "prophet, oracle, and the archetypal 'Medicine Man of Old.'" Glover lambasts Jung, in particular, for his discarding of what Glover considers one of the hallmarks of Freudian thought—the latent content of dreams (or the difference between the manifest and latent content in the dream-work). For Jung, says Glover, dreams are predictive of the present as well as the future, and they were read in terms of the archetypal figures for which Jung became so well known. In her discussion of the fiction of Alan Garner (a writer of children's literature and a Jungian), Jacqueline Rose takes Glover's discussion a step further. She argues that, unlike Freud, Jung's interest was in the history of the human race; "He saw the unconscious as a repository of a set of myths and symbols which our culture has destroyed" (p. 18). An appeal to Jung, notes Rose, is "in line with a mystification that places childhood at the origin of all human history." Finally, Rose concludes, "The dispute between Freud and Jung is not about just childhood; it is more crucially about the question of language and whether meaning is stable." For the latter, she says, "Meaning was no more divided than subjectivity itself."

18. Kawai's second talk in 2001, "The Wisdom of Stories" (*Ohanashi no Chie*).

19. The difference Kawai is inscribing here between wisdom and knowledge is between something that is experience driven, and something that may have little to do with experience. Moreover, it should not be overlooked that the interpersonal relations (*ningen kankei*) to which Kawai refers are none other than the vaunted basis on which rests one of the core differences of Japanese society.

20. In the latter part of this chapter, in my analysis of the report headed by Kawai Hayao on "The Structure of the Twenty-First Century: Japan's Frontier Is within Japan," I will argue that in this use of the "frontier" imagery and the turn to the individual, by way of a psychology of myth as history, there is a turning inward that suggests a new means of control, and, if you will, neoliberalism wedded closer than ever to a newly fortified discourse of national culture.

21. For a reading of the Ohira plan for "an age of culture" in the 1980s, see Harry Harootunian, "Visible Discourses/Invisible Ideologies."

22. Teruhisa Horio, *Educational Thought and Ideology in Modern Japan*.

23. This committee produced two sets of findings (*daiichi, daini tōshin*); I will be principally interested in the reportings of the second.

24. This is of course never seamless in any nation as thoroughly implicated in the discourses of the modern as Japan. Throughout the period about which I am speaking here (from the 1980s through the present), different kinds of direct forms of repressive control were exercised, none of them with long-lasting efficacy, a point that I make with regard to the new rights and responsibilities focus of Chapter Five.

25. Harry Harootunian, "National Narratives/Spectral Happenings." The FLE was promulgated in March 1947 to replace the Imperial Rescript on Education (Kyōiku Chokugo, 1890), which was judged by postdefeat American Occupation forces to represent, in its imperial-centered doctrine, one of the foundations of Japan's wartime militarism. The intention of the FLE that replaced the Rescript as the legal foundation for education was to move the people into the place that the emperor had held as the bearer of the right to have what Teruhisa Horio has called an education freer from the exigencies of the state (whether military or economically initiated). For an in-depth discussion of the Imperial Rescript, the FLE, and the "Image of the Ideal Japanese," see Horio's *Educational Thought and Ideology in Modern Japan.* Also, for an interesting discussion of the problems faced by teachers in making the switch from the prewar Rescript to the postwar FLE, see Inoue Kyoko's *Individual Dignity in Modern Japanese Thought,* chapter 2.

26. Ibid.

27. Kosugi, Takashi, *Ushinatta Kokoro no Kyōiku.* Here Kosugi also explained that the bullying (*ijime*) and school refusal (*tōkōkyohi*) that continue to plague Japanese schools could be ameliorated through the improvement of manner training in the home and the teaching of form (*sahō*) in the schools.

28. Referred to as "declining academic ability" (*gakuryoku teika*), this large reduction of core curriculum has been met by parents and many teachers alike with anxieties for the future of math and science in particular in Japan. It has also, as I argue in Chapter Five, been an area that has not unintentionally allowed the supplementary education industry to benefit as well from the reforms.

29. As I mentioned in the previous chapter, the question of smaller class size has been raised enthusiastically by parent's groups taking the idea of individualized education at its word. Their efforts, unfortunately, had (as of the winter of 2002) been in vain, due in large part to the kind of logic employed by Ken Terawaki and others in the ministry about whose responsibility the full implementation of this individualized education will really be.

30. Imai Elementary is the subject of my discussion of "schools, homes, and *hōkai*" in Chapter Four.

31. Sometime afterward, in one of the many conversations I was fortunate enough to have with principal Majima, he informed me that he was in his last year before retirement (and so, he let it fall, felt freer than before to express his opinions about things). One of the things we talked about on this occasion was his concern that the reforms were projecting an image of a completely failed past, an image with which he could not totally agree. There were things that he thought had been successful about Japanese schooling, along with the problems, but he wondered if this sudden move to blame the past was really the key to a more successful and open future.

32. As a member of the PTA, I helped collect and compile the participant survey (*anketo*) that was taken after this session with the principal. Most who attended

expressed their concerns afterwards. Some responded that they were worried as to whether this reform would help out with the college entrance examinations, which despite all the talk about relaxed education still loomed large (even larger than before for some parents, as I discuss in Chapter Five); others said that they left the meeting with the same level of anxiety about the upcoming changes that they had entered with. Yet some seemed to appreciate principal Majima's frankness about what he didn't yet know.

33. Following this gathering, I was asked by another teacher, with whom I had become friendly, what I had thought about this experience of different cultures. When I ventured briefly that I was not sure how much about other cultures the kids had gotten from smelling rice and comparing everything to Japan, she mentioned without hesitation that, of course, it was clear that anything connected with *kokusaika* (internationalization) was actually a program to strengthen the students' knowledge and attachment to Japan first, and then through this knowledge they could go out and understand others (and their own difference) better. Of course there is another side to the kind of investigative learning proposed under the name of comprehensive studies, but most kids don't have the time to engage in what clearly requires extra work at home. I know this, because my older daughter was one of the only ones in her class who became enthusiastically involved in what was, for the most part, homework, not having the time commitment of after-school lessons or the pressure and worries of entrance exams.

34. I want to thank Hiromi Nakano, homeroom teacher of this fifth grade class, for allowing me to participate in what was certainly a difficult experience for her, made no easier by the presence of a stranger like myself. We talked about her difficulty with this class afterwards, and she said that she had agreed to have me with her for the day to see what kinds of challenges the staff faces in schools like Tomuro, the socioeconomic facets of which don't often enough reach the headlines.

35. The proposals, social commentary, and criticism of the people's committee's report are now massive in length and, because of the significance of the future impact of this report on the postwar Constitution, continue to appear in the papers and larger academic discussions. I will not attempt here to cover the whole range of these but instead will highlight what I understand to be the most influential (and, to many, controversial) of their proposals.

36. This decision appeared to be in line for most proponents and critics of this plan with the same year's harshening of the juvenile law, by lowering the age at which young offenders could face adult criminal charges from eighteen to fourteen, the age of the Kobe youth at the time of his arrest. This does not make Japan exceptional in its harshening of this law, compared to the United States, for example, but several legal commentators on this change regarded it as the possible beginning of a slippery slope, given that it was the first revision of the juvenile law in Japan since its inception at the time of the immediate postwar reforms.

37. This discussion and the opposition to it continued full-fledged up until August 2001; the only things that seem to have redirected media attention away from it were the terrorist attacks in the United States in September 2001 and other successive and troubling world events. Concern that the government would take advantage of the media's preoccupation with other issues and continue to move in lower-level ways on the issue of revising the FLE though the discussions of revisions despite this is high among leftist groups, like the Shinjujinkai (New Women's Association) and the Kodomo to Kyōkasho Netto (The Child and Text-book Network).

38. The term *battle royale* is associated with the "battle" to the end in professional wrestling, where all contestants (combatants?) enter the ring at one time and battle until only one is left standing at the end.

39. Although it is nowhere mentioned as such, it is interesting to speculate on the Deweyian overtones of the idea of the "frontier" that Kawai employs here. Writing about transnationalism and the limits of liberalism, Kathryne Mitchell, a geographer at the University of Washington, notes that, for Dewey, "the frontier can be read as a metonym for the endlessly expandable 'spaces' of democracy within the confines of the nation-state project." As the literal spaces of the frontier closed up by the 1930s, Dewey advocated a "substitute," in the form of a "moral frontier," in the sense of seeing unused resources as human rather than material. See Kathryn Mitchell, "Education for Democratic Citizenship"; and John Dewey, *Democracy and Education*.

40. My interpretation of the "neoliberalism" of Kawai's message here, and for that matter, in the greater tone and direction of the reforms, is informed Thomas Lemke's, "The Birth of Bio-Politics"; Andrew Barry, Thomas Osborne, and Nikolas Rose "Introduction" to (and various articles in) *Foucault and Political Reason*; and Colin Gordon, "Governmental Rationality."

41. The idea of cultures having their own unique personalities, is, as I have argued in Chapter Two, a product of the complicated crossings of discourse that have occurred between Japan and the West (in principal the United States) as the American cultural anthropology of Franz Boas and his students' originally radical idea turned on them in the rapidly changing political realities of the postwar era to which they were not entirely politically attuned.

42. From the second public lecture that I attended in May 2001.

43. Throughout this section on "The Structure of Japan in the Twenty-First Century," I will be focusing on the opening essay in this report by Kawai Hayao, "The Frontier Within." I have combined here a strategy of paraphrasing and citing Kawai and, wherever the latter is the case, have set off the phrase, as is customary, in quotation marks.

44. Kawai Hayao, "The Frontier Within," 1.

45. Kawai does not make explicit here what he means by *Nihon no yosa*, and it is arguable that he does not have to. For the target Japanese audience, the body

of ideas contained in this notion of *yosa* connects directly to national identity discourse and its psychological traits of dependency, homogeneity, restraint (*gaman*), inside and outside (*omote* and *ura*), division of duties and responsibilities (*kejime*), implicit communication style, and many more that have been written so thoroughly into the social lexicon over the past several decades that many Japanese, if queried, point to these as the markers of difference between them and the Western world, in particular the United States. I would also like to note that the English summary of the "Frontier Within" is poignantly free of the subtexts invoked here, using terms like "individual empowerment" that, one might argue, suggest the sphere of discursive influence, a corporate U.S. one, which has certainly on many levels influenced the Kawai text in reverse.

46. Kawai Hayao, "The Frontier Within," 1.

47. It is interesting that Kawai stays away here from the more obvious references to the relationship between the public and the private (*ōyake to watakushi*), where the former would probably be better rendered as "traditional authority," according to J. Victor Koschmann, due to the specificities of the developments of these terms and relationships in the Japanese and Western spheres. For more on this, see, J. Victor Koschmann, "'*Ko to Shi*,' Idioms of Contemporary Japan X," and Harry D. Harootunian, "National Narratives/Spectral Happenings," 24–27.

48. Kawai Hayao, "The Frontier Within," 25.

49. Ibid.

50. Ibid., 27–28. The term that Kawai uses here, *shinayakana*, has various renderings in English, among which are *supple* and *flexible*. Although *flexible* would be a good choice for its implications of the flexible worker demanded by the ever-changing, ever-deterritorializing nature of late capitalism, I have intentionally chosen *supple* to also pick up on the physical and perhaps even youthful overtones that Kawai suggests will be necessary here.

51. Ibid., 32.

52. Ibid., 37–38.

53. Ibid., 42–43.

54. These comments of Miyazaki's and others about the film, to which I have referred here, have been taken from a series on NHK (Japanese public television) that featured Miyazaki engaging a number of prominent writers about the themes of his new film that closely repeat many recent issues. Among the well-known participants were psychologist and social commentator Keigo Okonogi, of *Moratoriamu Ningen no Jidai* (1978) fame; Banana Yoshimoto, who was also promoting a new book of hers about childhood memories and her recent collaboration with globally known artist Nara Yoshimoto; and others. In the course of these conversations, Miyazaki, who in his past film of worldwide acclaim, *Mononokehime*, had an agenda that he widely noted informed the setting and thematics of that film, responded to the questions that so obviously begged themselves about the timeliness of *Sen to Chihiro* by insisting that he had no clear political message in mind

here but was merely trying "to make a film about children and the recent troubles they are facing."

CHAPTER FOUR

1. This is an excerpt from a conversation I had with Kawakami about his book *School Collapse*. Pleasure in killing or the idea of killing as a game (*hito wa koroshite mitai*) first erupted on the national scene in the messages of the junior high student from Kobe (Youth A), who in 1997 was convicted of heinous crimes against other school-aged children. Reenunciated by the perpetrators of a series of juvenile crime incidents in the spring of 2000, the idea of a terrible lack in the overall training of the Japanese child emerged as a central theme in Japan. I describe this 1997 event, my fieldwork in Kobe in its aftermath, and its social and political effects in Chapter Two.

2. Kawakami, "*Kodomo ga hen da*" [The child is strange], 95. Used as a verb, *hen* or *henka*, can also refer to a change, so, depending on the context, I sometimes include this notion of change with strange because the idea of transformation into something unknown or unfamiliar is key to the expression of *Kodomo ga hen da* and other expressions of uneasiness. I want to emphasize that the field of discourse on the problem with the child is broad and diverse. The view of the strange child (and variations thereof) occupied a significant portion of the discursive field of the recessionary period.

3. Much of the attraction of Kawakami's message was the view he presents of classroom teacher. In particular in the aftermath of a series of violent incidents involving school-aged children, from the infamous Kobe Youth A killings in 1997 through the early 2000s, the Japanese public was anxious for precise information about child behavior. Chapter Two goes into detail about the Youth A incident of 1997, the public and governmental response that followed, and what was left out of all the reporting about this youth, his family, and the recessionary changes in the city of Kobe.

4. Yoshikuni Igarashi, *Bodies of Memory*.

5. From my interviews with Kawakami and repeated in his book *Gakkō Hōkai*, 24.

6. Although a number of age differentiating terms for children exist, such as *jidō* (young child and term used in pediatrics), *shōnen* (young teen and term used in juvenile law), and *seishonen* (older teens and young [legal] adults), *kodomo* (child) was the main term used in the discourse of problem and strangeness (*kodomo ga hen da*), fears of the dangers of and to the child (*kodomo ga abunai*), and the child problem (*kodomo no mondai*).

7. Ryu Murakami, Introduction to *AERA* Special (#45) *Kodomo ga Abunai* (The Child Is Dangerous). Also see Murakami Ryu, *Kyoiku no Hōkai to iu Uso*. Murakami's position shifted often during this period. He published a number of essays

together with Hayao Kawai in the early 2000s. Later on he wrote about exodus and hope. For more on Murakami and his interest in the younger generation and education, see Adrienne Hurley, *Revolutionary Suicide and Other Desperate Measures*.

8. Jacqueline Rose, *The Case of Peter Pan or The Impossibility of Children's Fiction*.

9. Naoki Oki, *Kodomo no Kiki wo Do Miru ka*. I attended a large conference in Tokyo in 2001 on "classroom collapse" sponsored by the *Asahi Newspaper* at which Oki was one of two main speakers. Oki has written several books about trouble in the schools. He is from the Osaka area and has conducted a number of surveys in this area as well as in Tokyo.

10. In his discussions of the danger of and to the child, Oki in distinction to Kawakami tends to see the child as victim, in utterances such as "behind these heinous incidents [*jiken*] are the cries [*sakebi*] of children" or in removing the child's involvement from the scene altogether in injunctions like "fix the child and cure the anxiety [*fuan*] of the nation."

11. See Shoko Yoneyama, "The Era of Bullying: Japan under Neoliberalism."

12. Another way of seeing these outbursts is, as my eighteen-year-old Japanese niece pointed out to me, of losing yourself, or being "cut," disappearing, in line with the literal meaning of the verb *kireru*. Thanks to Azumi Arai for discussing this with me and directing me to the manga in which it appears.

13. "*Hiko shōnen to futsu no ko no kyōkai ga kiwamete aimai ni natta.*" Meticulous researcher of the historical record regarding the relationship between the occurrence of delinquent acts and school problems and the public response to them, Teruyuki Hirota insists that "there were far more dangerous youth in the 60s than today," though their acts were not understood as "heinous" (*kyoaku*); in fact, this terminology did not exist according to Hirota for reference to youth crime. Of course, as Hirota notes, when they did occur, they seemed to occur far from what was considered the center of the population. Moreover, when they did occur, there was little blaming of the school: "*Gakkozo no Henyo to Kyōiku Mondai.*"

14. This metamorphosis was poignantly depicted on the cover of the special issue of *Bessatsu Takarajima* (1991, 95), *Purokyōshi no Kai, Kodomo ga Hen Da* (The Child Is Turning Strange), in the figure of a male junior high student who is sitting at his desk holding a pencil, as half his body is in the process of turning into something strange and unrecognizable—in this case a green, evil-eyed monster.

15. During the first half of the year 2000, a new string of juvenile crime incidents reignited the terror that emerged with the Kobe Youth A incident. What appeared to be most frightening about these new incidents (*jiken*), which ranged from the extortion of huge sums of money (equivalent to $50,000), a bus-jacking, murder, and a frenzied murder rampage of several students by another with a baseball bat, was that they all seemed to reproduce through their actions and expressions the same "pleasure in killing," or disregard for life, that appeared to characterize the Youth A events.

16. The assumption made here is that mothers, because of the uniqueness of their bond with the child, should be the primary caretakers of the child's emotional, moral, and sociocultural development. For a critical discussion of these assumptions made about the Japanese mother, see Ueno Chizuko's "Collapse of the Japanese Mother," and Megan McKinlay's "Unstable Mothers."

17. Teruyuki Hirota, *Shitsuke ga Suitai Shita Ka*. There is a huge body of work on *shitsuke* (Japanese manner training) that Hirota refers to here, and although his coverage of the literature seems exhaustive, confined by his own (academic) disciplinary boundaries, he does not, I believe, take adequate account of how this literature is appropriated, sometimes written about as in the case of Hara and Wagatsumi's well-known book by the same name in the discourse on the Japanese (*Nihonjinron*).

18. Teruyuki Hirota, *Gendai no Hahaoya wa Dame ni Natta no Ka?* The increasingly unclear boundaries between child abuse and manner training that emerged at this time in Japan is a fascinating subject.

19. *Gendai no Kyōiku, Dai ni Maki, "Gakkōzo no Henyo,"* February, 1998. The expression that Hirota uses here is *"susunda gakkō, okureta chiiki."*

20. In Chapters Five and Six, I focus on the role that the exam preparation cram schools and other forms of supplementary education played in these changing attitudes as well as how changes that begin earlier become noticeable at a particular time because of other changing circumstances.

21. Shortly after the publication of Hirota's book debunking the romantic view of the traditional home, another book called *Nihonjin no Shitsuke* was published that tied the home to the school in the relay that was supposed to have existed between these two. Arichi Tōru, *Nihonjin no shitsuke* [Japanese manner training].

22. I am grateful to the members of the Purokyōshi for allowing me to join them at their meetings, for engaging with me in conversation about their ideas, and for their open sharing of their writings. I especially want to thank Ryōichi Kawakami for his help over the entire period of my observations at Jonan Junior High, for enduring my many questions, and for all of our fascinating conversations. Kawakami, in return, asked little of me, only that I not deal with the child problem in Japan as an isolated issue peculiar to Japan but consider its larger historical background, as the Purokyōshi believe they are doing.

23. The physical health care facility (*hokenshitsu*) is a busy place, with a fascinating history. Over the past decade this facility had a new and challenging set of demands placed on it. Mental health until recently was not seen as under the jurisdiction of the school, and problems that exceeded the bounds of the physical became the responsibility, by default, of the health care room. The subject of the mental health or inner mind (*naimen*) of the child, however, as I have previously suggested, became a hot subject, elevated from the marginally academic to the mainstream within a matter of several years. The widespread yearning (and

demand) for a means of explaining the seemingly inexplicable acts of the youth has provided the necessary impetus for the development of a nationwide nascent counseling program in the junior high schools. This age was judged in the aftermath of the Kobe incident of 1997 to be the most elusive—and in need of an industry of "counselors."

24. I believe that my status as a Fulbright fellow affiliated with Tokyo University and a graduate student at Columbia University had something to do with Kawakami's motivation to provide me with this kind of access. He also appeared curious about my position as wife to a Japanese national and educating our two daughters bilingually in Japan and the United States.

25. Wherever possible, I spoke to the teachers of the many lessons that I observed afterwards in the teacher's room or outside on breaks. Some of them had the impression that the students were a little better behaved (tense [*kinchō shita*] due to my presence), but overall they did not report reacting differently themselves to the commotion when I was not there. It appears that Kawakami had assured them that I was not affiliated in any way with the bureaucracy and was there to learn about the situation in the schools and the teacher's side of things. Some of them even seemed to welcome the chance to talk to me about their views and their complaints.

26. Some teachers still do engage in hitting, and I witnessed some small examples of this, which of course made me think that this behavior was inhibited by my presence. There are not a few teachers and parents who believe that a return to this form of teacher-imposed corporal punishment would not be a bad idea; anything to restore discipline. The MOE, however, is officially opposed to corporal punishment, having been drawn into lawsuits and negative publicity over this, the problem of bullying in the schools, and other issues.

27. In the English-language literature on the presecondary school in Japan, discussions of peer policing are absent for the most part. When the question of the assigning of authority to students in elementary schools has been attended to, it has been addressed in relativizing terms that shed a generally positive light on this aspect of the difference of the Japanese school system and classroom management.

28. Discourse on classroom collapse and the strange child has given rise to a surfeit of social and political discourse on art as opposed to science and math, physical education in terms of the weakening of the child's body and loss of corporeal discipline, and the health center and its connections to the emerging program of counseling in the junior high schools. These sub (if you will) discourses all add back into the overarching anxiety over collapse and the changing child.

29. For more on anime and manga in contemporary Japan, see Anne Allison, *Permitted and Prohibited Desires*; and Susan J. Napier, *Anime*.

30. Although they publish under the name of the Purokyōshi, the formal name for their study group is the Saitama Kyōiku Juku (The Saitama Education Study Group), and this was their 134th meeting with these members.

31. It occurred to me that a group of this sort, were it to convene over this length of time in the United States, would most likely be focused on curriculum, salary, or other practical political issues. This is not to say that the child's education is not a heated political topic in the United States; far from it, as Sharon Stephens, Lauren Berlant, and many others have pointed out. Yet, it seemed unimaginable for a group of American teachers to be as devoted as these men were to trying to understand educational problems and the student–teacher relationship.

32. This is an excerpt from the first of several interviews with Ryōichi Kawakami at his school, Jonan Middle School, Kawagoe, Japan.

33. This is an excerpt from their gathering on February 17, 2001.

34. Maruyama Masao was perhaps the most prominent social theorist to emerge in the immediate postwar period. His name became synonymous for the public with the creation of a more democratic Japan by abolishing the elements of the prewar past that had led to the imperialism and fascism of the Second World War. The aim was to create a new Japan on the basis of new (and more complete) social institutions. For an in-depth discussion of Maruyama's thought, see J. Victor Koschmann, *Revolution and Subjectivity in Postwar Japan.* Also see Harry Harootunian's "Dialectical Optics" essay in his *History's Disquiet* for a short but helpful understanding of the shortcomings of Maruyama's position.

35. The public writings of the Purokyōshi differ substantially from the discussions of their closed group meetings and internal magazine, in which they have been circulating the products of their studies for the last couple of decades.

36. From a conversation on a bus back to Tokyo from Kawagoe between myself and a young NHK producer, who had been invited along with me on this particular afternoon to take part in the Purokyōshi meeting.

37. Kawakami in particular professed to me that he was suspicious of the direction proposed by the MOE to create what is called "an independent individual" (*jiritsutekina kojin*). This, he says, is just more of the same modernity. He also confessed to me that he doesn't see the strength of the view of psychologists like Kawai Hayao, who have become such a dominant voice in the new reforms. Kawakami has written about his participation as the only practicing teacher on the high-level education committee convened in the aftermath of the juvenile crime incidents of the year 2000.

38. In the fall of 1999, I made a prefieldwork trip to Tokyo to look for a "returnee" school for my two half-Japanese daughters, who along with my husband would be accompanying me to Japan. What I found, after visiting over fifteen of the schools listed as having large programs, was that these programs were vibrant on paper (or on the MOE website only), but floundering, due to drastically reduced budgets, in practice. Imai was the exception to this rule, and that was primarily due to the principal Keikichi Majima and his assistant, Atsuko Kono.

39. I am tremendously grateful for the reception that both I and my family received from Imai Elementary and its exceptionally farsighted principal (at the time) Majima. My children's stay at the school and my own observations were also greatly aided by the freedom that Principal Majima allowed me, a freedom about which his own teachers were sometimes taken aback. I also wish to thank the teacher in charge of the "international study room" (*kokusaishitsu*), Ms. Kono, for serving as the mediator between the principal and the teachers, with their concerns about their own classrooms. Beyond this, I owe a great debt to all the teachers, who endured my presence and questions over a long period of time and at times when they may have preferred not to have an observer following them around.

40. In total, I observed in four elementary schools and two junior highs. I have chosen to describe at length in this chapter my observations at Jonan and Imai, as these were the two schools at which I spent the largest amount of time and because they were presented to me as contrasting examples of the phenomenon of collapse.

41. I say this advisedly, having spent a great quantity of time in alternative elementary classrooms in the United States, in which the students are not expected to conform to a particular classroom demeanor and as a result can seem quite disorderly.

42. Prior writings on the school have documented these roles in mostly glowing terms as one of the ways that students learn responsibility in the classroom without the teacher having to discipline them. The situation has been, I believe, much more complex than this, especially given what I have come to understand as the method of internalized self- and peer policing has broken down, such that only the retributive side of it remains. Children in these roles use the power that is given them to reprimand or shame other students in a way that has become counterproductive to maintaining order.

43. Teachers depart the room often during the day, leaving the kids alone. This is due, I was told, to the mountains of administrative work for which they are also responsible, and perhaps it is simply to get some quiet time away from the students. Unfortunately, these were times when it would have been possible to view the conflicts that were developing among the students and perhaps informally ward some of them off. However, with everything that one teacher was expected to handle on his or her own (including managing not to let on that things were out of control in the classroom), it was hard to imagine them doing more than they were already doing.

44. These extra-academic things include the famed "sports day" (*undōkai*), which under the present circumstances I found to be much changed from the past, when it was a huge family event. Now families in many urban areas come for only a short time, or arrive late, purchasing ready-made foods, rather than porting the homemade delicacies of the *obento*, of which Anne Allison has written. In addition,

the big events at the school, which include sports, art, music, and science exhibits, and the graduation ceremony require a magnitude of planning, the subject of which I will return to shortly.

45. I will continue to cite from individual conversations with mothers at Imai, small group meetings, and a "study group" on the child problem, consisting of mothers from across the Kawasaki area that I joined. This group called the "Katei Kyōiku Gakkyû" (Study-group on education in the home) was organized by Mrs. Mitsuboshi. I am grateful to her for allowing me to participate in the group and for introducing me to a number of other places and persons in the Kawasaki area, including the "child's rights committee."

46. Whereas the subject of bullying (*ijime*) within Japanese schools has attracted a fair amount of attention, there have been few studies that actually look at the structures of order and discipline in the schools. Perhaps the best documentation of the existence of bullying has come from the larger literature on "school refusal" (*tōkōkyohi*) in Japan. For more on the phenomenon of school refusal and its relation to bullying, see Margaret Lock "A Nation at Risk"; and Shoko Yoneyama, "Student Discourse on Tōkōkyohi (School Phobia/Refusal)."

47. Although I did not have an opportunity to spend entire days with the first graders at Imai, from the reports of a first grade teacher whom I had befriended, I learned that the younger grades have become more challenging than ever. At this younger age, children are expected to absorb the procedures, routines, and structures of the school days, such that lessons, outings, and extra-academic activities can proceed without a great deal of disturbance. There is a great deal to do to teach a class of close to thirty children to function well on their own, without a great deal of instruction or questioning, as well as to integrate themselves smoothly, on command, into the group for both small and larger group activities.

48. At an elementary school that I visited in Kobe, an informal survey of the kids done within the framework of their health studies that day produced the results that most sixth graders in the class were getting no more than six hours of sleep a night, due to their late return from exam preparation school, extra homework from the school, and then late night TV, snacks, and video games used to calm down them down before bed.

49. Amidst the many concerns over education that attracted media attention during my fieldwork was the problem of "teacher school refusal" (*tannin futōkō*). From the national television specials that were aired during the period of my fieldwork, stress-related conditions among homeroom teachers were on the rise (though no numbers were explicitly given). Stress-related conditions it seemed had resulted in teachers' physical and psychological aversions to entering school. These news programs did not go into specifics about the on-the-ground conditions facing teachers, choosing instead to focus on the intensity of aversion reactions. It was, however, not hard to imagine how problems of in-class control, extra hours, and deteriorating relations with parents had all contributed to teachers' distress.

50. At one point, my older daughter became the brunt of some small kinds of ostracism and wanted to stay home from school for several days. Given our unique position in the school community, the administration was anxious, more anxious than usual as many afterwards told us, to resolve the situation with my daughter. They advised us that they thought she was going through an emotional phase very usual at this age, and that with some individual counseling she would overcome what were to their minds clearly individual issues of hers. At one closed meeting of her teachers, my daughter, my husband, and myself, her teachers asked her to tell them frankly what she thought was the one thing that could be changed about the class, that would make her want to return. She blurted out, quite suddenly, that she wished for the destruction of all the *juku*, to the seeming shock of her teachers.

51. In general these teachers were worried about the upcoming reforms (*kaikaku*). They reported being confused about how to implement the new course of study, *sōgō gakushū*, in these already difficult conditions, having a lack of training themselves and wondering where they were to find the time for all these new things, given the constant budget cuts and staff shortages.

52. I report on the connection of this incident to the import of psychological language in which it was eventually couched and provide an account of my fieldwork in Kobe in Chapter Two.

53. The inability to produce value or the effect of value is also articulated with the companion concerns of the dwindling numbers of births, known as *shoshika* (low birth). As my sister-in-law from Nagano expressed in exasperated tones, "This will be the end of the Japanese race." They (today's children) not only cannot but will not reproduce the race.

54. Diane Negra and Yvonne Tasker, eds., *Gendering the Recession*, 16.

CHAPTER FIVE

1. Excerpt from an expo put on by one of the largest cram school companies, Nichinoken, in 2000.

2. Takagi Mikio's *Jibun no Kodomo wa Jibun de Mamore* (2002) was a best-selling book written by one of the managers of Nichinoken, a nationwide (and the largest of its kind) chain of supplementary schools specializing in junior high entrance exam preparation. The idea expressed in this title, that parents had only themselves to depend on and that on their own with such a weighty responsibility formerly assumed by the state would welcome help, appeared repeatedly in the various advertisements that we received.

3. Jacques Donzelot, *The Policing of Families*, 225.

4. Ibid., xxv.

5. Norma Field, "The Child as Laborer and Consumer."

6. Anne Allison, *Nightwork*.

7. From a nationwide survey of participation in after-school schools by the MOE (1994). The problem of choice that I alluded to earlier obtains in ever more poignant terms to the case of the child.

8. It is important to add that the heightened appeal of the supplementary education industry to parents did not begin during the economic crisis. The lifeblood of the *juku* has been the conflicting narrative of groupism, noncompetition, equality in the schools, and the homogeneity in the society at large. This narrative has always been in stark opposition to the exam (*juken*) system, the height of competition and selectivity.

9. Information on how the industry is doing during these stark economic times comes from my interviews with managers of various branches of the large exam preparation schools. I was also informed of the overall fiscal strength of these schools by the head of the elementary curriculum division at the largest producer of home-use materials, Benesee (or Challenge, as it is known to children and families), with whom I met several times.

10. *Kyōsō no jidai wa mo oshimai* (The End of the Age of Competition) is the subtitle of a book on the reform program by the MOE's chief spokesman on the new reforms, Ken Terawaki. Beyond these written announcements, Terawaki appeared on a ten-part show on NHK in 2001 on *kyōiku mondai* (education problems), describing at length the government's vision for ending the competition. Many parents and teachers with whom I spoke were hopeful but dubious about these promises. I have discussed this television series, Terawaki's publications, and the promise to "end the competition" in Chapter One.

11. Paralleling the MOE's complaints about the pressure put on Japanese children and their parents by the supplementary schooling industry are the exam school's spoofs and critiques of the ministry's plans for reform. The question that is begged here, which almost never rises to the forefront of discussions, is whether the government truly wishes to eliminate "exam hell" or whether, within the new formation of order that is being fashioned, the supplementary industry will continue to occupy an important structural position as it has until now in the constitution of sociopolitical order.

12. Tomiko Yoda, "A Roadmap to Millennial Japan."

13. *Holonic society* is a term used by Harry D. Harootunian in "Visible Discourse/Invisible Ideologies," in *Postmodernism and Japan* (1989) to refer to the kind of unmediated forms of communication said to be exclusively available to Japanese by virtue of their inhabiting (regarded as automatic and similarly mandatory) a system of comportments and dispositions discursively produced as uniquely Japanese.

14. Hiyoshi is a small but upscale area, two train stops (about a five-minute train ride) from where we lived in Musashi Kosugi and about one hour outside Tokyo. It is also the site of Keio University's main campus. The free testing and parent information session that we attended was specially designed to entice parents to enroll their children a full year prior to the beginning of exam preparation

classes for the purpose of what is referred to at Nichinoken as learning the correct postures *(shisei)*, dispositions, and study skills that children of this age are no longer getting at regular school. My younger daughter, who was in the third grade at the time at our local elementary school, agreed to accompany me and take the test.

15. I was truly surprised to see that out of the close to 500 parents in attendance at the information session on this early Sunday morning, over a fourth were fathers. Most of the other parent events that I attended were predominantly made up of mothers, and this seemed to be attributable in part at least to their weekday timing. It also occurred to me that although mothers continue to bear the burden for the decisions, arrangements, and overall concerns of extra schooling, as well as the responsibility for the success or failure of their kids, fathers, when available, are called in for their input in areas in which mothers profess to feeling inadequate, such as high-level math and science.

16. Nichinoken, *Hogosha Setsumei Kai—Gakuryokukenko Shindan*, June, 2000, Hiyoshi.

17. There is a new kind of popularity for these religion-based schools for girls. Talking to a friend of mine, whose daughters attend a Christian girls' school, about whether she thought there was any potential clash between the Christian morality that her daughter and others would most certainly be absorbing at this school and her own idea of morality, she announced simply that Japan and the Japanese have absorbed many kinds of outside influences over the years, but this has not affected the inner core of Japanese culture.

18. The idea of *nobiru*, referred to by the Futaba administrators, refers to a concept of child rearing that became popular among the "education conscientious" mothers in the mid-1980s. In retrospect the ideas and practices that informed *nobinobi kyōiku* (develop-at-your-own-speed education) have been repudiated of late for giving an excuse to mothers to abdicate the training of their children. The idea of free development continues to be invoked, albeit in a revised fashion, by the exam preparation and private schools that suggest how the idea of freedom can be applied in a restricted fashion to promote the potential and encourage the motivation of the child.

19. Though I have focused my discussion here on Nichinoken, parent information sessions that I attended at several other secondary exam preparation schools were similar in their endeavor to demonstrate their superior command of information about the child abilities and ultimately about how to obtain from them the greatest potential, while maintaining supervision over them. This combined function speaks strongly to the burden of responsibility, which has grown exponentially in the midst of the crisis atmosphere surrounding the child, and of which parents seem thankful to be relieved.

20. My early contacts in the capacity of researcher at Nichinoken went surprisingly smoothly compared to how cumbersome my interactions with the staff became as my observations proceeded. I conducted an initial set of in-class

observations in the summer of 2000 and then again in the winter and spring of 2001. By the time of this latter set, Mr. Hasegawa, who had given the approval for my presence there, had been transferred, and I was told that this kind of unfettered access to lessons was unusual. Because it had been preapproved, they felt required, though not altogether pleased, to let me proceed. My desire to view a variety of levels for successive periods of time did not sit well with the staff, who appeared to view my continued presence with some disdain.

21. The idea of *mendō miru* (to look after) and which school did the best job of looking after children, which is to say of relieving the mother of some of the burden of work and responsibility for this process, turned out to be the main criterion in choosing a school. As I discovered in my conversations with women in Kobe who had enrolled their children in exam preparation schools, several schools were competing with Nichinoken on these very grounds of offering to look after more of the child's exam process, including keeping them for longer hours at the *juku* to finish their homework, providing more advising and individual attention, and even organizing sports activities on the weekends before and after studies.

22. Perhaps to let me know that there were indeed further extremes to which all of this could go, and perhaps also to emphasize to me that this is not just a phenomenon of mothers, one of my respondents related to me the now famous "wig" (*katsura*) episode of almost a decade ago. Though she said that she once considered this situation completely bizarre, now that she herself was deep within the process with her own child, she acknowledged that her sympathy for this parent now far outweighed her sense of the outlandishness of his action. The episode involved a father whose daughter was attempting to enter one of the higher-ranking schools (*hensachi* 70), who disguised himself as his daughter and went to the test site to take the test for her. "You have to be in this situation to know," she said. "You can laugh from the outside. If the girl's mother went, she might not have been able to pass the test, because the kids have training for years to solve (*toku*) these problems, and the parents don't have this training. With such a high-level test, it was probably the father who must have helped her with her homework."

23. In another example, an acquaintance of mine in Kobe was literally besieged daily by a mother, formerly a friend of hers, for whom the stress of not knowing was so great that she would appear on the doorstep of her house, or constantly phone, looking for solace. My acquaintance, finding no easy way out, began to hide in her own house until the woman would leave. This mother had been a schoolteacher who had quit her job to focus on her child's *juken*. She wanted her son to go to Nada, the school in Kobe renowned for the high percentage of its graduates who are accepted to Tokyo University, which prior to the mid-1990s recession drove entrance to this school. With each week's level-adjusting tests, this woman's emotions would swing wildly.

24. The leading schools and materials producers are well aware of the importance of the parent's role in presenting the exam and its rewards to their kids. To

this end, Nichinoken, Benesee (the largest producer of home-use materials about which I will have more to say in the following discussion), Sapix, and others publish their own magazines chock full of how-to tips for parents.

25. The Kumon program has spread to the United States and focused here from the first on the anxiety of American parents over the lack of adequate mathematics instruction in the schools. Of late, they have begun in some cities to offer reading help as well, but in the absence of a nationally constructed language curriculum as in Japan, Kumon's progress in this area may be for the time being somewhat restricted.

26. Those who choose the route of home-use materials, while avoiding the pressures and expenses of junior high exam entrance preparation, are all the same looking ahead to the huge hurdle that their children face in high school entrance. The challenge to home-use materials companies is to keep the price down while holding children's interest at varying ages and thus keeping families subscribing all the way to college entrance.

27. I had firsthand experience with the "Challenge" materials because my daughters asked to try them for a free trial period. The free gifts that came with the materials, which friends of ours cautioned us to withhold until the lessons were completed, enthralled my younger daughter, She, however, soon lost interest in the extra lessons, finding it repetitive of what she was learning in school. The point that was, of course, lost on her, was that while these lessons were similar in format and content to her school assignments, each month she completed moved her a month ahead of her school studies, such that, by the time the public school introduced these materials, whether math or Japanese language, the child doing "Challenge," would already be well familiar with it.

28. To complicate matters even further, the coach was also one of the heads of our neighborhood association (*chōnaikai*); in this capacity, he and I often found ourselves at similar gatherings related to the problems in schools and homes.

29. It should be noted that many of these mothers felt constrained in their opposition to the coach's methods. There were few opportunities available in our area for young girls to participate on a team, and many of their children's friends were busy with *juku*.

CHAPTER SIX

1. Interview with Japanese college student, Tokyo, Japan, spring 2009.

2. For a reminder of the financial dimensions of the financial and real estate bubble's bursting in Japan, please see the Introduction.

3. Conversation with Japanese exchange student who had just arrived in Seattle from Tokyo, University of Washington, October 2013. His response, "All we know is depression," was in English and in answer to a question of mine about the key issue for his generation in Japan. As he explained in his choice of the word

depression, he was thinking of the Japanese word for economic downturn, *fukeiki*, which I have followed others in rendering as *recession*, as well as the ongoing effects of the depressed state of society. I was preparing for my winter class, "Changing Generations in Japan and East Asia," at the time and regularly solicited the views of incoming Japanese and other East Asian exchange students.

4. John Pemberton, personal communication, 2004.

5. Kiyoshi Kurosawa, "Bright Future" (*Akarui Mirai*, 2003) and "Tokyo Sonata" (*Tōkyō saonata*, 2008).

6. Takehiko Kariya, "From Credential Society to 'Learning Capital' Society". A number of young Japanese interlocutors of mine have suggested that the need for credential is not gone, as the MOE slogans of "ending competition" (Chapter Two) or psychologically informed language like "frontiers within" and "independent individual" suggest. What they experience in their everyday life are the uncharted requirements of self-development and rearticulation in a national community and subjectivity through notions, like the heart, that have moved responsibility into their hands.

7. William Kelly, "Finding a Place in Metropolitan Japan"; Amy Borovoy, "Japan as Mirror"; and Andrew Gordon, *The Wages of Affluence*.

8. Iwama Natsuki, *Why Has the Work Consciousness of the Youth Changed? [Wakamono no Hataraku Ishiki ga Naze Kawatta no Ka]*, 10.

9. Ibid., 12.

10. Mary Brinton, *Lost in Transition*; and Amy Borovoy, "Japan as Mirror."

11. Personal communication with Tom Looser, September 2013, Seattle, Washington.

12. Yoshitaka Mori, "New Art and Culture in the Age of the 'Freeter' in Japan," 52.

13. Anne Allison, *Precarious Japan*; and Gabriella Lukacs, "Dreamwork."

14. Andrea G. Arai, "The Wild Child of 1990s Japan."

15. In several very particular instances, students remarked about how reading my "Wild Child in Japan" piece reminded them of how childhood and youth violence was portrayed in Japan. Andrea G. Arai, "The Wild Child of 1990s Japan."

16. The course was designed for international programs and made up of a section of University of Washington international studies students and an exchange student program from the international studies program at Waseda University.

17. Personal communication with mothers in Kobe who had done this work.

18. I have been amazed at the frequency with which these terms have replaced the older ones, uttered by young Japanese with little or no surprise to speak about themselves, their futures, and their nation.

19. Takehiko Kariya, "From 'Credential' Society to 'Learning Capital' Society," 88.

20. Interviews in Yokohama, Tokyo, and Kobe in June 2010 and August 2011.

21. Yokohama, June 2010.

22. Tokyo, August 2011.
23. Michael Feher, "Self-Appreciation."
24. Ibid., 25.
25. Ibid., 26.
26. Ibid., 28.
27. Ibid., 29.
28. The 1947 Japanese National Constitution contains an antiaggression clause, known as Article 9. Article 9 prohibits Japan from maintaining a standing or permanent army that can lawfully wage war. Article 9 has been a point of pride and contention since its enactment. Conservative Japanese governments have tried to repeal the antiaggression clause since the early 1950s, but because such a repeal requires a two-thirds national referendum, it has eluded the conservative party, the LDP (Liberal Democratic Party). However, from 1999 on, many education reform committee members began to talk about using the FLE revisions they were working to push through (and eventually succeeded in doing in 2006) to repeal Article 9 of the Japanese Constitution as well. These members' rationale was that the child problem necessitated these changes. The Japanese child was no longer "normal" (*futsu*) because neither was the nation, lacking the ability to prosecute war!
29. Many people have talked about the resonances between the recent American film, *The Hunger Games*, and *Battle Royale*. They share a focus on young people being forced by the government into a battle to the death against their peers. *Battle Royale*, however, is not set in some fantasized future. It is set against the backdrop of a recession in Japan and a problem with the Japanese child. The "BR Law" (*BR Ho*), which decrees the random selection each year of one junior high school class to battle to the death is explained in *Battle Royale* as part of the newly revised education law.
30. The young female victor's strangely bloodstained smiling face reminds the viewer of the menacing female child images of Yoshitomo Nara. See Marilyn Ivy's "The Art of Cute Little Things."
31. See Tomiko Yoda's "A Roadmap to Millennial Japan."
32. Takehiko Kariya, "From 'Credential' Society to 'Learning Capital' Society," 98.
33. Ibid., 94.
34. Ibid.
35. Michael Feher, "Self-Appreciation," 25.
36. Jacques Donzelot, "Michel Foucault and Liberal Intelligence."
37. Anna Tsing, "How to Make Resources and Then Destroy Them (and Then Save Them?) on the Salvage Frontier," 51–74.
38. One of the more salient terms was *inner recesses* or *naimen*, a term that had been unfamiliar to the general public prior to its usage in the 1990s. It is my contention that the psychological knowledge and discourse introduced in this

period became wedded with the neoliberal language of self-responsibility and self-appreciation.

39. The "child," childhood, and youth are often identified as the focus of future potential, in particular in national programs of reform, repair, and revitalization as well as in moments of national crisis and private industry's appeals to families. For more on how the child and childhood have been transposed into resource frontiers and objects of future potential for the nation, even as the subjects of these objectifications are no longer provided with the promises of future guarantees and protections by the state, see Claudia Casteneda, *Figurations: Child, Bodies, Worlds*; Jacqueline Rose, *The Case of Peter Pan or the Impossibility of Children's Literature*; Ann Anagnost, "Children and National Transcendence in China"; and Andrea G. Arai, "Notes to the Heart."

40. Anna Tsing, "How to Make Resources and Then Destroy Them (and Then Save Them?) on the Salvage Frontier," 51–74.

41. *Furītā* or *freeter* is the main name used for the part-time, irregular labor force in Japan. It is a neologism made up the English *free* and the German *arbeiter* or part-timer. In the early 2000s, society blamed members of the recessionary generation for their inability to get full-time jobs. Reiko Kosugi and Genda Yuji have written at length about the plight of the *freeter* as well as the increase in dispatch work (*haken*) with all the insecurities it involves. I have also written at length about the relationship of educational reform and the creation of this reserve army of youth labor. See Reiko Kosugi, "The Problems of Freeters and 'NEETS' Under the Recovering Economy"; Yuji Genda, *A Nagging Sense of Job Insecurity*; and Andrea Arai, *The Neoliberal Subject of Lack and Potential*.

42. This is even more prominent in South Korea, something that became apparent during a collaborative project of mine on the contemporary parallels and coincident realities of Japan and South Korea.

43. I would like to express my thanks to my friend and Dr. Mari Fujino. Dr. Fujino's knowledge of the local foods movement, self-sufficiency, and the *moretsu shaiin* has been extremely helpful.

44. *Inaka de Kosodate* [Child-rearing in the Countryside], 12–13.

45. Theodore Adorno and Max Horkheimer, *Dialectic of Enlightenment*.

46. Interview, Kokage, summer 2012.

47. Teruhisa Horio, *Educational Thought and Ideology in Japan*, 44.

48. There is a long history in modern Japan to returning to the land to revalue and revitalize rural and local communities. Kyodaimura, a farm commune started by Tachibana near his native city of Mito in Ibaragi Prefecture, is one example of what Stephen Vlastos calls "radical agrarianism." See Stephen Vlastos, "Agrarianism without Tradition," 88.

49. My use of the term *a* history as opposed to *the* history comes from Stefan Tanaka's *New Times in Modern Japan*. See especially his opening Prelude, "Time, Pasts, History."

50. Marilyn Ivy, *Discourses of the Vanishing,* 21

51. Ibid.

52. Gary Snyder, *The Gary Snyder Reader,* 55.

53. Andy Couturier, *A Different Kind of Luxury.*

54. *Turns,* October 2012.

55. Thanks to Ann Anagnost for her discussion comments on a paper I gave at the American Association for Asian Studies, San Diego, 2013.

56. Takehiko Kariya, "The End of Egalitarian Education."

CONCLUSION

1. Wendy Brown, *Undoing the Demos.*

2. Ibid.

References

Filmography

Akarui mirai [Bright Future]. DVD. Directed by Kiyoshi Kurosawa. Japan, 2003.
Batoru rowaiaru [Battle Royale]. DVD. Directed by Kinji Fukusaku. Japan, 2000.
Kaze tachinu [The Wind Rises]. DVD. Directed by Hayao Miyazaki. Japan, 2013.
Kibō no kuni [Land of Hope]. DVD. Directed by Sono Sion. Japan, 2012.
Manin Densha [The Crowded Streetcar]. DVD. Directed by Kon Ichikawa, 1957.
Mitsubachi no haoto to chikyū no kaiten [Ashes to Honey]. DVD. Directed by Hitomi Kamanaka. Japan. 2010.
Tōkyō sonata [Tokyo Sonata]. DVD. Directed by Kiyoshi Kurosawa. Japan, 2008.

Bibliography

Abe, Shinzo. "Japanese Prime Minister Address to Joint Meeting of Congress" (speech). C-SPAN. April 29, 2015; available at www.c-span.org/video/?325576-2/japanese-prime-minister-shinzo-abe-addresses-joint-meeting-congress.
Abelmann, Nancy, Jung-Ah Choi, and So Jin Park. *No Alternative? Experiments in South Korean Education*. Berkeley: University of California Press, 2012.
"Abenomics, Nationalism, and the Challenge to China." *The Economist* (May 18–24, 2013): 13, 24–26.
Adorno, Theodore, and Max Horkheimer. *The Dialectic of Enlightenment*. Brooklyn, NY: Verso Books, 1997.
Allison, Anne. *Nightwork: Sexuality, Pleasure, and Corporate Masculinity in a Tokyo Hostess Club*. Chicago: University of Chicago Press, 1994.
———. *Permitted and Prohibited Desires: Mothers, Comics and Censorship in Japan*. Berkeley: University of California Press, 2000.
———. *Precarious Japan*. Durham, NC: Duke University Press, 2013.

Ambaras, David. *Bad Youth: Juvenile Delinquency and the Politics of Everyday Life in Modern Japan.* Berkeley: University of California Press, 2006.

Anagnost, Ann. "Children and National Transcendence in China," in *Constructing China: The Interaction of Culture and Economics,* edited by Kenneth Lieberthal, Lin Shuen-fu, and Ernest P. Young, 195–219. Ann Arbor: Center for Chinese Studies, University of Michigan Press, 1997.

———. "Introduction: Life-Making in Neoliberal Times," in *Global Futures in East Asia: Youth, Nation, and the New Economy in Uncertain Times,* edited by Ann Anagnost, Andrea Arai, and Hai Ren. Stanford, CA: Stanford University Press, 2012.

Anagnost, Ann, Andrea Arai, and Hai Ren, eds. *Global Futures in East Asia: Youth Nation, and the New Economy in Uncertain Times.* Stanford, CA: Stanford University Press, 2012.

Anderson, Benedict. *Imagined Communities: Reflections on the Origin and Spread of Nationalism.* Brooklyn, NY: Verso Books, 2006.

Arai, Andrea. "The Neoliberal Subject of Lack and Potential: Developing 'the Frontier Within' and Creating a Reserve Army of Labor in 21st Century Japan." *Rhizomes: Cultural Studies in Emerging Knowledge,* 10 (Spring 2005); available at www.rhizomes.net/issue10/index.html.

———. "The Wild Child of 1990s Japan." In *Japan after Japan: Social and Cultural Life from the Recessionary 1990s to the Present,* edited by Tomiko Yoda and Harry Harootunian, 216–238. Durham, NC: Duke University Press. 2006.

———. "Notes to the Heart: New Lessons in National Sentiment and Sacrifice," in *Global Futures in East Asia: Youth, Nation, and the New Economy in Uncertain Times,* edited by Ann Anagnost, Andrea Arai, and Hai Ren, 174–196. Stanford, CA: Stanford University Press, 2013.

Arai, Andrea Gevurtz, and Sorensen Clark W. "Introduction: Movement, Collaboration, Spaces of Difference, in Clark W. Sorensen and Andrea Gevurtz Arai, *Spaces of Possibility: Korea and Japan, In, Between and Beyond the Nation.* Seattle: University of Washington Press, forthcoming.

Aries, Philippe. *Centuries of Childhood: A Social History of Family Life.* New York: Vintage Books, 1962.

Barry, Andrew, Thomas Osborne, and Nikolas Rose. *Foucault and Political Reason: Liberalism, Neo-liberalism, and Rationalities of Government.* Chicago: University of Chicago Press, 1996.

Benedict, Ruth. *The Chrysanthemum and the Sword.* Boston, MA: Houghton Mifflin, 1989 (reprint edition).

———. *Patterns of Culture.* Boston, MA: Houghton Mifflin Co., 1934.

Benedict, Ruth, and Margaret Mead, eds. *An Anthropologist at Work.* Cambridge, MA: The Riverside Press, 1959.

Benjamin, Gail. *Japanese Lessons: A Year in the Japanese School through the Eyes of an American Anthropologist and Her Children.* New York: New York University Press, 1997.

Boas, Franz. *Race, Language, and Culture.* Chicago: University of Chicago Press, 1940.

Borovoy, Amy. "Doi Takeo and the Rehabilitation of Particularism in Postwar Japan." *Journal of Japanese Studies* 38, no. 2 (Summer 2012): 263–295.

———. "Japan as Mirror: Neoliberalism's Promise and Costs," in *Ethnographies of Neoliberalism,* edited by Carol J. Greenhouse, 60–76. Philadelphia: University of Pennsylvania Press, 2010.

Bose, Pradip Kumar. "Sons of the Nation: Child Rearing in the New Family," in *Texts of Power: Emerging Disciplines in Colonial Bengal,* edited by Partha Chatterjee, 118–144. Minneapolis: University of Minnesota Press, 1995.

Brinton, Mary. *Lost in Transition: Youth, Work, and Instability in Postindustrial Japan.* Cambridge, UK: Cambridge University Press, 2011.

Brown, Wendy. *Undoing the Demos: Neoliberalism's Stealth Revolution.* New York: Zone Books, 2015.

Büscher, Bram. *Transforming the Frontier: Peace Parks and the Politics of Neoliberal Conservation in Southern Africa.* Durham, NC: Duke University Press, 2013.

Casteneda, Claudia. *Figurations: Child, Body, Worlds.* Durham, NC: Duke University Press, 2002.

Cave, Peter. "Education after the 'Lost Decade(s)': Stability or Stagnation?" in *Capturing Contemporary Japan: Differential and Uncertainty,* edited by Satsuki Kawano, Glenda S. Roberts, and Susan Orpett Long, 271–299. Honolulu: University of Hawai'i Press, 2014.

Ching, Leo. "'Give me Japan and Nothing Else!' Postcoloniality, Identity, and the Traces of Colonialism," in *Japan after Japan: Social and Cultural Life from the Recessionary 1990s to the Present,* edited by Tomiko Yoda and Harry Harootunian, 142–166. Durham, NC: Duke University Press, 2006.

Cooper, Melinda, and Martjin Konings (special editors). "Contingency and Foundation," in *Rethinking Money, Debt and Finance after the Crisis.* SAQ (The South Atlantic Quarterly), 239–250. Durham, NC: Duke University Press, 2015.

Couturier, Andy. *A Different Kind of Luxury: Japanese Lessons in Simple Living.* Berkeley, CA: Stone Bridge Press, 2010.

Creighton, Millie. "The Shifting Image of Childhood among Consumer Affluence," in *Child Development and Education in Japan,* edited by Harold W. Stevenson, Hiroshi Azuma, and Kenji Hakuta. New York: W. H. Freeman, 1986.

Cruikshank, Barbara. "Revolutions Within: Self-Government and Self-Esteem," in *Foucault and Political Reason,* edited by Andrew Barry, Thomas Osborne, and Nicholas Rose, 231–252. Chicago: University of Chicago Press, 1996.

Cunningham, Hugh. *The Children of the Poor: Representations of Childhood since the Seventeenth Century.* Oxford, UK: Blackwell, 1991.

Deleuze, Gilles. "Foreword," in *The Policing of Families*, edited by Jacques Donzelot, ix–xvii. New York: Pantheon Books, 1979.

Derrida, Jacques. *Of Grammatology.* Baltimore, MD: Johns Hopkins University Press, 1994.

Dewey, John. *Democracy and Education.* New York: Free Press, 1924.

Dohse, Knuth, Ulrich Ju_rgens, and Thomas Malsch. *From "Fordism" to "Toyotism"? The Social Organization of the Labour Process in the Japanese Automobile Industry.* Berlin: International Institute for Comparative Social Research/Labor Policy, Wissenschaftszentrum, 1984.

Doi Takeo. *The Anatomy of Dependence.* Tokyo: Kodansha International, 1973.

Donzelot, Jacques. "Michel Foucault and Liberal Intelligence." *Economy and Society* 37, no. 1 (February 2008): 115–134.

Donzelot, Jacques. *The Policing of Families.* New York: Pantheon Books, 1979.

Feher, Michael. "Self-Appreciation; or, The Aspirations of Human Capital." *Public Culture* 21, no. 1 (Winter 2009): 21–41.

Field, Norma. "The Child as Laborer and Consumer: The Disappearance of Childhood in Contemporary Japan," in *Children and the Politics of Culture*, edited by Sharon Stephens, 51–78. Princeton, NJ: Princeton University Press, 1995.

———. *In the Realm of the Dying Emperor.* New York: Vintage Books, 1993.

Foucault, Michel. *Discipline and Punish: The Birth of the Prison.* New York: Pantheon Books, 1977.

———. "Governmentality," in *The Foucault Effect: Studies in Governmentality*, edited by Graham Burchell, Colin Gordon, and Peter Miller, 87–104. Chicago: University of Chicago Press, 1991.

———. *Lectures on the Will to Know*, edited by Daniel Defert. New York: Picador, 2011.

———. "The Subject and Power," in *Michel Foucault: Beyond Structuralism and Hermeneutics*, edited by Hubert L. Dreyfus and Paul Rabinow. Chicago: University of Chicago Press, 1983.

Foucault, Michel, Donald F. Bouchard, and Sherry Simon. *Language, Counter-Memory, Practice: Selected Essays and Interviews.* Ithaca, NY: Cornell University Press, 1977.

Fujitani, Takashi. *Splendid Monarchy: Power and Pageantry in Modern Japan.* Berkeley: University of California Press, 1996.

Gao, Bai. *Japan's Economic Dilemma.* Cambridge, MA: Cambridge University Press, 2001.

Gao, Helen. "China's Education Gap." *New York Times*, September 7, 2014.

Genda, Yuji. *A Nagging Sense of Job Insecurity: The New Reality Facing Japanese Youth*. Tokyo: International House Press, 2006.

Gerow, Aaron. "Consuming Asia, Consuming Japan: The New Neonationalist Revisionism in Japan," in *Censoring History: Citizenship and Memory in Japan, Germany, and the United States*, edited by Laura Hein and Mark Selden, 74–95. London: M. E. Sharpe, 2000.

Glover, Edward. *Freud or Jung*. Evanston, IL: Northwestern University Press, 1950.

Gluck, Carol. *Japan's Modern Myths*. Princeton, NJ: Princeton University Press, 1985.

———. "*Sekinin*: Responsibility in Modern Japan," in *Words in Motion: Towards a Global Lexicon*, edited by Carol Gluck and Anna Tsing, 83–108. Durham, NC: Duke University Press, 2009.

Goodman, Roger. *Japan's "International Youth": The Emergence of a New Class of Schoolchildren*. Oxford, UK: Oxford University Press, 1990.

———. "Shifting Landscapes: The Social Context of Youth Problems in an Ageing Nation," in *A Sociology of Japanese Youth: From Returnees to NEETs*, edited by Roger Goodman, Yuki Imoto, and Tuukka Toivonen. London: Nissan Institute/ Routledge Japanese Studies Series, 2012.

———. "The What, Why and How of Education Reform in Japan," in *Can the Japanese Change Their Education System?*, edited by Roger Goodman and David Phillips. Oxford, UK: Symposium Books, 2003.

Gordon, Andrew. *The Wages of Affluence: Labor and Management in Postwar Japan*. Cambridge, MA: Harvard University Press, 1998.

Gordon, Colin. "Government Rationality: An Introduction," in *The Foucault Effect: Studies in Governmentality*. Chicago: Chicago University Press, 1991.

Harootunian, Harry. "Japan's Long Postwar: The Trick of Memory and the Ruse of History," in *Japan after Japan: Social and Cultural Life from the Recessionary 1990s to the Present*, edited by Tomiko Toda and Harry Harootunian, 98–121. Durham, NC: Duke University Press, 2006.

———. "National Narratives/Spectral Happenings: Formations of the Subject and Self," in *Modern Japan, Kodansha Series on Japanese History*, Vol. 24. Tokyo.

———. *Overcome by Modernity: History, Culture, and Community in Interwar Japan*. Princeton, NJ: Princeton University Press, 2000.

———. "Visible Discourses/Invisible Ideologies," in *Postmodernism and Japan*, edited by Masao Miyoshi and Harry Harootunian, 63–92. Durham, NC: Duke University Press, 1989.

Heiman, Rachel. *Driving after Class: Anxious Times in an American Suburb*. Oakland: University of California Press, 2015.

Herz, Ansel. "Does Media Coverage of School Shootings Lead to More School Shootings? Copycat Killers, Media Coverage, and the Fight over Footage of the Seattle Pacific University Shooting." *The Stranger*, August 13, 2014, 11–16.

Hideo Kojima, "Childrearing Concepts as a Belief-Value System of the Society and the Individual," in *Child Development and Education in Japan*, edited by Harold W. Stevenson et al., 39–54. New York: W. H. Freeman, 1986.

Higashi, Julie. "The *Kokoro* Education: Landscaping the Minds and Hearts of Japanese," in *Social Education in Asia: Critical Issues and Multiple Perspectives*, edited by David L. Grossman and Joe Tin-Yau Lo, 13–38. Charlotte, NC: Information Age Publishing, 2008.

Hood, Christopher P. "The Third Great Reform of the Japanese Education System: Success in the 1980s Onwards," in *Can the Japanese Change Their Education System*, edited by Roger Goodman and David Phillips. Oxford, UK: Symposium Books, 2003.

Hook, Glen, and Takeda Hiroko, "Self-responsibility and the Nature of the Postwar Japanese State: Risk through the Looking Glass." *Journal of Japanese Studies*, 33, no. 1 (2007): 93–123.

Horio, Teruhisa. *Educational Thought and Ideology in Modern Japan: State Authority and Intellectual Freedom*. Tokyo: University of Tokyo Press, 1988.

Igarashi, Yoshikuni. *Bodies of Memory: Narratives of War in Postwar Japanese Culture, 1945–xr1970*. Princeton, NJ: Princeton University Press, 2000.

Iida, Yumiko. "Between the Technique of Living an Endless Routine and the Madness of Absolute Degree Zero." *Positions* 8, no. 2 (2000): 423–464.

Inoue, Kyoko. *Individual Dignity in Modern Japanese Thought: The Evolution of the Concept of Jinkaku in Moral and Educational Discourse*. Ann Arbor: University of Michigan Press, 2001.

Ishimure, Michiko, and Bruce Allen. *Lake of Heaven: An Original Translation of the Japanese Novel*. Lanham, MD: Lexington Books. 2008.

Ito, Takatoshi. "Retrospective on the Bubble Period and Its Relationship to Development in the 1990s," in *Japan's Lost Decade: Origins, Consequences, and Prospects for Recovery*, edited by G. Savonhouse and R. Stern, 17–19. Oxford, UK: Blackwell Publishing, 2004.

Ivy, Marilyn J. "The Art of Cute Little Things: Nara Yoshitomo's Parapolitics." *Mechademia* 5, no. 1 (2010): 3–29.

———. "Benedict's Shame," *Cabinet Magazine*, no. 31 (Fall, 2008). Available at http://cabinetmagazine.org/issues/31/ivy.php.

———. "Critical Texts, Mass Artifacts: The Consumption of Knowledge in Postmodern Japan," in *Postmoderism and Japan*, edited by Masao Miyoshi and Harry Harootunian, 21–46. Durham, NC: Duke University Press, 1989.

———. *Discourses of the Vanishing: Modernity, Phantasm, Japan*. Chicago: Chicago University Press, 1995.

———. "Revenge and Recapitation in Recessionary Japan," in *Japan after Japan: Social and Cultural Life from the Recessionary 1990s to the Present*, edited by Tomiko Yoda and Harry Harootunian, 195–215. Durham, NC: Duke University Press, 2006.

Johnson, Frank. *Dependency and Japanese Socialization.* New York: New York University, 1993.

Jones, Mark. *Children as Treasures: Childhood and the Middle Class in Early Twentieth-Century Japan.* Cambridge, MA: Harvard University Asia Center, 2010.

Jung, Carl. *Man and His Symbols.* New York: Laurel Books, 1964.

Kariya, Takehiko. "The End of Egalitarian Education," in *Challenges to Japanese Education: Economics, Reform, and Human Rights*, edited by June Gordon, Hidenori Fujita, Takehiko Kariya, and Gerald LeTendre, 54–66. New York: Teachers College Press, 2010.

———. "From 'Credential' Society to 'Learning Capital' Society: A Rearticulation of Class Formation in Japanese Education and Society," in *Social Class in Contemporary Japan*, edited by Hiroshi Ishida and David Slater, 87–113. New York: Routledge, 2010.

Kawashima, Ken C. *The Proletarian Gamble: Korean Workers in Interwar Japan.* Durham, NC: Duke University Press, 2009.

Kelly, William. "Finding a Place in Metropolitan Japan: Ideologies, Institutions, and Everyday Life," in *Postwar Japan as History*, edited by Andrew Gordon, 189–238. Berkeley: University of California Press, 1995.

Kim, Misook. "Private Institutions as Educational Sedatives," in *No Alternative: Experiments in South Korean Education*, edited by Nancy Abelmann, Jung-ah Choi, and So-Jin Park, 97–114. Berkeley: University of California Press, 2012.

Kitanaka, Junko. *Depression in Japan: Psychiatric Cures for a Society in Distress.* Princeton, NJ: Princeton University Press, 2011.

Kojin, Karatani. *The Origins of Modern Japanese Literature.* Durham, NC: Duke University Press, 1993.

Kondo, Sumio. "Off We Go to Our Lessons." *The Japan Interpreter: A Journal of Social and Political Ideas* IX, no. 1 (Spring 1974): 15–32.

Koo, Se-Woong. "How South Korea Enslaves Its Students." *New York Times*, August 1, 2014; available at www.nytimes.com/2014/08/02/opinion/sunday/south-koreas-education-system-hurts-students.html?module=Search&mabReward=relbias&.

Kosaku, Yoshino. *Cultural Nationalism in Contemporary Japan: A Sociological Enquiry.* London: Routledge, 1992.

Koschmann, Victor. "'*Ko to Shi*,' Idioms of Contemporary Japan X," in Japanese Life-Styles IX, 3 (Winter 1975).

———. "Modernization and Democratic Values: The 'Japanese Model' in the 1960s," in *Staging Growth: Modernization, Development and the Global Cold War*, edited by David Engerman, Neil Gilman, Mark Haefele, and Michael Latham, 225–250. Amherst: University of Massachusetts Press, 2003.

Kosugi, Reiko. "The Problems of Freeters and 'NEETS' under the Recovering Economy." *The Social Science Research Journal of Japan* (2005): 5–7.

Latham, Michael. "Introduction: Modernization, International History, and the Cold War World," in *Staging Growth: Modernization, Development, and the Global Cold War*, edited by David Engerman, Neil Gilman, Mark Haefele, and Michael Latham, 1–24. Amherst: University of Massachusetts Press, 2003.

Lebra, Takie. *Japanese Patterns of Behavior, Becoming Japanese.* Honolulu: University of Hawaii Press, 1976.

Lemke, Thomas. "'The Birth of Bio-Politics': Michel Foucault's Lecture at the Collège de France on Neoliberal Governmentality." *Economy and Society* 30 (May 2001): 190–207.

Lewis, Catherine C. *Educating Hearts and Minds: Reflections on Japanese Preschool and Elementary Education.* Cambridge, UK: Cambridge University Press, 1995.

Lock, Margaret M. "A Nation at Risk: Interpretations of School Refusal," in *Biomedicine Examined*, edited by Margaret M. Lock and Deborah Gordon, 377–414. Dordrecht: Kluwer Academic Publishers, 1988.

Lukacs, Gabriella. "Dreamwork: Cell Phone Novelists, Labor and Politics in Contemporary Japan." *Cultural Anthropology* 28, no. 1 (2013): 44–64.

———. *Scripted Affects, Branded Selves: Television, Subjectivity, and Capitalism in 1990s Japan.* Durham, NC: Duke University Press, 2010.

Lukose, Ritty. *Liberalization's Children: Gender, Youth, and Consumer Citizenship in Global India.* Durham, NC: Duke University Press, 2009.

Masuda, Yoneji. *The Information Society as Post-Industrial Society.* Washington, DC: World Future Society, 1981.

Matthews, Gordon, and Bruce White. *Japan's Changing Generations: Are Young People Creating a New Society?* New York: Routledge, 2003.

McCormack, Gavan. *The Emptiness of Japanese Affluence* (revised edition). New York: M. E. Sharpe, 2001.

McKinlay, Megan. "Unstable Mothers: Redefining Motherhood in Contemporary Japan." *Intersections: Gender, History and Culture in the Asian Context*, no. 7 (March, 2002); available at http://intersections.anu.edu.au/issue7/mckinlay .html.

Mead, Margaret. "Theoretical Setting—1954," in *Childhood in Contemporary Cultures*, edited by Margaret Mead and M. Wolfenstein. Chicago: University of Chicago Press, 1955.

Miller, Peter, and Nikolas Rose. *Governing the Present: Administering Economic, Social and Personal Life.* Malden, MA: Polity Press, 2008.

Mitchell, Kathryn."Education for Democratic Citizenship: Transnationalism, Multiculturalism, and the Limits of Liberalism." *Harvard Educational Review* 71 (Spring 2001): 1.

Miura, Atsushi. *The Rise of Sharing: Fourth-Stage Consumer Society in Japan.* Translated by Dana Lewis. Tokyo: International House of Japan, 2014.

Miyazaki, Hirokazu. "The Temporality of No Hope," in *Ethnographies of Neoliberalism*, edited by C. J. Greenhouse, 238–250. Philadelphia: University of Pennsylvania Press, 2010.

Miyoshi, Masao. "Japan Is Not Interesting," in *Trespasses: Masao Miyoshi, Selected Writings*, edited by Eric Cazdyn, 189–204. Durham, NC: Duke University Press, 2010.

Mori, Yoshitaka. "New Art and Culture in the Age of the 'Freeter' in Japan: On the Young Part Time Workers and the Ideology of Creativity." *Kontur*, nr. 20 (2010): 48–53 ; available at http://kontur.au.dk/fileadmin/www.kontur.au.dk/Kontur_20/Microsoft_Word_-_VAM-MORI_MOD2.pdf.

Morris-Suzuki, Tessa. *Beyond Computopia: Information, Automation, and Democracy in Japan.* New York: Kegan Paul Publishers, 1988.

Nandy, Ashis. "Reconstructing Childhood: A Critique of the Ideology of Adulthood," in *Traditions, Tyranny, and Utopias: Essays in the Politics of Awareness*, 56–76. Oxford, UK: Oxford University Press, 1987.

Nathan, John. *Japan Unbound: A Volatile Nation's Quest for Pride and Purpose.* Boston, MA: Houghton Mifflin, 2004.

Negra, Diane, and Tasker, Yvonne. "Introduction: Gender and Recessionary Culture," in *Gendering the Recession: Media and Culture in an Age of Austerity*, edited by Diane Negra and Yvonne Tasker, 1–30. Durham, NC: Duke University Press, 2014.

Nelson, Christopher T. *Dancing with the Dead: Memory, Performance and Everyday Life in Postwar Okinawa.* Durham, NC: Duke University Press, 2008.

Okano Kaori and Motonori Tsuchiya. *Education in Contemporary Japan: Inequality and Diversity.* Cambridge, UK: Cambridge University Press, 1999.

Park, So-Jin. "Mother's Anxious Management of the Private After-school Education Market," in *No Alternative: Experiments in South Korean Education*, edited by Nancy Abelmann, Jung-ah Choi, and So-Jin Park, 115–131 . Berkeley: University of California Press, 2012.

Peck, Jamie, and Adam Tickell. "Neoliberalizing Space." *Antipode* (2002): 380–404.

Pemberton, John. *On the Subject of "Java."* Ithaca, NY: Cornel University Press, 1994.

Penny, Matthew. "Miyazaki Hayao's *Kaze Tachinu* (The Wind Rises). *Asia-Pacific Journal* 11, Issue 30, no. 2 (August 15, 2013); available at www.japanfocus.org/-Matthew-Penney/3976.

———. "Why on Earth Is Something as Important as This Not in the Textbooks: Teaching Supplements, Student Essays, and History Education in Japan." *Asia-Pacific Journal* 12, no. 1 (January 6, 2014); available at www.japanfocus.org/-Matthew-Penney/4055.

Riggs, Lynne. *"Ranjuku Jidai"* [The Idioms of Contemporary Japan XVIII] (in English). Tokyo: Japan Center for International Exchange, Spring, 1977.

Riley, Denise. *War in the Nursery: Theories of the Child and Mother.* London: Virago Press, 1983.

Rohlen, Thomas K. *Japan's High Schools.* Berkeley: University of California Press, 1983.

———. "The *Juku* Phenomenon: An Exploratory Essay." *Journal of Japanese Studies* 6, no. 2 (Summer 1980): 207–242.

Rose, Jacqueline. *The Case of Peter Pan or the Impossibility of Children's Fiction.* Philadelphia: University of Pennsylvania Press, 1984.

Rosenberger, Nancy, ed. *The Japanese Sense of Self.* Cambridge, UK: Cambridge University Press, 1992.

Ryang, Sonia. *Japan and National Anthropology: A Critique.* New York: Routledge, 2004.

Samuels, Andrew. *Jung and the Post-Jungians.* London: Routledge, 1985.

Santner, Eric L. *My Own Private Germany: Daniel Paul Schreber's Secret History of Modernity.* Princeton, NJ: Princeton University Press, 1996.

Sato, Manabu. "Imagining Neo-Liberalism and the Hidden Realities of the Politics of Reform: Teachers and Students in a Globalized Japan," in *Reimagining Japanese Education,* edited by David Willis and Jeremy Rappeleye, 225–246. Oxford, UK: Symposium Books, 2011.

Saxonhouse, Gary R., and Robert M. Stern. *Japan's Lost Decade: Origins, Consequences, and Prospects for Recovery.* Oxford, UK: Blackwell Publishing, 2004.

Sharma, Sarah. *In the Meantime: Temporality and Cultural Politics.* Durham, NC: Duke University Press, 2014.

Slater, David H., "The New Working Class of Urban Japan," in *Social Class in Contemporary Japan,* edited by Hiroshi Ishida and David H. Slater, 137–169. New York: Routledge, 2010.

Snyder, Gary. *The Gary Snyder Reader: Prose, Poetry, Translations (1952–99) Vol.1.* Berkeley, CA: Counterpoint Press, 1999.

Splinder, George D, ed. *The Making of Psychological Anthropology.* Berkeley: University of California Press, 1978.

Steedman, Carolyn. *Strange Dislocations: Childhood and the Idea of Human Interiority 1780–1930.* Cambridge, MA: Harvard University Press, 1995.

Stenson, Leah, and Asao Sarukawa Aroldi. *Reverberations from Fukushima: 50 Japanese Poets Speak Out.* Portland, OR: Inkwater Press, 2014.

Stephens, Sharon. "Children and the Politics of 'Late Capitalism.'" In *Children and the Politics of Culture*, edited by Sharon Stephens, 3–48. Princeton, NJ: Princeton University Press, 1995.

Stocking, George W. Jr., ed. *Race, Culture, and Evolution: Essays in the History of Anthropology*. Chicago: University of Chicago Press, 1968.

Stolz, Robert. *Bad Water: Nature, Pollution, and Politics in Japan, 1870–1950*. Durham, NC: Duke University Press, 2014.

Takeyama, Keita. "Reconceptualizing the Politics of Education.," in *Reimagining Japanese Education*, edited by David Willis and Jeremy Rappeleye, 247–280. Oxford, UK: Symposium Books, 2011.

Tanaka, Stefan. "Childhood: Naturalization of Development into a Japanese Space," in *Cultures of Scholarship*, edited by Sally Humphreys, 22–54. Ann Arbor: University of Michigan Press. 1998.

———. *New Times in Modern Japan*. Princeton, NJ: Princeton University Press, 2004.

Tiberghien, Yves. "Thirty Years of Neo-Liberal Reforms in Japan," in *The Great Transformation of Japanese Capitalism*, edited by Sébastien Lechevalier. New York: Nissan Institute/Routledge Japanese Studies, 2014.

Tsing, Anna. "How to Make Resources and Then Destroy Them (and Then Save Them?) on the Salvage Frontier." In *Histories of the Future*, edited by Daniel Rosenberg and Susan Harding, 51–74. Durham, NC: Duke University Press, 2005.

Tsuneyoshi Ryoko. "Junior High School Entrance Exams in Metropolitan Tokyo," in *Japanese Education in an Era of Globalization*, edited by Gary DeCoker and Christopher Bjork. New York: Teachers College Press, 2013.

———. "The New Japanese Educational Reforms and the Achievement 'Crisis' Debate." *Educational Policy* 18, no. 2 (May, 2004): 364–394.

Ueno Chizuko. "Collapse of the Japanese Mother." *US–Japan Women's Journal, English Supplement* no. 10 (June, 1996): 42–63.

Uno, Kathleen, S. *Passages to Modernity: Motherhood, Childhood, and Social Reform in Early Twentieth-Century Japan*. Honolulu: University of Hawai'i Press, 1999.

Vlastos, Stephen. "Agrarianism without Tradition: The Radical Critique of Prewar Japanese Modernity," in *Mirror of Modernity: Invented Traditions of Modern Japan*, edited by Stephen Vlastos, 79–94. Berkeley: University of California Press, 1998.

Vogel, Ezra. *Japan as Number One: Lessons for America*. Boston, MA: Harvard University Press, 1979. New York : Harper & Row, 1980.

White, Merry. *The Japanese Educational Challenge: A Commitment to Children*. New York: Free Press, 1987.

———. *Perfectly Japanese: Making Families in an Era of Upheaval*. Berkeley: University of California Press, 2002.

Yoda, Tomiko. "The Rise and Fall of Maternal Society," in *Japan after Japan: Social and Cultural Life from the Recessionary 1990s to the Present*, edited by Tomiko Yoda and Harry Harootunian, 16–53. Durham, NC: Duke University Press, 2006.

———. "A Roadmap to Millennial Japan," in *Japan after Japan: Social and Cultural Life from the Recessionary 1990s to the Present*, edited by Tomiko Yoda and Harry Harootunian, 239–274. Durham, NC: Duke University Press.

Yoneyama, Shoko. *The Japanese High School: Silence and Resistance*. London and New York: Routledge, 1999,

Zizek, Slavoj. *The Sublime Object of Ideology*. London: Verso, 1989.

Japanese-Language Sources

Arichi Tōru. *Nihonjin no shitsuke: Katei kyōiku to gakkō kyōiku no hensen to kōsaku* [Japanese manner training: Home education and school education transition and intertwining]. Kyoto: Hōritsubunkasha, 2000.

Asahi Shinbun Osaka Shakaibu. *Kurai mori: Kobe renzoku jidō sasshō jiken* [Dark forest: The Kobe serial killing and wounding incident]. Osaka: Asahi Shinbunsha, 1998.

Asahi Shinbunsha Shakaibu. *Naze gakkō wa hōkai suru no ka* [Why are schools collapsing?]. Tokyo: Asahi Shinbunsha, 1999.

Batoru Rouiaru Kenkyū Iinkai. *Batoru rowaiaru The MOVIE: Kanzen kōryaku gaidobukku* [Battle royale]. Tokyo: Kadogawa Shoten, 2000.

Bungei Shunjūsha. "Kodomo ga hen da!" [The child is turning strange]. Special issue, *Bungei Shunjū* 75, no. 12 (1997).

———. "Shōnen A hanzai no zenbō" [Youth A the entirety of his crime]. *Bungei Shunjū* 76, no. 3 (1998): 94–160.

Doi Takeo. *"Amae" no kōzō* [The structure of dependence]. Tokyo: Kōbundō, 1972.

Hirota Teruyuki. *Nihonjin no shitsuke wa suitaishita ka: "Kyōikusuru kazoku" no yukue* [Has Japanese manner training really declined?]. Tokyo: Kodansha, 1999.

Hirota Teruyuki and Itō Shigeki. *Kyōiku mondai wa naze machigatte katarareru no ka? "Wakatta tsumori" kara no dakkyaku* [Why are educational problems depicted incorrectly?] Tokyo: Nihon Tosho Sentā, 2010.

"Kobe shōgakusei satsugai jiken: Jiken no haikei to kore kara no kyōiku o kangaeru" [The killing of Kobe elementary school children incident: The incident's background and thinking about education in the aftermath]. *Jidō Shinri* (1997).

Kawai Akira and Muroi Tsutomu. *Kyōiku kihonhō rekishi to kenkyū* [Historical research on the fundamental law of education]. Tokyo: Shin Nihon Shuppansha, 1999.

———. *Kokoro no kyōiku no jūjitsu ni mukete* [Toward a Solid Emotional education]. Kobe: Kokoro no Kyōiku Kyūkyū Kaigi, 1997.

———. *Nihon bunka no yukue* [The direction of Japanese culture]. Tokyo: Iwanami Shoten, 2000.

———. "The Structure of Japan in the 21st Century," in *Nihon no furontia wa Nihon no naka ni aru* [Japan's frontier is within Japan], edited by Hayao Kawai. Tokyo: Kodansha, 2000.

———. *Ohanashi no chie* [The wisdom of stories]. Tokyo: Asahi Shinbunsha, 2000.

Kawakami Ryōichi. *Futsū no kodomotachi no hōkai* [The collapse of ordinary children]. Tokyo: Bungei Shunjū, 1999.

———. *Gakkō hōkai* [School collapse]. Tokyo: Sōshisha, 1999.

———. *Kyōiku kaikaku kokumin kaigi de nani ga ronjirareta ka* [What was discussed in the citizen's committee on education reform]. Tokyo: Sōshisha, 2000.

"Kodomo ga abunai." [The child is dangerous]. Special issue, *AERA* 10, no. 45 (1997).

Kosugi Takashi. *Ushinawareta "kokoro no kyōiku" o motomete: 21 seiki ni okuru kyōiku kaikaku* [Seeking the lost emotional education: Toward twenty-first-century education reform]. Tokyo: Dasiyamondosha, 1997.

Monbukagakushō [Ministry of education, sports, science and technology]. *Kyōiku kaikaku kokumin kaigi saishū hōkoku: Kyōiku o kaeru 17 no teigen* [The final report of the citizen's committee on education reform: Changing education 17 suggestions]. Tokyo: Monbukagakushō, 2000.

Monbukagakushō Chūō Kyōiku Shingikai [Ministry of education, sports, science and technology central council for education]. *Chūō Kyōiku Shingikai Tōshin: Yōji ki kara no kokoro no kyōiku no arikata ni tsuite* [Central education committee report: the method of emotional education from childhood on]. Tokyo: Gyōsei, 1998.

Murakami Ryū. *"Kyōiku no hōkai" to iu uso* [The illusion of education collapse]. Tokyo: NHK Shuppan, 2001.

Natsuki, Iwama. *Wakamono no Hataraku Ishiki ga Naze Kawatta no Ka* [Why Has the Work Consciousness of the Youth Changed?] Tokyo: Minerva Press, 2010.

Noguchi Yoshikuni. *Soredemo shōnen o basshimasu ka* [Under the circumstances, will you still punish the youth?]. Tokyo: Kyōdō Tsūshinsha, 1998.

Oki Naoki. *Kodomo no kiki o dō miru ka* [How to view the child crisis]. Tokyo: Iwanami Shoten, 2000.

Sawanobori Toshio. *Shōnenhō: Kihon rinen kara kaisei mondai made.* [Juvenile justice law: From the fundamental philosophy to the problem of revision]. Tokyo: Chūō Kōron Shinsha, 1999.

Takagi Mikio. *Jibun no kodomo wa jibun de mamore: "Gakuryoku" tte nan darō, Nichinōken wa kō kangaeru.* [Protecting your own child on your own: What is academic ability? What Nichinoken thinks about it]. Tokyo: Kodansha, 2002.

Takami Kōshun. *Batoru rowaiaru.* [Battle royale]. Tokyo: Ōta Shuppan, 1999.

Terawaki Ken. *21 seiki e kyōiku wa kawaru: Kyōsō no jidai wa mō oshimai* [Toward the twenty-first-century educational change]. Tokyo: Kindai Bungeisha, 1997.

Tetsuya Takahashi. *"Kokoro" to Sensō* ["Heart" and war]. Tokyo: Shobunsha, 2003.

Yoneyama, Shoko, "The Era of Bullying: Japan Under Neoliberalism," *The Asia-Pacific Journal,* 1-3-09 (December 31, 2008).

Za, Chūgaku. "Kyōshi: Kodomo ga hen da: Kodomo wa mohaya, anata no shitteiru kodomo de wa nai? [The junior high student: The child is turning strange: The child is no longer what you think it is]." *Bessatsu takarajima,* no. 129 (March 1991, 1995).

Index

Abe Shinzō: economic policies, 37–38, 46, 173; education policies, 8, 10, 38, 39–40, 46, 73, 144–45, 157, 174; and neoliberalism, 153; speech to U.S. Congress, 173–74

academic ability, 110, 116, 119, 120, 124; and exam preparation schools, 103, 104, 105, 112, 115

Allison, Anne, 11, 111, 144, 197n44

alternative spaces, 19, 37, 156–59, 174, 177

alternatives, 15, 143, 153, 186, 192

Ambaras, David, 22

Anagnost, Ann, 206n39; *Global Futures in East Asia*, 182n44

Anderson, Benedict: on configuration of national imaginings, 5–6; on imagined communities, 2, 5–6, 23

anime, 95; *see also* comics

Aum Shinrikyō (Supreme Truth), 52–53, 77

bankruptcy, 3, 39, 40, 147, 156–57

Barry, Andrew: *Foucault and Political Realism*, 179n26, 190n40

Battle Royale (*Batoru Rowaiaru*), 73–74, 149–50, 171, 190n38, 205n29

Benedict, Ruth, 180n6; *Chrysanthemum and the Sword*, 24–25, 26, 27, 180n11; on Japanese child rearing, 24–25; on mother-child relationship, 25; *Patterns of Culture*, 23–24

Benesee company, 203n24; "Challenge" materials, 135–36, 200n9, 203n26

Boas, Franz, 7, 180nn6,7, 190n41

body, the: and language, 6–7, 18, 32, 36, 83–84; and the mind, 97, 98–99; the national body, 23, 36, 108; *see also kokutai*

Borovoy, Amy, 12

Bright Future (*Akarui Mirai*), 140, 150–51, 171

Brinton, Mary, 12

Brown, Wendy, 175

bullying (*ijime*), 12, 45, 51, 68, 74, 87, 95, 119, 188n27, 195n27, 198n46

Büscher, Bram, 63

capitalism, 5, 20, 22, 27, 53, 112, 150, 179n32, 191n50; and the frontier, 63–64, 155; in Japan, 2, 9, 16, 26, 35, 41, 48, 63–64, 68, 81, 86, 141–42, 155, 168–69, 174. *See also* globalization; modernity, the child as figure of; neoliberalism; value creation

Casteneda, Claudia, 5, 22; *Figurations*, 206n39

Central Committee on Education (Chūō Kyōiku Shigikai), 68, 75, 187n23

certainty production, 2–3, 4, 5, 6

the child problem (*kodomo no mondai*), 4, 6–9, 12–13, 16–17, 21, 46, 47, 66, 74, 142, 154, 159, 160, 172–73, 174, 183n1, 192nn2,6, 195n28, 198n45; Kawakami on, 6–7, 13, 18, 82, 83–84, 85, 89, 96, 193n14, 194n22;

150, 171, 183n45, 206n38; of parents,
40, 44–45, 51, 52, 115, 201n19; for self-
development, 7, 28, 35, 61, 86, 96–97,
140–41, 152, 170, 206n38; as self-
responsibility, 1, 7, 8, 14, 15, 28, 35, 39,
44, 144, 148, 150, 171, 173; shifted to
individual, 1, 6, 7, 17, 28, 34, 35, 37, 39,
40, 44, 51, 59, 61, 65, 79, 87, 112, 115,
138, 140, 150, 152, 154–55, 156, 170,
171, 186n16
restructuring (*ristora*), 3, 40, 71, 93, 140,
145, 146, 147, 156–57, 173
"returnee" (*kikokushijo*) schools, 100,
196n38
reverse migrants (Uturn, Iturn)
158–71
Riley, Denise, 22
risk, 16, 19, 48, 78, 97, 117, 145, 153, 155,
173, 183n45; shifted to individual, 1,
15, 17, 28, 34, 35, 60, 61, 112, 138, 150,
152, 170
Robertson, Jennifer, 181n21
Rohlen, Thomas, 11
Rose, Jacqueline, 22, 86; on children,
1, 2, 3; *The Case of Peter Pan*, 186n17,
206n39
Rose, Nikolas, 177n5; *Foucault and Political Realism*, 179n26, 190n40
Ryang, Sonia, 25, 180n11

salaryman families, 5, 31–34, 61
Samuels, Andrew: *Jung and the Post-
Jungians*, 187n17
Sapix, 203n24
Sasai, Toru, 51, 185n35 ?
Sato, Manabu, 12, 46, 47, 48
school collapse. *See* classroom/school
collapse (*gakkyū hōkai*)
school refusal (*futokō, tōkōkyohi*), 45, 69,
74, 87, 188n27, 198n46
Schoppa, Leonard: immobility thesis,
46–47
self-development, 8, 9, 14, 30, 37, 40,
81–82, 143, 145, 148–49, 153, 154, 173,
204n6; as individual responsibility, 7,
15, 28, 61, 86, 96–97, 112, 140–41, 149,
152, 159–60, 170, 171, 204n6; prodigies, 33–34, 35, 133; skills (*nōryoku*),
28, 32, 35, 37, 138, 147, 151, 152

Shinjujinkai (New Women's Association), 190n37
Showa period, 21
skills (*nōryoku*), 28, 32, 35, 37, 138, 147,
151, 152
Slater, David, 12
Snyder, Gary: on the Tribe, 169
social class, 5, 11, 29; divided society
(*kakusa shakai*), 114, 142, 152–53,
156, 173; and extra supplementary
schooling, 156, 173; middle class, 38,
52, 54, 111, 120–21, 137, 142, 145,
146, 156
social engineering, 4, 9, 16, 20, 30, 45
Sōri, Katsuyoshi: "Hyogo Trial Week
and Children," 58
South Korea, 159, 177n7, 180n36,
206n42
spatiality, 14, 16, 19–20, 21, 22, 23, 63,
139–40, 156–64, 168–71
*Spirited Away (Sen to Chihiro no Kami-
kakushi)*, 78–79, 191n54
standard deviation curve, 121
Steedman, Carolyn, 22
Stephens, Sharon, 196n31
Stocking, George, 180n6,7
Stolz, Robert: *Bad Water*, 180n33
"strength to live" (*ikiru chikara*), 41, 43,
45, 67, 69, 73, 117, 118, 140
"Structure of Japan in the Twenty-First
Century, The," 18, 58–59, 75–78, 154,
186n9, 187n20, 190n43
student movement of 1960s, 81, 97, 99
subjectivity, 52, 53, 57, 74, 82, 97, 111,
128, 140, 141, 149, 151, 153, 174,
184n22, 187n17, 204n6
suicide, 147
supplementary education industry,
180n36, 184n26, 188n28, 200n9;
and class divisions, 156, 173; and
differences in academic ability, 103,
104, 105, 112, 115; exam preparation
schools (*gakushū/shingakujuku*)11,
15–16, 18–19, 32, 54, 85, 89, 91, 103,
104, 105, 108–9, 110–38, 194n20,
198n48, 199nn2,50, 200nn11,14,
201nn15,18,19,20, 202n21, 203n24;
Kumon, 34, 113, 135, 179n36, 203n25;
vs. public school system, 18–19,

.

supplementary education industry
(*continued*)
108–9, 114, 119, 120, 125, 127, 129,
131; and recessionary effects, 15–16,
18–19, 39–40, 84, 85, 112, 114, 126–27,
146, 173; relations with government,
114–15, 119; relations with parents,
19, 40, 54, 123, 124, 126, 127–29;
remedial-type schools (*hoshūjuku*),
113; Sylvan Learning Centers,
180n36
supplementary education materials, 102,
103, 110, 112, 114, 135–36, 198n48,
203n26
sustainability, 170–71
Suwa, Tetsuji, 97–98
Sylvan Learning Centers, 180n36

Tachibana, Kozaburo, 168, 206n48
Taisho period, 21
Takagi Mikio: *Jibun no Kodomo wa Jibun de Mamore*, 199n2
Takeshi, Kitano (Beat), 73–74
Takeyama, Keita, 46–47
Tanaka, Stefan, 21, 22; *New Times in Modern Japan*, 206n49
Tasker, Yvonne, 109
teachers, 9, 54, 111, 188n25, 197n39; attitudes regarding education reforms, 71–72, 73, 115, 199n51; homeroom teachers, 18, 58, 69, 102, 103, 104, 105, 189n34, 198n49; Purokyōshi (Professional Teachers' Association), 18, 78, 81–83, 85, 92, 97–100, 107–8, 194n22, 196nn30,31,35; relations with parents, 91, 106–7, 198n49; relations with students, 7, 31, 33, 51, 70–72, 86, 87, 88, 93–95, 96, 98, 99–100, 101–5, 117–18, 128–29, 131, 132–33, 189n34, 195nn25,26, 196n31, 197n43, 198nn47,49. *See also* Kawakami Ryōichi
temporality, 5, 14, 16, 19–20, 32, 63–64, 67, 146, 160, 165, 168; and the child, 3, 4, 15, 19, 21–23, 34, 141, 155; and neoliberalism, 139–40, 141, 143–44, 153, 171; and the recessionary generation, 143–44, 171
Terawaki Ken, 42–45, 48, 58, 65, 183nn4,9,10, 188n29, 200n10

Teruyuki, Hirota, 35, 186n8, 193n13
Tetsuya Takahashi, 145, 179n27, 181n21
Thatcher, Margaret, 34, 87
Tickell, Adam: "Neoliberalizing Space," 34, 35, 178n15
Tohoku area, 16
Tokugawa period, 21, 66
Tokyo Sonata, 31–34, 35, 36–37, 61, 90, 138, 140, 149, 150, 151, 154
Tomuro Elementary, 71–72, 189n34
"Toward a Solid Emotional Education," 56–57
Tsing, Anna, 63; on resource frontiers, 154, 155–56
Tsuneyoshi, Ryoko, 12
Turns, 170

United Kingdom vs. Japan, 34, 35, 47, 81–82, 87
United States: *Anpō* with Japan, 97; vs. Japan, 10–11, 25, 35, 40, 44, 47, 70–71, 81–82, 87, 96, 100, 113, 150, 155, 159–60, 174, 178n11, 180n36, 189n36, 191n45, 196n31, 197n41, 203n25; private schooling services in, 180n36, 203n25; recessionary conditions in, 109
University of Tokyo, 52, 114, 153, 202n23
University of Washington, 32–33, 145, 159–60, 182n36, 203n3, 204n16

value creation, 61, 154, 155, 199n53
verticality, 27
Vlastos, Stephen, 206n48

Wagatsumi, Hiroshi, 194n17
Waseda University, 204n16
White, Merry: *The Japanese Educational Challenge*, 11
whole child practices, 11
"wig" (*katsura*) incident, 202n22

Yoda, Tomiko, 9, 115
Yoneyama, Shoko, 12
Yoshimoto, Banana, 191n54
youth, 13–15, 17, 22, 38, 40, 45, 46, 51, 53, 72, 91, 95, 96, 99, 100, 108, 130, 142–144, 147, 151, 152, 154, 155, 157, 160, 193n13, 204n15, 206nn39,41